The College Panda

SAT Math

Advanced Guide and Workbook

ISBN: 978-0-9894964-2-1

*SAT is a registered trademark of the College Board, which does not endorse this product.

For more information, visit thecollegepanda.com

Discounts available for teachers and companies. Please contact thecollegepanda@gmail.com for details.

To Mom and Dad

Introduction

The best way to do well on any test is to be experienced with the material. Nowhere is this more true than on the SAT, which is standardized to repeat the same question types again and again. The purpose of this book is to teach you the concepts and battle-tested approaches you need to know for all these questions types. If it's not in this book, it's not on the test. The goal is for every SAT question to be a simple reflex, something you know how to handle instinctively because you've seen it so many times before.

You won't find any cheap tricks in this book, simply because there aren't any that work consistently. Don't buy into the idea that you can improve your score significantly without hard work.

Format of the Test

There are two math sections on the SAT. The first contains 20 questions to be done in 25 minutes without a calculator. The second contains 38 questions to be done in 55 minutes and a calculator is permitted.

Some topics only show up in the calculator section. I've made sure to accurately divide the practice questions into non-calculator and calculator components.

How to Read this Book

For a complete understanding, this book is best read from beginning to end. That being said, each chapter was written to be independent of the others as much as possible. After all, you may already be proficient in some topics yet weak in others. If so, feel free to jump around, focusing on the chapters that are most relevant to your improvement.

All chapters come with exercises. Do them. You won't master the material until you think through the questions yourself.

About the Author

Nielson Phu graduated from New York University, where he studied actuarial science. He has obtained perfect scores on the SAT and on the SAT math subject test. As a teacher, he has helped hundreds of students throughout Boston and Hong Kong perform better on standardized tests. Although he continues to pursue his interests in education, he is now an engineer in the Boston area.

Table of Contents

1

Exponents & Radicals

Here are the laws of exponents you should know:

Law	Example
$x^1 = x$	$3^1 = 3$
$x^0 = 1$	$3^0 = 1$
$x^m \cdot x^n = x^{m+n}$	$3^4 \cdot 3^5 = 3^9$
$\dfrac{x^m}{x^n} = x^{m-n}$	$\dfrac{3^7}{3^3} = 3^4$
$(x^m)^n = x^{mn}$	$(3^2)^4 = 3^8$
$(xy)^m = x^m y^m$	$(2 \cdot 3)^3 = 2^3 \cdot 3^3$
$\left(\dfrac{x}{y}\right)^m = \dfrac{x^m}{y^m}$	$\left(\dfrac{2}{3}\right)^3 = \dfrac{2^3}{3^3}$
$x^{-m} = \dfrac{1}{x^m}$	$3^{-4} = \dfrac{1}{3^4}$

Many students don't know the difference between

$$(-3)^2 \text{ and } -3^2$$

Order of operations (PEMDAS) dictates that parentheses take precedence. So,

$$(-3)^2 = (-3) \cdot (-3) = 9$$

Without parentheses, exponents take precedence:

$$-3^2 = -3 \cdot 3 = -9$$

The negative is not applied until the exponent operation is carried through. Make sure you understand this so you don't make this common mistake. Sometimes, the result turns out to be the same, as in:

$$(-2)^3 \text{ and } -2^3$$

Make sure you see why they yield the same result.

EXERCISE 1: Evaluate WITHOUT a calculator. Answers for this chapter start on page 254.

1. $(-1)^4$

2. $(-1)^5$

3. $(-1)^{10}$

4. $(-1)^{15}$

5. $(-1)^8$

6. -1^8

7. $-(-1)^8$

8. $(-3)^3$

9. -3^3

10. $-(-3)^3$

11. $-(-6)^2$

12. $-(-4)^3$

13. $2^3 \times 3^2 \times (-1)^5$

14. $(-1)^4 \times 3^3 \times 2^2$

15. $(-2)^3 \times (-3)^4$

16. 3^0

17. 6^{-1}

18. 4^{-1}

19. 5^0

20. 3^2

21. 3^{-2}

22. 5^3

23. 5^{-3}

24. 7^2

25. 7^{-2}

26. 10^3

27. 10^{-3}

EXERCISE 2: Simplify so that your answer contains only positive exponents. Do NOT use a calculator. The first two have been done for you. Answers for this chapter start on page 254.

1. $3x^2 \cdot 2x^3 = 6x^5$

2. $2k^{-4} \cdot 4k^2 = \dfrac{8}{k^2}$

3. $5x^4 \cdot 3x^{-2}$

4. $7m^3 \cdot -3m^{-3}$

5. $(2x^2)^{-3}$

6. $-3a^2b^{-3} \cdot 3a^{-5}b^8$

7. $\dfrac{3n^7}{6n^3}$

8. $(a^2b^3)^2$

9. $\left(\dfrac{xy^4}{x^3y^2}\right)$

10. $-(-x)^3$

11. $(x^2y^{-1})^3$

12. $\dfrac{6u^4}{8u^2}$

13. $2uv^2 \cdot -4u^2v$

14. $\dfrac{x^2}{x^{-3}}$

15. $\dfrac{3x^4}{(x^{-2})^2}$

16. $\dfrac{x^{\frac{3}{2}}}{x^{\frac{1}{2}}}$

17. $x^2 \cdot x^3 \cdot x^4$

18. $(x^2)^{-3} \cdot 2x^3$

19. $(2m)^2 \cdot (3m^3)^2$

20. $(a^{-1} \cdot a^{-2})^2$

21. $(b^{-2})^{-3} \cdot (b^3)^2$

22. $\dfrac{(m^2n)^3}{(mn^2)^2}$

23. $\dfrac{1}{x^{-2}}$

24. $\dfrac{mn}{m^2n^3}$

25. $\dfrac{k^{-2}}{k^{-3}}$

26. $\left(\dfrac{m^2}{n^3}\right)^3$

27. $\left(\dfrac{x^2y^3z^4}{x^{-3}y^{-4}z^{-5}}\right)$

EXAMPLE 1: If $3^{x+2} = y$, then what is the value of 3^x in terms of y?

A) $y + 9$ B) $y - 9$ C) $\dfrac{y}{3}$ D) $\dfrac{y}{9}$

Let's avoid the trouble of finding what x is. Here we notice that the 2 in the exponent is the only difference between the given equation and what we want. So using our laws of exponents, let's extract the 2 out:

$$3^{x+2} = 3^x \cdot 3^2 = y$$

$$3^x = \frac{y}{9}$$

The answer is $\boxed{(D)}$.

EXAMPLE 2: If $3^{a+1} = 3^{-a+7}$, what is the value of a?

Here we see that the bases are the same. The exponents must therefore be equal.

$$a + 1 = -a + 7$$

$$2a = 6$$

$$a = \boxed{3}$$

EXAMPLE 3: If $2a - b = 4$, what is the value of $\dfrac{4^a}{2^b}$?

Realize that 4 is just 2^2.

$$\frac{4^a}{2^b} = \frac{(2^2)^a}{2^b} = \frac{2^{2a}}{2^b} = 2^{2a-b} = 2^4 = \boxed{16}$$

Square roots are just fractional exponents:

$$x^{\frac{1}{2}} = \sqrt{x}$$

$$x^{\frac{1}{3}} = \sqrt[3]{x}$$

But what about $x^{\frac{2}{3}}$? The 2 on top means to square x. The 3 on the bottom means to cube root it:

$$\sqrt[3]{x^2}$$

We can see this more clearly if we break it down:

$$x^{\frac{2}{3}} = (x^2)^{\frac{1}{3}} = \sqrt[3]{x^2}$$

The order in which we do the squaring and the cube-rooting doesn't matter.

$$x^{\frac{2}{3}} = (x^{\frac{1}{3}})^2 = (\sqrt[3]{x})^2$$

The end result just looks prettier with the cube root on the outside. That way, we don't need the parentheses.

EXAMPLE 4: Which of the following is equal to $\sqrt[4]{x^5}$?

A) x B) $x^5 - x^4$ C) $x^{\frac{5}{4}}$ D) $x^{\frac{4}{5}}$

The fourth root equates to a fractional exponent of $\dfrac{1}{4}$, so

$$\sqrt[4]{x^5} = x^{\frac{5}{4}}$$

Answer $\boxed{(C)}$.

The SAT will also test you on simplifying square roots (also called "surds"). To simplify a square root, factor the number inside the square root and take out any pairs:

$$\sqrt{48} = \sqrt{2 \cdot 2 \cdot 2 \cdot 2 \cdot 3} = \sqrt{\boxed{2 \cdot 2} \cdot \boxed{2 \cdot 2} \cdot 3} = 2 \cdot 2\sqrt{3} = 4\sqrt{3}$$

In the example above, we take a 2 out for the first $\boxed{2 \cdot 2}$. Then we take another 2 out for the second pair $\boxed{2 \cdot 2}$. Finally, we multiply the two 2's outside the square root to get 4. Of course, a quicker route would have looked like this:

$$\sqrt{48} = \sqrt{\boxed{4 \cdot 4} \cdot 3} = 4\sqrt{3}$$

Here's one more example:

$$\sqrt{72} = \sqrt{\boxed{2 \cdot 2} \cdot \boxed{3 \cdot 3} \cdot 2} = 2 \cdot 3\sqrt{2} = 6\sqrt{2}$$

To go backwards, take the number outside and put it back under the square root as a pair:

$$6\sqrt{2} = \sqrt{6 \cdot 6 \cdot 2} = \sqrt{72}$$

EXAMPLE 5: If $4\sqrt{3} = \sqrt{3x}$, what is the value of x?

A) 4   B) 12   C) 16   D) 48

Solution 1: Moving the 4 back inside, we get

$$4\sqrt{3} = \sqrt{3 \cdot 4 \cdot 4} = \sqrt{48}$$

Now equating the stuff inside the square roots,

$$\sqrt{48} = \sqrt{3x}$$
$$48 = 3x$$
$$16 = x$$

Answer $\boxed{(C)}$.

Solution 2: Square both sides:

$$(4\sqrt{3})^2 = (\sqrt{3x})^2$$
$$16 \cdot 3 = 3x$$
$$16 = x$$

EXERCISE 3: Simplify the radicals or solve for x. Do NOT use a calculator. Answers for this chapter start on page 254.

1. $\sqrt{12}$

2. $\sqrt{96}$

3. $\sqrt{45}$

4. $\sqrt{18}$

5. $2\sqrt{27}$

6. $3\sqrt{75}$

7. $\sqrt{32}$

8. $\sqrt{200}$

9. $\sqrt{8}$

10. $\sqrt{128}$

11. $5\sqrt{2} = \sqrt{x}$

12. $3\sqrt{x} = \sqrt{45}$

13. $2\sqrt{2} = \sqrt{4x}$

14. $4\sqrt{6} = 2\sqrt{3x}$

15. $3\sqrt{14} = \sqrt{6x}$

16. $4\sqrt{3x} = 2\sqrt{6}$

17. $3\sqrt{8} = x\sqrt{2}$

18. $x\sqrt{x} = \sqrt{216}$

CHAPTER EXERCISE: Answers for this chapter start on page 254.

A calculator should NOT be used on the following questions.

1

If $a^{-\frac{1}{2}} = 3$, what is the value of a?

A) -9

B) $\dfrac{1}{9}$

C) $\dfrac{1}{3}$

D) 9

(handwritten: $\frac{1}{\sqrt{a}} = 3$, $1 = 3\sqrt{a}$, $(\frac{1}{3})^2 = a = \frac{1}{9}$)

2

$$n = 1^2 + 1^4 + 1^6 + 1^8 + \ldots + 1^{50}$$

What is the value of n?

A) 10

B) 20

C) 25

D) 30

3

If $4^{2n+3} = 8^{n+5}$, what is the value of n?

A) 6

B) 7

C) 8

D) 9

(handwritten: $4^{2n} \cdot 4^3 = 8^n \cdot 8^5$)

4

If $\dfrac{2^x}{2^y} = 2^3$, then x must equal

A) $y + 3$

B) $y - 3$

C) $3 - y$

D) $3y$

5

If $3^x = 10$, what is the value of 3^{x-3}?

A) $\dfrac{10}{3}$

B) $\dfrac{10}{9}$

C) $\dfrac{10}{27}$

D) $\dfrac{27}{10}$

6

If $x^2 y^3 = 10$ and $x^3 y^2 = 8$, what is the value of $x^5 y^5$?

A) 18

B) 20

C) 40

D) 80

7

If a and b are positive even integers, which of the following is greatest?

A) $(-2a)^b$

B) $(-2a)^{2b}$

C) $(2a)^b$

D) $2a^{2b}$

8

Which of the following is equivalent to $x^{\frac{2a}{b}}$, for all values of x?

A) $\sqrt[b]{ax^2}$

B) $\sqrt[b]{x^{2a}}$

C) $\sqrt[b]{x^{a+2}}$

D) $\sqrt[2a]{x^b}$

9

If $x^2 = y^3$, for what value of z does $x^{3z} = y^9$?

A) -1

B) 0

C) 1

D) 2

10

If $2^{x+3} - 2^x = k(2^x)$, what is the value of k?

A) 3

B) 5

C) 7

D) 8

11

If $\sqrt{x\sqrt{x}} = x^a$, then what is the value of a?

A) $\dfrac{1}{2}$

B) $\dfrac{3}{4}$

C) 1

D) $\dfrac{4}{3}$

12

$$2\sqrt{x+2} = 3\sqrt{2}$$

If $x > 0$ in the equation above, what is the value of x?

A) 2.5

B) 3

C) 3.5

D) 4

13

If $x^{ac} \cdot x^{bc} = x^{30}$, $x > 1$, and $a + b = 5$, what is the value of c?

A) 3

B) 5

C) 6

D) 10

A calculator is allowed on the following questions.

14

If $n^3 = x$ and $n^4 = 20x$, where $n > 0$, what is the value of x?

15

If $x^8y^7 = 333$ and $x^7y^6 = 3$, what is the value of xy?

Percent

First, let's find the total number of questions he got correct:

$$50\% \times 30 = \frac{1}{2} \times 30 = 15$$

$$90\% \times 50 = \frac{9}{10} \times 50 = 45$$

So he got $15 + 45 = 60$ questions correct out of a total of $30 + 50 = 80$ questions. $\frac{60}{80} = \frac{3}{4} = \boxed{75}\%$

Here's the technique for dealing with these "series of percent change" questions. Let the original price be p. When p is increased by 20%, you multiply by 1.20 because it's the original price plus 20%. When it's decreased by 40%, you multiply by .60 because 60% is what's left after you take away 40%. Our final price is then

$$p \times 1.20 \times .60 \times 1.25 = .90p$$

The final price is $\boxed{90\%}$ of the original price.

Example 2 shows the MOST IMPORTANT percent concept by far on the SAT. Never ever calculate the prices at each step. String all the changes together to get the end result.

It's important to know why this works. Imagine again that the original price is p and we want to increase it by 20%. Normally, we would just take p and add 20% of it on top:

$$p + .20p$$

But realize that

$$p + .20p = p(1 + .20) = 1.20p$$

And now we want to decrease this new price by 40%:

$$1.20p - (.40)(1.20p) = (1.20p)(1 - .40) = (1.20p)(0.60) = (1.20)(0.60)p$$

which proves we can calculate the final price directly by using this technique. Now we're set up to tackle the inevitable compound interest questions on the SAT.

EXAMPLE 3: Jonas has a savings account that earns 3 percent interest compounded annually. His initial deposit was $1000. Which of the following expressions gives the value of the account after 10 years?

A) $1000(1.30)^{10}$ B) $1000 + 30(10)$ C) $1000(1.03)(10)$ D) $1000(1.03)^{10}$

A 3 percent interest rate compounded annually means he earns 3 percent on the account once a year. Keep in mind that this isn't just 3% on the original amount of $1000. This is 3% of whatever's in the account at the time, including any interest that he's already earned in previous years. This is the meaning of **compound interest**. So if we're in year 5, he would earn 3% on the original $1000 and 3% on the total interest deposited in years 1 through 4.

If we try to calculate the total after each and every year, this problem would take forever. Let's take what we learned from Example 3 and apply it here:

Year 1 total: $1000(1.03) = 1000(1.03)^1$
Year 2 total: $1000(1.03)(1.03) = 1000(1.03)^2$
Year 3 total: $1000(1.03)(1.03)(1.03) = 1000(1.03)^3$
Year 4 total: $1000(1.03)(1.03)(1.03)(1.03) = 1000(1.03)^4$

See the pattern? Each year is an increase of 3% so it's just 1.03 times whatever the value was last year. Note that we're not doing any calculations out. Think of it as the price of a dress being increased by 3% ten times.

Therefore, the Year 10 total is $1000(1.03)^{10}$, answer $\boxed{(D)}$.

Most of these compound interest questions can be modeled by the equation $A = P(1 + r)^t$, where A is the total amount accumulated, P is the principal or the initial amount, r is the interest rate, and t is the number of times interest is received.

EXAMPLE 4: Jay puts an initial deposit of $400 into a bank account that earns 5 percent interest each year, compounded semiannually. Which of the following equations gives the total dollar amount, A, in the account after t years?

A) $A = 400(1 + 0.05t)$ B) $A = 400(1 + 0.1t)$ C) $A = 400(1.05)^t$ D) $A = 400(1.025)^{2t}$

The interest is compounded *semiannually*. That means twice a year. So interest is received $2t$ times. However, we don't receive a full 5% each time interest is received. The 5% interest rate is a yearly figure. We have to divide it by 2 to get the semiannual rate: 2.5%. The answer is $\boxed{(D)}$.

Note that semiannual compounding is better than annual compounding. Why? With annual compounding, you just get 5% on the initial amount after one year. That's just like 2.5% on the initial amount and then another 2.5% on the initial amount. But with semiannual compounding, you get 2.5% on the initial amount and then you get 2.5% on the mid-year amount, which is greater than the initial amount because it includes the first interest payment. Because you've already earned interest before the end of the year, you get a little extra. This might not seem like a lot, but over many years, it can make a huge difference. The more times interest is compounded, the more money you accumulate.

If interest is compounded more than once a year, the previous formula can be generalized to

$$A = P\left(1 + \frac{r}{n}\right)^{nt}$$

where A is the total amount accumulated, P is the principal or initial amount, r is the interest rate, t is the number of years, and n is the number of times the interest is compounded each year. You don't need to memorize these formulas if you understand the underlying math.

Now that we've shown you how to handle compound interest questions, let's take a step back to bring up **simple interest**. While compound interest lets you earn interest on interest you've earned, simple interest means you get the same amount each time. Interest is earned only on the original amount, not on any interest you've earned.

EXAMPLE 5: An investor decides to offer a business owner a $20,000 loan at simple interest of 5% per year. Which of the following functions gives the total amount, A, in dollars, the investor will receive when the loan is repaid after t years?

A) $A = 20,000(1.05)^t$ B) $A = 20,000(1 + 0.05^t)$ C) $A = 20,000(1.05t)$ D) $A = 20,000(1 + 0.05t)$

At a simple interest of 5%, the investor will receive $20,000(0.05)$ in interest each year. That amount does not change because the 5% always applies to the original $20,000 under simple interest. So after t years, he will receive a total of $20,000(0.05)t$ in interest.

The amount he will be repaid after t years is then

$$A = \text{Original amount} + \text{Total interest}$$
$$= 20,000 + 20,000(0.05)t$$
$$= 20,000(1 + 0.05t)$$

Notice how we factored out the 20,000 in the last step. The answer is $\boxed{(D)}$. The answer would have been (A) under compound interest.

For simple interest, the formula is
$$A = P(1 + rt)$$

where A is the total amount accumulated, P is the principal or initial amount, r is the interest rate, and t is the number of times interest is earned (typically the number of years).

EXAMPLE 6: This year, the chickens on a farm laid 30% less eggs than they did last year. If they laid 3,500 eggs this year, how many did they lay last year?

$$\text{This Year} = (.70)(\text{Last Year})$$
$$3,500 = (.70)(\text{Last Year})$$
$$\boxed{5,000} = \text{Last Year}$$

Percent change (a.k.a. percent increase/decrease) is calculated as follows:

$$\% \text{ change} = \frac{\text{new value} - \text{old value}}{\text{old value}} \times 100$$

For example, if the price of a dress starts out at 80 dollars and rises to 90 dollars, the percent change is:

$$\frac{90 - 80}{80} \times 100 = 12.5\%$$

If percent change is positive, it's a percent increase. Negative? Percent decrease. It's important to remember that percent change is always based on the original value.

EXAMPLE 7: In a particular store, the number of TVs sold the week of Black Friday was 685. The number of TVs sold the following week was 500. TV sales the week following Black Friday were what percent less than TV sales the week of Black Friday (rounded to the nearest percent)?

A) 17%   B) 27%   C) 37%   D) 47%

$$\frac{500 - 685}{685} \approx -0.27$$

We put the difference over 685, NOT 500. Answer $\boxed{(B)}$.

EXAMPLE 8: In a particular store, the number of computers sold the week of Black Friday was 470. The number of computers sold the previous week was 320. Which of the following best approximates the percent increase in computer sales from the previous week to the week of Black Friday?

A) 17%   B) 27%   C) 37%   D) 47%

$$\frac{470 - 320}{320} \approx 0.47$$

This time, the week of Black Friday is not the "original" basis for the percent change. We put the difference over the previous week's number, 320. The answer is $\boxed{(D)}$.

A few more examples involving percent:

> **EXAMPLE 9:** The number of students at a school decreased 20% from 2010 to 2011. If the number of students enrolled in 2011 was k, which of the following expresses the number of students enrolled in 2010 in terms of k?
>
> A) $0.75k$ B) $1.20k$ C) $1.25k$ D) $1.5k$

The answer is NOT $1.20k$. Percent change is based off of the original value (from 2010) and not the new value. Let x be the number of students in 2010,

$$.80x = k$$

$$x = 1.25k$$

Therefore, there were 25% more students in 2010 than in 2011. Answer $\boxed{(C)}$.

> **EXAMPLE 10:** Among 10th graders at a school, 40% of the students are Red Sox fans. Among those Red Sox fans, 20% are also Celtics fans. What percent of the 10th graders at the school are both Red Sox fans and Celtics fans?

We don't know the number of 10th graders at the school so let's suppose that it's 100.

$$\text{Red Sox fans} = 40\% \text{ of } 100 = 40$$

$$\text{Celtics \& Red Sox fans} = 20\% \text{ of } 40 = 8$$

The answer is then $\dfrac{8}{100} = \boxed{8\%}$

A common strategy in percent questions is to make up a number to represent the total, typically 100.

CHAPTER EXERCISE: Answers for this chapter start on page 258.

A calculator is allowed on the following questions.

1

In March, a city zoo attracted 32,000 visitors to its polar bear exhibit. In April, the number of visitors to the exhibit increased by 15%. How many visitors did the zoo attract to its polar bear exhibit in April?

A) 32,150

B) 32,480

C) 35,200

D) 36,800

2

Miguel is following a recipe for marinara sauce that requires half a tablespoon of vinegar. If one cup is equivalent to 16 tablespoons, approximately what percent of a cup of vinegar is the amount required by the recipe?

A) 2.3%

B) 3.1%

C) 9.4%

D) 12.5%

3

If x is 50% larger than z, and y is 20% larger than z, then x is what percent larger than y?

A) 15%

B) 20%

C) 25%

D) 30%

4

Veronica has a bank account that earns m% interest compounded annually. If she opened the account with $200, the expression $200(x)^t$ represents the amount in the account after t years. Which of the following gives x in terms of m?

A) $1 + .01m$

B) $1 + m$

C) $1 - m$

D) $1 + 100m$

5

A charity organization collected 2,140 donations last month. With the help of 50 additional volunteers, the organization collected 2,690 donations this month. To the nearest tenth of a percent, what was the percent increase in the number of donations the charity organization collected?

A) 20.4%

B) 20.7%

C) 25.4%

D) 25.7%

6

The discount price of a book is 20% less than the retail price. James manages to purchase the book at 30% off the discount price at a special book sale. What percent of the retail price did James pay?

A) 42%

B) 48%

C) 50%

D) 56%

7

Each day, Robert eats 40% of the pistachios left in his jar at that time. At the end of the second day, 27 pistachios remain. How many pistachios were in the jar at the start of the first day?

A) 75

B) 80

C) 85

D) 95

8

Joanne bought a doll at a 10 percent discount off the original price of $105.82. However, she had to pay a sales tax of x% on the discounted price. If the total amount she paid for the doll was $100, what is the value of x?

A) 2

B) 3

C) 4

D) 5

9

In 2010, the number of houses built in Town A was 25 percent greater than the number of houses built in Town B. If 70 houses were built in Town A during 2010, how many were built in Town B?

10

Over a two week span, John ate 20 pounds of chicken wings and 15 pounds of hot dogs. Kyle ate 20 percent more chicken wings and 40 percent more hot dogs. Considering only chicken wings and hot dogs, Kyle ate approximately x percent more food, by weight, than John. What is x (rounded to the nearest percent)?

A) 25

B) 27

C) 29

D) 30

11

Jane is playing a board game in which she must collect as many cards as possible. On her first turn, she loses 18 percent of her cards. On the second turn, she increases her card count by 36 percent. If her final card count after these two turns is n, which of the following represents her starting card count in terms of n?

A) $\dfrac{n}{(1.18)(0.64)}$

B) $(1.18)(0.64)n$

C) $\dfrac{n}{(1.36)(0.82)}$

D) $(0.82)(1.36)n$

12

Due to deforestation, researchers expect the deer population to decline by 6 percent every year. If the current deer population is 12,000, what is the approximate expected population size 10 years from now?

A) 4800

B) 6460

C) 7240

D) 7980

13

Kyle bought a $2,000 government bond that yields 6% in simple interest each year. Which of the following equations gives the total amount A, in dollars, Kyle will receive when he sells the bond after t years?

A) $A = 2,000(1 + .06)t$

B) $A = 2,000(1 + 0.06t)$

C) $A = 2,000(1 + 0.06)^t$

D) $A = 2,000(1 + 0.06^t)$

14

A small clothing store sells 3 different types of accessories: 20% are scarves, 60% are ties, and the other 40 accessories are belts. If half of the ties are replaced with scarves, how many scarves will the store have?

15

Daniel has $1000 in a checking account and $3000 in a savings account. The checking account earns him 1 percent interest compounded annually. The savings account earns him 6 percent interest compounded annually. Assuming he leaves both these accounts alone, which of the following represents how much more interest Daniel will have earned from the savings account than from the checking account after 5 years?

A) $3,000(1.06)^5 - 1,000(1.01)^5$

B) $3,000(1.06)(5) - 1,000(1.01)(5)$

C) $(3,000(1.06)^5 - 3,000) - (1,000(1.01)^5 - 1,000)$

D) $(3,000(1.06)(5) - 3,000) - (1,000(1.01)(5) - 1,000)$

16

Kristen opens a bank account that earns 4% interest each year, compounded once every two years. If she opened the account with k dollars, which of the following expressions represents the total amount in the account after t years?

A) $k(1.04)^{2t}$

B) $k(1.04)^{\frac{t}{2}}$

C) $k(1.08)^t$

D) $k(1.08)^{\frac{t}{2}}$

17

$$P\left(1 + \frac{r}{100}\right)^5$$

The expression above gives the population of leopards after five years during which an initial population of P leopards grew by r percent each year. Which of the following expressions gives the percent increase in the leopard population over these five years?

A) $\left(1 + \dfrac{r}{100}\right)^5$

B) $\dfrac{\left(1 + \dfrac{r}{100}\right)^5 - 1}{\left(1 + \dfrac{r}{100}\right)^5} \times 100$

C) $\left[\left(1 + \dfrac{r}{100}\right)^5 - 1\right] \times 100$

D) $\left(1 + \dfrac{r}{100}\right)^5 \times 100$

3

Exponential vs. Linear Growth

The population of ants doubling every month. A bank account earning 5 percent every year. These are examples of **exponential growth**, which occurs when the amount at each stage is multiplied by a number greater than 1. In the case of the ants, this number is 2. In the case of the bank account, it's 1.05. When exponential growth happens, we can model it as a function that looks like

$$y = ax^t$$

where y is the final amount after t time intervals, a is the initial amount, and x is the rate that we multiply by. So if we started off with 100 ants, our equation would be

$$y = 100(2)^t$$

where t is the number of months that have gone by. And if our bank account started off with $200, our equation would look like

$$y = 200(1.05)^t$$

where t is the number of years. You've seen this already in the previous chapter.

Graphs of exponential growth have the following shape:

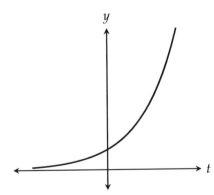

Notice how the graph creeps up slowly at first but then shoots up faster and faster over time. That's exponential growth.

Exponential decay, however, is the opposite. Imagine a radioactive element that loses mass over time. It loses a lot of its mass at first but then loses it more slowly over time.

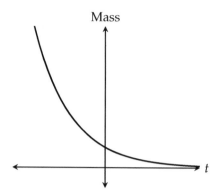

Memorize the shape of these graphs for exponential growth and decay. The SAT will test you explicitly on them.

The equation for exponential decay is the same as the equation for exponential growth:

$$y = ax^t$$

The only difference is that the rate, x, is less than 1. So in the case of radioactive decay, the equation might look like

$$y = 400(0.6)^t$$

where y is the final mass, 400 is the initial amount, and t is the number of years that have gone by.

Now compare exponential growth and decay to linear growth and decay. As you may already know, **linear growth** can be modeled by a line with a positive slope. For example, if Ann has a piggybank with 50 dollars already in it, and she adds 10 dollars every month, the total amount in the piggybank can be modeled by

$$A = 10t + 50$$

where A is the total amount, t is the number of months, and 50 (the y-intercept) is the initial amount.

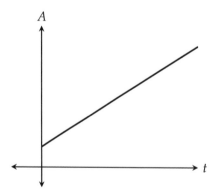

Unlike exponential growth, **linear growth** doesn't have moments when it slows down or speeds up. Growth is constant. It goes up by the same amount each time.

The same holds for **linear decay**. Imagine Ann now takes 10 dollars every month out of her piggybank, which initially contained 100 dollars. The final amount A would be

$$A = 100 - 10t$$

The decrease is at a constant rate, and the slope is negative.

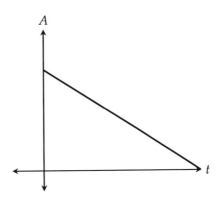

Both exponential decay and linear decay are examples of a **negative association** between two things. As one thing increases, the other thing decreases. For example, the number of absences over the semester and final exam scores:

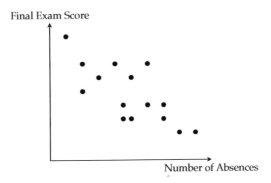

When the data points are close to forming a smooth line or graph that shows the negative relationship, we can say there is a **strong** negative association.

A **positive association** happens when one thing increases, the other thing also increases. We saw this with exponential growth and linear growth. For example, the number of hours spent studying and final exam scores:

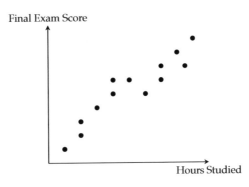

The graph above shows a positive association that is quite strong.

CHAPTER EXERCISE: Answers for this chapter start on page 260.

A calculator should NOT be used on the following questions.

1

If the initial population of rats was 20 and grew to 25 after the first year, which of the following functions best models the population of rats P with respect to the number of years t if the population growth of rats is considered to be exponential?

A) $P = 5t + 20$

B) $P = 20(1.25)^t$

C) $P = 20(5)^t$

D) $P = 5t^2 + 20$

2

If the initial population of pandas was 100 and grew to 125 after the first year, which of the following functions best models the population of pandas P with respect to the number of years t if the population growth of pandas is considered to be linear?

A) $P = 25t + 100$

B) $P = 100(1.25)^t$

C) $P = 100(1.2)^t$

D) $P = 20t^2 + 5t + 100$

3

The population of trees in a forest has been decreasing by 6 percent every 4 years. The population at the beginning of 2015 was estimated to be 14,000. If P represents the population of trees t years after 2015, which of the following equations gives the population of trees over time?

A) $P = 14,000(0.06)^{\frac{t}{4}}$

B) $P = 14,000 + 0.94(4t)$

C) $P = 14,000(0.94)^{4t}$

D) $P = 14,000(0.94)^{\frac{t}{4}}$

A calculator is allowed on the following questions.

4

Which scatterplot shows the strongest positive association between x and y?

A)

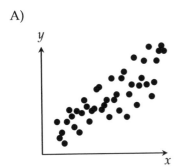

B)

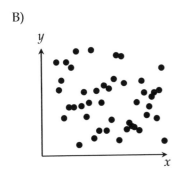

C)

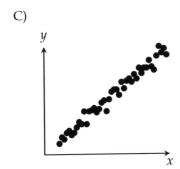

D)

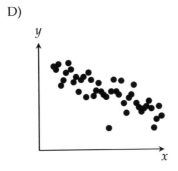

5

Jamie owes Tina some money and decides to pay her back in the following way. Tina receives 3 dollars the first day, 6 dollars the second day, 18 dollars the third day, and 54 dollars the fourth day. Which of the following best describes the relationship between time and the total amount of money (cumulative) Tina has received from Jamie over the course of these four days?

A) Increasing linear

B) Decreasing linear

C) Exponential growth

D) Exponential decay

6

Albert has a large book collection. He decides to trade in two of his used books for one new book each month at a local bookstore. Which of the following best describes the relationship between time (in months) and the total number of books in Albert's collection?

A) Increasing linear

B) Decreasing linear

C) Exponential growth

D) Exponential decay

7

A scientist counts 80 cells in a petri dish and finds that each one splits into two new cells every hour. He uses the function $A(t) = cr^t$ to calculate the total number of cells in the petri dish after t hours. Which of the following assigns the correct values to c and r?

A) $c = 40, r = 2$

B) $c = 80, r = 0.5$

C) $c = 80, r = 1.5$

D) $c = 80, r = 2$

8

Of the following scenarios, which one would result in linear growth of the square footage of a store?

A) The owner increases the square footage by 0.75% each year.

B) The owner increases the square footage by 5% each year.

C) The owner expands the store by 5% of the original square footage each year.

D) The owner alternates between adding 200 square feet one year and 300 square feet the next year.

Proportion

Imagine we have a triangle. We know that the area of a triangle is $A = \frac{1}{2}bh$.

Now let's say we triple the height. What happens to the area?

Well, if we triple the height, the new height is $3h$. The new area is then

$$A_{new} = \frac{1}{2}b(3h) = 3\left(\frac{1}{2}bh\right) = 3A_{old}$$

See what happened? The terms were rearranged so that we could clearly see the new area is three times the old area. We put the "3" out in front of the old formula.

This technique is extremely important because it saves us time on tough proportion problems. We could've made up numbers for the base and the height and calculated everything out, and while that's certainly a strategy you should have in your toolbox, it would've taken much longer and left us more open to silly mistakes.

Let's do a few more complicated examples.

EXAMPLE 1: The radius of a circle is increased by 25%. By what percent does the area of the circle increase?

Let the original area be A_{old}. If the original radius is r, then the new radius is $1.25r$.

$$A_{new} = \pi(1.25r)^2 = (1.25)^2(\pi r^2) = 1.5625(\pi r^2) = 1.5625A_{old}$$

We can see that the area increases by $\boxed{56.25\%}$.

The idea is to get a number in front of the old formula. In the previous example, that number turned out to be 1.5625. Also note that the $1.25r$ was wrapped in parentheses so that the whole thing gets squared. It would've been incorrect to have $A_{new} = \pi(1.25)r^2$ because we wouldn't be squaring the new radius.

EXAMPLE 2: The length of a rectangle is increased by 20%. The width is decreased by 20%. Which of the following accurately describes the change in the area of the rectangle?

A) Increases by 10%   B) Decreases by 10%   C) Decreases by 4%   D) Stays the same

Originally, $A = lw$. Now,

$$A_{new} = (1.20l)(0.80w) = 0.96lw = 0.96A_{old}$$

The area has decreased by 4%. Answer $\boxed{(C)}$. Most students think the answer is (D). It's not.

EXAMPLE 3:

$$F = \frac{9q_1q_2}{r^2}$$

The force of attraction between two particles can be determined by the formula above, in which F is the force between them, r is the distance between them, and q_1 and q_2 are the charges of the two particles. If the distance between two charged particles is doubled, the resulting force of attraction is what fraction of the original force?

A) $\frac{1}{2}$ B) $\frac{1}{4}$ C) $\frac{1}{8}$ D) $\frac{1}{16}$

$$F_{new} = \frac{9q_1q_2}{(2r)^2} = \left(\frac{1}{2}\right)^2 \left(\frac{9q_1q_2}{r^2}\right) = \frac{1}{4}\left(\frac{9q_1q_2}{r^2}\right) = \frac{1}{4}F_{old}$$

Answer $\boxed{(B)}$. Notice how we do not let constants like the "9" in the formula affect the result. In getting a number out front, students often make the mistake of mixing that number up with numbers that were originally in the formula.

EXAMPLE 4: The volume of a cube is tripled. The length of each side must have been increased by approximately what percent?

A) 3%   B) 12%   C) 33%   D) 44%

Now we have to solve backwards. Keep in mind that the volume of a cube is $V = s^3$ where s is the length of each side. Even though this problem is a little different, we can still apply the same process as before: increase each side by some factor and rearrange the terms to extract a number. Only this time, we have to use x.

$$V_{new} = (xs)^3$$
$$V_{new} = x^3s^3 = x^3V_{old}$$

Notice how we were still able to extract something out in front, x^3. That x^3 must be equal to 3 if the new volume is to be triple the old volume:

$$x^3 = 3$$
$$x = \sqrt[3]{3} \approx 1.44$$

Each side must have been increased by approximately 44%. Answer $\boxed{(D)}$.

CHAPTER EXERCISE: Answers for this chapter start on page 261.

A calculator is allowed on the following questions.

1

$$P = \frac{V^2}{R}$$

Electric power P is related to the voltage V and resistance R by the formula above. If the voltage were halved, how would the electric power be affected?

A) The electric power would be 4 times greater.

B) The electric power would be 2 times greater.

C) The electric power would be halved.

D) The electric power would be a quarter of what it was.

2

Julie has a square fence that encloses her garden. She decides to expand her garden by making each side of the fence 10 percent longer. After this expansion, the area of Julie's garden will have increased by what percent?

A) 20%

B) 21%

C) 22%

D) 25%

3

A right circular cone has a base radius of r and a height of h. If the radius is decreased by 20 percent and the height is increased by 10 percent, which of the following is the resulting percent change in the volume of the cone?

A) 10% decrease

B) 12% decrease

C) 18.4% decrease

D) 29.6% decrease

4

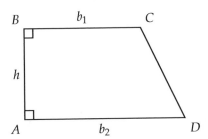

The area of the trapezoid above can be found using the formula $\frac{1}{2}(b_1 + b_2)h$. If lengths BC and AD are halved and the height is doubled, how would the area of the trapezoid change?

A) The area would be increased by 50 percent.

B) The area would stay the same.

C) The area would be decreased by 25 percent.

D) The area would be decreased by 50 percent.

5

Calvin has a sphere that is four times bigger than the one Kevin has in terms of volume. The radius of Calvin's sphere is how many times greater in length than the radius of Kevin's sphere (rounded to the nearest hundredth)?

A) 1.44

B) 1.59

C) 1.67

D) 2.00

6

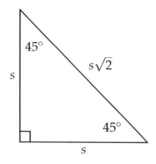

In the triangle above, the lengths of the sides relate to one another as shown. If a new triangle is created by decreasing s such that the area of the new triangle is 64 percent of the original area, s must have been decreased by what percent?

A) 8%

B) 20%

C) 25%

D) 30%

▼

Questions 7-8 refer to the following information.

$$L = 4\pi d^2 b$$

The total amount of energy emitted by a star each second is called its luminosity L, which is related to d, its distance (meters) away from Earth, and b, its brightness measured in watts per square meter, by the formula above.

7

If one star is three times as far away from Earth as another, and twice as bright, its luminosity is how many times greater than that of the other star?

A) 8

B) 9

C) 16

D) 18

8

Astronomers see two equally bright stars, Star A and Star B, in the night sky, but the luminosity of Star A is one-ninth the luminosity of Star B. The distance of Star A from Earth is what fraction of the distance of Star B from Earth?

A) $\dfrac{1}{27}$

B) $\dfrac{1}{9}$

C) $\dfrac{1}{3}$

D) $\dfrac{2}{3}$

▲

5
Rates

I've found rate problems to be pretty polarizing—some students just "get" them intuitively, others get completely lost. Most of the rate problems on the SAT will be pretty straightforward, but for the ones that aren't, I highly recommend using conversion factors to setup the solution (if you've gone through chemistry, you should know what I'm talking about). Conversion factors are a fool-proof way to approach a lot of these problems, but they can be slow-going for stronger problem solvers. I'll be covering both the straightforward, intuitive approaches and the conversion factor approach throughout the examples in this chapter.

EXAMPLE 1: A bicycle manufacturer can produce 20 bicycles per hour. How many hours would it take the manufacturer to produce 320 bicycles?

Easy enough. We divide the total by the rate to get $320 \div 20 = \boxed{16}$ hours.

EXAMPLE 2: A rocket has 360 gallons of fuel left after 2 hours of flight, and only 100 gallons after 6 hours of flight. It burns n gallons of fuel for every hour of flight, where n is a constant. What is the value of n?

Here, we are figuring out the rate. In $6 - 2 = 4$ hours of flight, the rocket burned $360 - 100 = 260$ gallons of fuel. Therefore, the rocket burns $\dfrac{260}{4} = \boxed{65}$ gallons of fuel every hour.

EXAMPLE 3: A box at the supermarket can hold 6 oranges each. Each orange costs 20 cents. Given that the supermarket has a budget of $500 to stock oranges, how many boxes will the supermarket be able to completely fill?

If each orange is 20 cents, then a dollar would be enough for 5 oranges. Five hundred dollars would be enough for $500 \times 5 = 2500$ oranges, which would fill $2500 \div 6 = 416.67$ boxes. Given that the question asks for full boxes, the answer is $\boxed{416}$.

The examples above were quite straightforward and didn't really call for writing out full conversion factors, but what if we wanted to use conversion factors for Example 3? What would've the solution looked like?

$$500 \text{ dollars} \times \frac{100 \text{ cents}}{1 \text{ dollar}} \times \frac{1 \text{ orange}}{20 \text{ cents}} \times \frac{1 \text{ box}}{6 \text{ oranges}} = 416.67 \text{ boxes}$$

The rest of the examples in this chapter are done with conversion factors to teach you how they're used, even though there may be more "casual" solutions.

EXAMPLE 4: A car can travel 1 mile in 1 minute and 15 seconds. At this rate, how many miles can the car travel in 1 hour?

In most rate problems, you'll start with what the question is asking for. We need to convert that 1 hour to a distance that the car travels. The car's rate is 1 mile every 75 seconds.

$$1 \text{ hour} \times \frac{60 \text{ minutes}}{1 \text{ hour}} \times \frac{60 \text{ seconds}}{1 \text{ minute}} \times \frac{1 \text{ mile}}{75 \text{ seconds}} = \frac{60 \times 60 \text{ miles}}{75} = \boxed{48} \text{ miles}$$

The units should cancel as you go along. If the units are canceling, chances are we're doing things right. Notice that the "miles" unit at the end is the unit we wanted to end up with. This is another sign that we've done things right.

EXAMPLE 5: Tom drives 30 miles at an average rate of 50 miles per hour. If Leona drives at an average rate of 40 miles per hour, how many more minutes will it take her to travel the same distance?

We have to figure out how long it takes Tom to drive 30 miles:

$$30 \text{ miles} \times \frac{1 \text{ hour}}{50 \text{ miles}} \times \frac{60 \text{ minutes}}{1 \text{ hour}} = 36 \text{ minutes}$$

Leona will take

$$30 \text{ miles} \times \frac{1 \text{ hour}}{40 \text{ miles}} \times \frac{60 \text{ minutes}}{1 \text{ hour}} = 45 \text{ minutes}$$

So,

$$45 - 36 = \boxed{9} \text{ minutes}$$

EXAMPLE 6: To prepare for class, Mr. Chu has to print a number of booklets with p pages per booklet. If every 5 pages cost c cents to print and he spent a total of d dollars, how many booklets did Mr. Chu print in terms of $p, c,$ and d?

A) $\frac{cp}{500d}$ B) $\frac{100d}{cp}$ C) $\frac{500d}{cp}$ D) $\frac{5d}{cp}$

$$d \text{ dollars} \times \frac{100 \text{ cents}}{1 \text{ dollar}} \times \frac{5 \text{ pages}}{c \text{ cents}} \times \frac{1 \text{ booklet}}{p \text{ pages}} = \frac{500d}{cp} \text{ booklets}$$

The answer is $\boxed{(C)}$.

CHAPTER EXERCISE: Answers for this chapter start on page 263.

A calculator should NOT be used on the following questions.

1

Tim's diet plan calls for 60 grams of protein per day. If Tim were to meet this requirement by only eating a certain protein bar that contains 30 grams of protein, how many protein bars would he have to buy to last a week?

2

An electronics company sells computer monitors and releases a new model every year. With each new model, the company increases the screen size by a constant amount. In 2005, the screen size was 15.5 inches. In 2011, the screen size was 18.5 inches. Which of the following best describes how the screen size changed between 2005 and 2011?

A) The company increases the screen size by 0.5 inch every year.

B) The company increases the screen size by 1 inches every year.

C) The company increases the screen size by 2 inches every year.

D) The company increases the screen size by 3 inches every year.

3

As a submarine descends into the deep ocean, the pressure it must withstand increases. At an altitude of -700 meters, the pressure is 50 atm (atmospheres), and at an altitude of -900 meters, the pressure is 70 atm. For every 10 meters the submarine descends, the pressure it faces increases by n, where n is a constant. What is the value of n?

A) 0.1

B) 1

C) 2

D) 10

4

An empty pool can be filled in 5 hours if water is pumped in at 300 gallons an hour. How many hours would it take to fill the pool if water is pumped in at 500 gallons an hour?

5

If a apples cost d dollars, which of the following expressions gives the cost of 20 apples, in dollars?

A) $\dfrac{20a}{d}$

B) $\dfrac{20d}{a}$

C) $\dfrac{a}{20d}$

D) $\dfrac{20}{ad}$

6

During a race on a circular race track, a racecar burns fuel at a constant rate. After lap 4, the racecar has 22 gallons left in its tank. After lap 7, the racecar has 18 gallons left in its tank. Assuming the racecar does not refuel, after which lap will the racecar have 6 gallons left in its tank?

A) Lap 13

B) Lap 15

C) Lap 16

D) Lap 19

7

By 1:00 PM, a total of 40 boxes had been unloaded from a delivery truck. By 3:30PM, a total of 65 boxes had been unloaded from the same truck. If boxes are unloaded from the truck at a constant rate, what is the total number of boxes that will have been unloaded from the truck by 7:00PM?

8

Amy buys d dollars worth of groceries each week and spends a fourth of those dollars on fruit. In terms of d, how many weeks will it take Amy to spend a total of $100 just on fruit?

A) $\dfrac{400}{d}$

B) $\dfrac{25}{d}$

C) $\dfrac{d}{25}$

D) $\dfrac{d}{400}$

A calculator is allowed on the following questions.

9

Henry drives 150 miles at 30 miles per hour and then another 200 miles at 50 miles per hour. What was his average speed, in miles per hour, for the entire journey, to the nearest hundredth?

A) 38.89

B) 40.00

C) 42.33

D) 43.58

10

A rolling ball covers a distance of 2400 feet in 4 minutes. What is the ball's average speed, in inches per second? (12 inches = 1 foot)

11

Idina can type 90 words in 2.5 minutes. How many words can she type in 12 minutes?

12

A painter can cover a circular region with a radius of 3 feet with paint in 2 minutes. At this rate, how many minutes will it take the painter to cover a circular region with a radius of 6 feet with paint?

13

A "slow" clock falls behind at the same rate every hour. It is set to the correct time at 4:00 AM. When the clock shows 5:00 AM the same day, the correct time is 5:08 AM. When the clock shows 10:30 AM that day, what is the correct time?

A) 11:02 AM

B) 11:18 AM

C) 11:22 AM

D) 12:18 PM

14

A salesman at a tea company makes a $15 commission on every $100 worth of products that he sells. If a jar of tea leaves is $20, how many jars would he have to sell to make $180 in commission?

15

A train covers 32 kilometers in 14.5 minutes. If it continues to travel at the same rate, which of the following is closest to the distance it will travel in 2 hours?

A) 54 kilometers

B) 265 kilometers

C) 364 kilometers

D) 928 kilometers

16

One liter is equivalent to approximately 33.8 ounces. Mark has plastic cups that can each hold 12 ounces of liquid. At most, how many of these plastic cups could a two liter bottle of soda fill?

A) 5

B) 6

C) 7

D) 8

17

Brett currently spends $160 each month on gas. His current car is able to travel 30 miles per gallon of gas. He decides to switch his current car for a new car that is able to travel 40 miles per gallon of gas. Assuming the price of gas stays the same, how much will he spend on gas each month with the new car?

A) $100

B) $120

C) $130

D) $140

18

An 8 inch by 10 inch piece of cardboard costs $2.00. If the cost of a piece of cardboard is proportional to its area, what is the cost of a piece of cardboard that is 16 inches by 20 inches?

A) $4.00

B) $8.00

C) $12.00

D) $16.00

19

Margaret can buy 4 jars of honey for 9 dollars, and she can sell 3 jars of honey for 15 dollars. How many jars of honey would she have to buy and then sell to make a total profit of 132 dollars?

20

In one hour, Jason can install at least 6 windows but no more than 8 windows. Which of the following could be a possible amount of time, in hours, that Jason takes to install 100 windows in a home?

A) 12

B) 16

C) 17

D) 18

21

$$1 \text{ fluid ounce} = 29.6 \text{ milliliters}$$
$$1 \text{ cup} = 16 \text{ fluid ounces}$$

A chemistry teacher is planning to run a class experiment in which each student must measure out 100 milliliters of vinegar in a graduated cylinder. The class is limited to using 6 cups of vinegar. Given the information above, what is the maximum number of students who will be able to participate in this experiment?

Expressions

Algebraic expressions are just combinations of numbers and variables. Both $x^2 + y$ and $\dfrac{3m - k}{2}$ are examples of expressions. In this chapter, we'll cover some fundamental techniques that will allow you to deal with questions involving expressions quickly and effectively.

1. Combining Like Terms

When combining like terms, the most important mistake to avoid is putting terms together that look like they can go together but can't. For example, you cannot combine $b^2 + b$ to make b^3, nor can you combine $a + ab$ to make $2ab$. To add or subtract, the variables have to completely match.

EXAMPLE 1:

$$2(2a^2 - 3a^2b^2 - 4b^2) - (a^2 + 5a^2b^2 - 10b^2)$$

Which of the following is equivalent to the expression above?

A) $-6a^2b^2$ B) $3a^2 - 11a^2b^2 - 18b^2$ C) $3a^2 - 11a^2b^2 + 2b^2$ D) $5a^2 + 2a^2b^2 + 2b^2$

$$2(2a^2 - 3a^2b^2 - 4b^2) - (a^2 + 5a^2b^2 - 10b^2) = 4a^2 - 6a^2b^2 - 8b^2 - a^2 - 5a^2b^2 + 10b^2$$
$$= 3a^2 - 11a^2b^2 + 2b^2$$

Answer $\boxed{(C)}$.

2. Expansion and Factoring

EXAMPLE 2:

$$2(x-4)(2x+3)$$

Which of the following is equivalent to the expression above?

A) $4x^2 - 10x - 24$ B) $4x^2 + 10x - 24$ C) $4x^2 + 10x + 24$ D) $8x^2 - 20x - 24$

Some people like to expand using a method called FOIL (first, outer, inner, last). If you haven't heard of it, that's totally fine. After all, it's the same thing as distributing each term. First, we distribute the "2."

$$2(x-4)(2x+3) = (2x-8)(2x+3)$$

Notice that it applies to just one of the two factors. Either one is fine, but NOT both.

$$(2x-8)(2x+3) = 4x^2 + 6x - 16x - 24$$
$$= 4x^2 - 10x - 24$$

Answer $\boxed{(A)}$.

Now when it comes to factoring and expansion, there are several key formulas you should know:

- $(a+b)^2 = a^2 + 2ab + b^2$
- $(a-b)^2 = a^2 - 2ab + b^2$
- $a^2 - b^2 = (a+b)(a-b)$

Memorize these forwards and backwards. They show up very often.

EXAMPLE 3: Which of the following is equivalent to $4x^4 - 9y^2$?

A) $(2x^2 + 9y)(2x^2 - y)$ B) $(4x^2 + 3y)(x^2 - 3y)$ C) $(x^2 + 3y)(4x^2 - 3y)$ D) $(2x^2 + 3y)(2x^2 - 3y)$

Part of what makes for a top SAT score is pattern recognition. Once you've done enough practice, you should be able to recognize the question above as a difference of two squares, a variation of the $a^2 - b^2$ formula. The SAT will rarely test you on those formulas in a straightforward way. Be on the lookout for variations that match the pattern. With more practice, you'll get better and better at noticing them.

Using the formula $a^2 - b^2 = (a+b)(a-b)$, we can see that $a = 2x^2$ and $b = 3y$. Therefore,

$$4x^4 - 9y^2 = (2x^2 + 3y)(2x^2 - 3y)$$

Answer $\boxed{(D)}$.

EXAMPLE 4:

$$16x^4 - 8x^2y^2 + y^4$$

Which of the following is equivalent to the expression shown above?

A) $(4x^2 + y^2)^2$ B) $(2x - y)^4$ C) $(2x + y)^2(2x - y)^2$ D) $(4x + y)^2(x - y)^2$

Using the formula $(a - b)^2 = a^2 - 2ab + b^2$ (in reverse), we can see that $a = 4x^2$ and $b = y^2$. Therefore,

$$16x^4 - 8x^2y^2 + y^4 = (4x^2 - y^2)^2$$

This is not in the answer choices. We have to take it one step further and apply the $a^2 - b^2$ formula to the expression inside the parentheses.

$$(4x^2 - y^2)^2 = [(2x + y)(2x - y)]^2 = (2x + y)^2(2x - y)^2$$

Answer $\boxed{(C)}$.

3. Combining Fractions

When you're adding simple fractions,

$$\frac{1}{3} + \frac{1}{4}$$

the first step is to find the least common multiple of the denominators. We do this so that we can get a common denominator. In a lot of cases, it's just the product of the denominators, as it is here, $3 \times 4 = 12$.

$$\frac{1}{3} + \frac{1}{4} = \frac{1}{3} \cdot \frac{4}{4} + \frac{1}{4} \cdot \frac{3}{3} = \frac{4}{12} + \frac{3}{12} = \frac{7}{12}$$

Now when we're adding fractions with expressions in the denominator, the idea is the same.

EXAMPLE 5:

$$\frac{1}{x + 2} + \frac{2}{x - 2}$$

Which of the following is equivalent to the expression above?

A) $\dfrac{3x - 2}{(x + 2)(x - 2)}$ B) $\dfrac{3x + 2}{(x + 2)(x - 2)}$ C) $\dfrac{3}{(x + 2)(x - 2)}$ D) $\dfrac{2}{(x + 2)(x - 2)}$

The common denominator is just the product of the two denominators: $(x + 2)(x - 2)$. So now we multiply the top and bottom of each fraction by the factor they don't have:

$$\frac{1}{x + 2} + \frac{2}{x - 2} = \frac{1}{x + 2} \cdot \frac{x - 2}{x - 2} + \frac{2}{x - 2} \cdot \frac{x + 2}{x + 2} = \frac{x - 2}{(x + 2)(x - 2)} + \frac{2(x + 2)}{(x + 2)(x - 2)} = \frac{(x - 2) + 2(x + 2)}{(x + 2)(x - 2)}$$

$$= \frac{3x + 2}{(x + 2)(x - 2)}$$

Answer $\boxed{(B)}$.

4. Flipping (Dividing) Fractions

What's the difference between $\dfrac{\frac{1}{2}}{3}$ and $\dfrac{1}{\frac{2}{3}}$?

The difference is where the longer fraction line is. The first is $\dfrac{1}{2}$ divided by 3. The second is 1 divided by $\dfrac{2}{3}$. They're not the same.

$$\frac{\frac{1}{2}}{3} = \frac{1}{2} \div 3 = \frac{1}{2} \times \frac{1}{3} = \frac{1}{6}$$

$$\frac{1}{\frac{2}{3}} = 1 \div \frac{2}{3} = 1 \times \frac{3}{2} = \frac{3}{2}$$

The shortcut is to flip the fraction that is in the denominator. So,

$$\frac{a}{\frac{b}{c}} = \frac{ac}{b}$$

If the fraction is in the numerator, then the following occurs:

$$\frac{\frac{a}{b}}{c} = \frac{a}{bc}$$

EXAMPLE 6: If $x > 1$, which of the following is equivalent to $\dfrac{x}{\dfrac{1}{x-1} + \dfrac{1}{x+1}}$?

A) $\dfrac{2x^2}{(x-1)(x+1)}$ B) $\dfrac{2}{(x-1)(x+1)}$ C) $\dfrac{x(x-1)(x+1)}{2}$ D) $\dfrac{(x-1)(x+1)}{2}$

First, combine the two fractions on the bottom with the common denominator $(x-1)(x+1)$.

$$\frac{1}{x-1} + \frac{1}{x+1} = \frac{x+1}{(x-1)(x+1)} + \frac{x-1}{(x-1)(x+1)} = \frac{2x}{(x-1)(x+1)}$$

Next, substitute this back in and flip it.

$$\frac{x}{\dfrac{2x}{(x-1)(x+1)}} = \frac{x(x-1)(x+1)}{2x} = \frac{(x-1)(x+1)}{2}$$

Answer $\boxed{(D)}$.

5. Splitting fractions

EXAMPLE 7: Which of the following is equivalent to $\dfrac{30 + c}{6}$?

A) $\dfrac{5 + c}{6}$ B) $\dfrac{10 + c}{2}$ C) $5 + c$ D) $5 + \dfrac{c}{6}$

We can split the fraction into two:

$$\frac{30 + c}{6} = \frac{30}{6} + \frac{c}{6} = 5 + \frac{c}{6}$$

The answer is $\boxed{D}$. This is just the reverse of adding fractions.

Note that while you can split up the numerators of fractions, you cannot do so with denominators. So,

$$\frac{3}{x + y} \neq \frac{3}{x} + \frac{3}{y}$$

In fact, you cannot break up a fraction like $\dfrac{3}{x + y}$ any further.

CHAPTER EXERCISE: Answers for this chapter start on page 265.

A calculator should NOT be used on the following questions.

1

Which of the following is equivalent to $6x^2y + 6xy^2$?

A) $6xy(x + y)$
B) $12xy(x + y)$
C) $6x^2y^2(y + x)$
D) $12x^3y^3$

2

If $a > 0$, then $\dfrac{1}{a} + \dfrac{3}{4}$ is equivalent to which of the following?

A) $\dfrac{3 + 4a}{4a}$

B) $\dfrac{4 + 3a}{4a}$

C) $\dfrac{7}{4a}$

D) $\dfrac{4}{a + 4}$

3

Which of the following is equivalent to $(x^2 + y)(y + z)$?

A) $x^2z + y^2 + yz$
B) $x^2y + x^2z + y^2 + yz$
C) $x^2y + y^2 + x^2z$
D) $x^2 + x^2z + y^2 + yz$

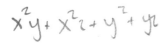

$$x^2y + x^2z + y^2 + yz$$

4

Which of the following is equivalent to $\dfrac{4 + 8x}{12x}$?

A) $\dfrac{1 + 8x}{3x}$

B) $\dfrac{4 + 2x}{3x}$

C) $\dfrac{1 + 2x}{3x}$

D) 1

5

Which of the following is equivalent to $3x^4 - 3$?

A) $3(x^2 + 1)^2$
B) $3(x^2 - 1)^2$
C) $3(x^3 - 1)(x + 1)$
D) $3(x^2 + 1)(x + 1)(x - 1)$

6

$$(x + 1)^2 + 2(x + 1)(y + 1) + (y + 1)^2$$

Which of the following is equivalent to the expression shown above?

A) $(x + y + 1)^2$
B) $(x + y + 2)^2$
C) $(x + y)^2 + 2$
D) $(x + y)^2 - x - y$

7

Which of the following is equivalent to $\dfrac{xy - x^2}{xy - y^2}$?

A) $-\dfrac{y}{x}$

B) $\dfrac{y}{x}$

C) $\dfrac{x}{y}$

D) $-\dfrac{x}{y}$

8

If $x > 1$, which of the following is equivalent to

$$\frac{1}{\dfrac{x-1}{2} + \dfrac{x+5}{3}}?$$

A) $\dfrac{5x+7}{6}$

B) $\dfrac{6}{2x+4}$

C) $\dfrac{6}{5x+7}$

D) $\dfrac{1}{30x+42}$

9

$$\frac{2 + \dfrac{1}{x}}{2 - \dfrac{1}{x}}$$

The expression above is equivalent to which of the following?

A) $\dfrac{2x-1}{2x+1}$

B) $\dfrac{2x+1}{2x-1}$

C) $\dfrac{4x^2-1}{x^2}$

D) -1

10

The expression $8x^2 - \dfrac{1}{2}y^2$ can be written in the form $8(x - cy)(x + cy)$, where c is a positive constant. What is the value of c?

A) $\dfrac{1}{16}$

B) $\dfrac{1}{8}$

C) $\dfrac{1}{4}$

D) $\dfrac{\sqrt{2}}{4}$

A calculator is allowed on the following questions.

11

$$3x^3 + 8x^2 - 4x$$
$$7x^2 - 11x - 7$$

Which of the following is the sum of the two polynomials above?

A) $3x^3 + x^2 - 15x - 7$

B) $3x^3 + 15x^2 - 15x - 7$

C) $10x^5 - 7x - 7$

D) $15x^4 + 3x^3 - 15x^2 - 7$

12

$$(5a + 3\sqrt{a}) - (2a + 5\sqrt{a})$$

Which of the following is equivalent to the expression above?

A) $-2a\sqrt{a}$

B) $a\sqrt{a}$

C) $3a - 2\sqrt{a}$

D) $3a + 8\sqrt{a}$

13

If $y \neq 0$, what is the value of $\dfrac{9(2y)^2 + 2(6y)^2}{8(3y)^2}$?

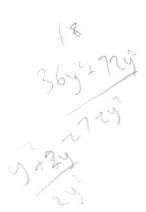

7

Constructing Models

Constructing model questions require you to represent real-life quantities as expressions, equations, and graphs. There's nothing new or difficult here, but you will have to combine what you've learned from the first 6 chapters. We'll do two examples and leave the rest to you in the chapter exercise.

EXAMPLE 1: At a school, there are a grade levels with b students in each grade. If the school buys n stickers to be distributed equally among the students, which of the following gives the number of stickers each student receives?

A) $\dfrac{ab}{n}$ B) $\dfrac{an}{b}$ C) $\dfrac{bn}{a}$ D) $\dfrac{n}{ab}$

The school has a total of $(a)(b) = ab$ students. To find the number of stickers each student receives, we divide the number of stickers n by the number of students: $\dfrac{n}{ab}$. Answer $\boxed{(D)}$.

EXAMPLE 2: Water was pumped into a tank at a constant rate until it was full. The tank was then drained at a slower rate than it had been filled. Which of the following graphs could represent the total amount of water in the tank versus time?

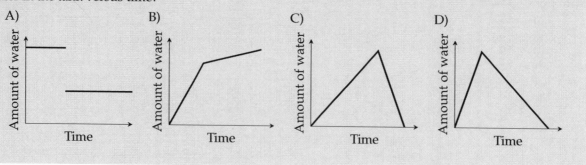

Water being pumped into the tank should be represented by a line going up and to the right (positive slope). Water being drained should be represented by a line going down and to the right (negative slope). That leaves us with answers C and D. Since the tank was drained at a slower rate than it was filled, the answer is $\boxed{(D)}$—the line going down is not as steep as the line going up.

CHAPTER EXERCISE: Answers for this chapter start on page 266.

A calculator should NOT be used on the following questions.

1

A carpenter lays x bricks per hour for y hours and then lays $\dfrac{x}{2}$ bricks for $2y$ more hours. In terms of x and y, how many bricks did he lay in total?

A) $2xy$

B) $\dfrac{5}{2}xy$

C) $5xy$

D) $\dfrac{3}{2}x + 3y$

2

An internet service provider charges a one time setup fee of \$100 and \$50 each month for service. If c customers join at the same time and are on the service for m months, which of the following expressions represents the total amount, in dollars, the provider has charged these customers?

A) $100c + 50m$

B) $100c + 50cm$

C) $150cm$

D) $100m + 50cm$

3

A manufacturing plant increases the temperature of a chemical compound by d degrees Celsius every m minutes. If the compound has an initial temperature of t degrees Celsius, which of the following expressions gives its temperature after x minutes, in degrees Celsius?

A) $\dfrac{mx + t}{d}$

B) $\dfrac{md + t}{x}$

C) $t + \dfrac{d}{mx}$

D) $t + \dfrac{dx}{m}$

4

At a shop for tourists, the price of one souvenir is a dollars. Each additional souvenir purchased after the first is discounted by 40 percent. If James buys n souvenirs, where $n > 1$, which of the following represents the total cost of the souvenirs?

A) $a + (n-1)(0.4a)$

B) $a + (n-1)(0.6a)$

C) $a + n(0.6a)$

D) $0.6an$

5

A cupcake store employs bakers to make boxes of cupcakes. Each box contains x cupcakes and each baker is expected to produce y cupcakes each day. Which of the following expressions gives the number of boxes needed for all the cupcakes produced by $3x$ bakers working for 4 days?

A) $12x^2y$

B) $\dfrac{3y}{4}$

C) $\dfrac{12x^2}{y}$

D) $12y$

6

At a math team competition, there are m schools with n students from each school. The host school wants to order enough pizza such that there are 2 slices for each student. If there are 8 slices in one pizza, which of the following gives the number of pizzas the host school must order?

A) $\dfrac{mn}{8}$

B) $\dfrac{mn}{4}$

C) $\dfrac{m+2n}{8}$

D) $2mn$

7

A retail store has monthly fixed costs of $3,000 and monthly salary costs of $2,500 for each employee. If the store hires x employees for an entire year, which of the following equations represents the store's total cost c, in dollars, for the year?

A) $c = 3,000 + 2,500x$

B) $c = 12(3,000 + 2,500x)$

C) $c = 12(3,000) + 2,500x$

D) $c = 3,000 + 12(2,500x)$

A calculator is allowed on the following questions.

8

On the release date, a vendor puts 8,000 tickets to a particular concert up for sale. After 5 hours, 38% of the tickets have been sold. If the tickets are sold at a constant rate, which of the following functions N models the number of tickets still available t hours after the vendor put them up for sale?

A) $N(t) = 8,000 - 482t$

B) $N(t) = 8,000 - 608t$

C) $N(t) = 8,000(0.38)^{\frac{t}{5}}$

D) $N(t) = 8,000(0.62)^{\frac{t}{5}}$

9

Day	Average speed, s (miles per hour)	Number of calories burned, c
Monday	7.2	616
Thursday	6.8	584
Friday	7.9	672
Saturday	8.5	720

On certain days of the week, Elaine runs for an hour on a treadmill. For each day that she ran in the last week, the table above shows the average speed s at which she ran, in miles per hour, and the number of calories c she burned during the run. If the relationship between c and s can be modeled by a linear function, which of the following functions best models the relationship?

A) $c(s) = 30s + 400$

B) $c(s) = 60s + 210$

C) $c(s) = 80s + 40$

D) $c(s) = 90s - 30$

10

Mike starts driving to work and records his distance from home, in miles, every 10 minutes. His distance from home increases slowly at first due to traffic, then increases more quickly as traffic clears up. Which of the following graphs could illustrate Mike's distance from home during his drive?

A)

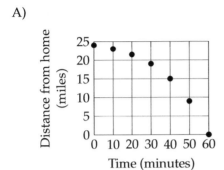

B)

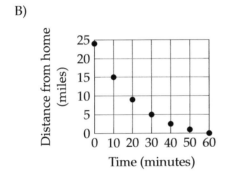

C)

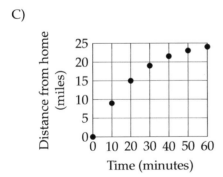

D)

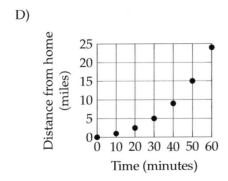

8

Manipulating & Solving Equations

On the SAT, there is a huge emphasis on equations. To get these types of questions right, you must learn how to isolate the variables and expressions you want. First, we'll cover several useful techniques in dealing with equations that you may already be familiar with.

1. Don't forget to combine like terms

You should be ruthless in finding like terms and combining them. Doing so will simplify things and allow you to figure out the next step.

> **EXAMPLE 1:** If $2(a + b + 2c + 3d + 1) = 3a + 2b + 4c + 6d$, find the value of a.

The same four variables are on both sides of the equation, a, b, c and d. That should tell you to distribute on the left side first and then **combine like terms**. Sounds simple but you won't believe how many students forget to do this, especially in the middle of a more complex problem.

$$2(a + b + 2c + 3d + 1) = 3a + 2b + 4c + 6d$$

The $b, c,$ and d variables cancel quite nicely.

$$2a + 2\!\!\!/b + 4\!\!\!/c + 6\!\!\!/d + 2 = 3a + 2\!\!\!/b + 4\!\!\!/c + 6\!\!\!/d$$

$$\boxed{2} = a$$

2. Square and square root correctly

When squaring equations to remove a square root, the most important thing to remember is that you're not squaring individual elements—you're squaring the entire side.

EXAMPLE 2:

$$\sqrt{ab} = a - b$$

If $a > 0$ and $b > 0$, the equation above is equivalent to which of the following?

A) $ab = a^2 - b^2$ B) $ab = a^2 + b^2$ C) $2ab = a^2 - b^2$ D) $3ab = a^2 + b^2$

The square root in the problem should scream to you that the equation should be squared. Most students know the square root should be eliminated, but here's the common mistake they make:

$$ab = a^2 - b^2$$

They square each individual element. However, this is WRONG. When modifying equations, you must apply any given operation to the entire SIDE, like so:

$$(\sqrt{ab})^2 = (a - b)^2$$

If it helps, wrap each side in parentheses before applying the operation. By the way, the same holds true for all other operations, including multiplication and division. When you multiply or divide both sides of an equation, what you're actually doing is wrapping each side in parentheses, but because of the distributive property, it just so happens that multiplying or dividing each individual element gets you the same result. For example, if we had the equation

$$x + 2 = y$$

and we wanted to multiply both sides by 3, what we're actually doing is

$$3(x + 2) = 3(y)$$

which turns out to be the same as

$$3x + 6 = 3y$$

Anyway, back to the problem

$$(\sqrt{ab})^2 = (a - b)^2$$
$$ab = a^2 - 2ab + b^2$$
$$3ab = a^2 + b^2$$

The answer is $\boxed{D}$.

Another common mistake is squaring each side before the square root is isolated on one side. For example,

$$\sqrt{x - 2} + 3 = x$$

Don't square each side until you've moved the "3" on the left to the right:

$$\sqrt{x - 2} = x - 3$$

And now we can square both sides and go from there.

Now, when it comes to taking the square root of an equation, most students forget the plus or minus ($\pm$).

Always remember that an equation such as $x^2 = 25$ has two solutions:

$$\sqrt{x^2} = \sqrt{25}$$
$$x = \pm 5$$

However, this only applies when you're taking the square root to **solve an equation**. By definition, square roots always refer to the positive root. So, $\sqrt{9} = 3$, NOT ± 3. And $\sqrt{x} = -3$ is not possible (except when working with non-real numbers, which we'll look at in a future chapter). The plus or minus is only necessary when the square root is used as a tool to solve an equation. That way, we get all the possible solutions to the equation.

EXAMPLE 3: If $(x+3)^2 = 121$, what is the sum of the two possible values of x?

$$(x+3)^2 = 121$$
$$\sqrt{(x+3)^2} = \pm\sqrt{121}$$
$$x+3 = \pm 11$$
$$x = -3 \pm 11$$

So x could be either 8 or -14. The sum of those two possibilities is $\boxed{-6}$.

3. Cross-multiply when fractions are set equal to each other

Whenever a fraction is equal to another fraction,

$$\frac{a}{b} = \frac{c}{d}$$

you can cross-multiply: $ad = bc$.

EXAMPLE 4: If $\frac{4}{5}x = \frac{10}{3}$, what is the value of x?

$$\frac{4}{5}x = \frac{10}{3}$$
$$12x = 50$$
$$x = \boxed{\frac{25}{6}}$$

EXAMPLE 5: If $\dfrac{5}{x-2} - \dfrac{3}{x+2} = 0$, what is the value of x?

$$\frac{5}{x-2} - \frac{3}{x+2} = 0$$
$$\frac{5}{x-2} = \frac{3}{x+2}$$
$$5(x+2) = 3(x-2)$$
$$5x + 10 = 3x - 6$$
$$2x = -16$$
$$x = \boxed{-8}$$

4. Factoring should be in your toolbox

Some equations have variables that are tougher to isolate. For a lot of these equations, you will have to do some shifting around to factor out the variable you want.

EXAMPLE 6:
$$b = \frac{a}{3a + c}$$

Which of the following expresses a in terms of b and c?

A) $\dfrac{bc}{1 - 3b}$ B) $\dfrac{bc}{3b + 1}$ C) $\dfrac{1 - 3b}{bc}$ D) $\dfrac{3b + 1}{bc}$

$$b = \frac{a}{3a + c}$$
$$b(3a + c) = a$$
$$3ab + bc = a$$
$$bc = a - 3ab$$
$$bc = a(1 - 3b)$$
$$\frac{bc}{1 - 3b} = a$$

See what we did? We expanded everything out and put every term containing a on the right side. Then we were able to factor out a and isolate it. The answer is $\boxed{(A)}$.

53

EXAMPLE 7:

$$x^4 + 3x^3 + x + 3 = 0$$

What is one possible real value of x for which the equation above is true?

$$x^4 + 3x^3 + x + 3 = 0$$

$$x^3(x+3) + (x+3) = 0$$

$$(x+3)(x^3+1) = 0$$

$$x = -3 \text{ or } -1$$

Once we factored out x^3 from the first two terms, further factoring was possible with the $(x+3)$ term. How would you know to do this? Experience.

5. Treat complicated expressions as one unit

EXAMPLE 8:

$$x^3 + x^2 + x = \frac{x\sqrt{x - \dfrac{1}{x}}}{m\left(x + \dfrac{1}{x}\right)}$$

Which of the following gives m in terms of x?

(A) $m = \dfrac{(x^4 + x^3 + x^2)\sqrt{x - \dfrac{1}{x}}}{\left(x + \dfrac{1}{x}\right)}$

(B) $m = \dfrac{\sqrt{x - \dfrac{1}{x}}}{(x^4 + x^3 + x^2)\left(x + \dfrac{1}{x}\right)}$

(C) $m = \dfrac{(x^3 + x^2 + x)\left(x + \dfrac{1}{x}\right)}{x\sqrt{x - \dfrac{1}{x}}}$

(D) $m = \dfrac{x\sqrt{x - \dfrac{1}{x}}}{(x^3 + x^2 + x)\left(x + \dfrac{1}{x}\right)}$

Don't let the big and complicated expressions freak you out. Treat these complicated expressions as one unit or variable, like so:

$$A = \frac{B}{mC}$$

Multiply both sides by m.

$$mA = \frac{B}{C}$$

Divide both sides by A.

$$m = \frac{B}{AC}$$

Finally, plug the original expressions back in.

$$m = \frac{x\sqrt{x - \dfrac{1}{x}}}{(x^3 + x^2 + x)\left(x + \dfrac{1}{x}\right)}$$

Answer $\boxed{(D)}$.

EXAMPLE 9:

$$(x + 1)^2 + 5(x + 1) - 24 = 0$$

If $x > 0$, for what real value of x is the equation above true?

Treat $(x + 1)$ as one unit and call it A.

$$(x + 1)^2 + 5(x + 1) - 24 = 0$$
$$A^2 + 5A - 24 = 0$$
$$(A + 8)(A - 3) = 0$$
$$(x + 1 + 8)(x + 1 - 3) = 0$$
$$(x + 9)(x - 2) = 0$$
$$x = -9 \text{ or } 2$$

Because the question stipulates that $x > 0$, the answer is $\boxed{2}$.

6. Be comfortable solving for expressions, rather than any one variable

EXAMPLE 10: If $3x + 9y = 9$, what is the value of $x + 3y$?

Get in the habit of looking for what you want **before** you solve for anything specific. Is there any way to get the answer without solving for x and y?

Yes! Dividing both sides of the given equation by 3 gives $x + 3y = \boxed{3}$.

EXAMPLE 11: If $\dfrac{x}{y} = 3$, what is the value of $\dfrac{y}{2x}$?

A) $\dfrac{1}{6}$ B) $\dfrac{1}{3}$ C) $\dfrac{2}{3}$ D) $\dfrac{3}{2}$

Here, we have no choice but to solve for the expression. We're given x over y but we want y over x. We can flip the given equation to get

$$\frac{y}{x} = \frac{1}{3}$$

Then we can divide both sides by 2 to obtain the $\dfrac{y}{2x}$ we're looking for.

$$\frac{y}{2x} = \frac{1}{2 \cdot 3} = \frac{1}{6}$$

The answer is $\boxed{(A)}$.

7. Guess and check when you're out of options

When all else fails and you don't have any answer choices or a calculator to work from, it never hurts to guess and check small numbers.

EXAMPLE 12:

$$x^2(x^3 - 4) = 4^x$$

If x is an integer, what is one possible solution to the equation above?

If you have to do a question this complicated without a calculator or any answer choices, you know it has to be solvable through basic guess and check. There's simply no other way.

It would be silly to show you every step of guess and check on this page. Just remember to start with numbers like 0, 1, 2, and -1. In this case, the answer is $\boxed{2}$.

EXERCISE 1: Isolate the variable in **bold**. Answers for this chapter start on page 267.

1. $A = \pi \mathbf{r}^2$

2. $C = 2\pi \mathbf{r}$

3. $A = \frac{1}{2}\mathbf{b}h$

4. $V = l\mathbf{w}h$

5. $V = \pi r^2 \mathbf{h}$

6. $V = \pi \mathbf{r}^2 h$

7. $c^2 = a^2 + \mathbf{b}^2$

8. $V = \mathbf{s}^3$

9. $S = 2\pi r \mathbf{h} + 2\pi r^2$

10. $\frac{\mathbf{a}}{b} = \frac{c}{d}$

11. $\frac{a}{b} = \frac{c}{\mathbf{d}}$

12. $y = m\mathbf{x} + b$

13. $m = \frac{\mathbf{y_2} - y_1}{x_2 - x_1}$

14. $m = \frac{y_2 - y_1}{x_2 - \mathbf{x_1}}$

15. $v^2 = u^2 + 2\mathbf{a}s$

16. $\frac{a}{b} = \frac{x}{\mathbf{y}^2}$

17. $t = 2\pi\sqrt{\dfrac{L}{\mathbf{g}}}$

18. $A = \pi r\sqrt{\mathbf{p} + q}$

19. If $X = \dfrac{X+1}{Y+Z}$, find X in terms of Y and Z.

20. If $x(y+2) = y$, find y in terms of x.

21. If $\dfrac{a}{b} = \dfrac{a+1}{2c}$, find a in terms of b and c.

22. If $t = \dfrac{2}{3}ax$, find ax in terms of t.

23. If $3x + 6y = 7z$, find $x + 2y$ in terms of z.

24. If $x + 5 = 2b$, find $2x + 10$ in terms of b.

25. If $\dfrac{a-1}{2t} = a$, find $4t$ in terms of a.

26. If $\dfrac{p-h}{p+h} = \dfrac{2}{3}$, find $\dfrac{p}{h}$.

27. If $\dfrac{1+2r}{1-t} = \dfrac{1}{2}$, find t in terms of r.

28. If $x^y = z$, then find x^{2y} in terms of z.

29. If $\dfrac{4^{x+1}}{x^3 - x^2} = p(x^5 - x^4)$, what is p in terms of x?

30. If $2^x\left(x^3 - \dfrac{1}{x}\right) = m(x^2 + 1) - \dfrac{1}{x^2}$, what is m in terms of x?

31. If $\dfrac{\sqrt{x}+1}{5x^2 - 3} - x^3 = \dfrac{1}{nx}$, what is n in terms of x?

32. If $a(b^2 + 2) + c = 5(c+1)^3$, what is a in terms of b and c?

33. If $k(x^2 + 4) + ky = \dfrac{7x^2 + 3}{2}$, what is k in terms of x and y?

34. If $ax + 3a + x + 3 = b$, what is x in terms of a and b?

6|9

CHAPTER EXERCISE: Answers for this chapter start on page 267.

A calculator should NOT be used on the following questions.

1

If $a + b = -2$, then $(a + b)^3 =$

A) 4

B) 0

C) −4

D) −8

2

For what value of n is $(n - 4)^2 = (n + 4)^2$?

3

If $\dfrac{1}{a} \times \dfrac{b}{c} = 1$, what is the value of $b - ac$?

A) −3

B) 0

C) 2

D) It cannot be determined from the information given.

4

If $3x - 8 = -23$, what is the value of $6x - 7$?

A) −5

B) −21

C) −30

D) −37

5

If $\dfrac{4}{9} = \dfrac{8}{3}m$, what is the value of m?

A) $\dfrac{1}{6}$

B) $\dfrac{2}{3}$

C) $\dfrac{5}{6}$

D) 6

6

If $3x + 1 = -8$, what is the value of $(x + 2)^3$?

A) −1

B) 1

C) 8

D) 125

7

If $\dfrac{4}{k + 2} = \dfrac{x}{3}$, where $k \neq -2$, what is k in terms of x?

A) $\dfrac{12 - 2x}{x}$

B) $\dfrac{12 + 2x}{x}$

C) $\dfrac{x}{12 + 2x}$

D) $12x - 2$

8

If $(x - 3)^2 = 36$ and $x < 0$, what is the value of x^2?

9

$$f = p\left(\frac{(1+i)^n - 1}{i}\right)$$

The formula above gives the future value f of an annuity based on the monthly payment p, the interest rate i, and the number of months n. Which of the following gives p in terms of f, i, and n?

A) $\dfrac{fi}{(1+i)^n - 1}$

B) $\dfrac{(1+i)^n - 1}{fi}$

C) $\dfrac{f - i}{(1+i)^n - 1}$

D) $fi + 1 - (1+i)^n$

10

If $\dfrac{m}{2n} = 2$, what is the value of $\dfrac{n}{2m}$?

A) $\dfrac{1}{8}$

B) $\dfrac{1}{4}$

C) $\dfrac{1}{2}$

D) 1

11

If $x < 0$ and $x^2 - 12 = 4$, what is the value of x?

A) -16

B) -8

C) -4

D) -2

12

If $x^2 + 7 = 21$, then what is the value of $x^2 + 3$?

13

$$x^2 + 5x - 24 = 0$$

If k is a solution of the equation above and $k < 0$, what is the value of $|k|$?

14

$$x^2(x^4 - 9) = 8x^4$$

If $x > 0$, for what real value of x is the equation above true?

15

If $\dfrac{2\sqrt{x+4}}{3} = 6$ and $x > 0$, what is the value of x?

16

$$20 - \sqrt{x} = \frac{2}{3}\sqrt{x} + 10$$

If $x > 0$, for what value of x is the equation above true?

A calculator is allowed on the following questions.

17

If $\dfrac{x}{6} = \dfrac{x+12}{42}$, what is the value of $\dfrac{6}{x}$?

A) $\dfrac{1}{3}$

B) 2

C) 3

D) 6

18

$$d = a\left(\dfrac{c+1}{24}\right)$$

Doctors use Cowling's rule, shown above, to determine the right dosage d, in milligrams, of medication for a child based on the adult dosage a, in milligrams, and the child's age c, in years. Ben is a patient who is in need of a certain medication. If a doctor uses Cowling's rule to prescribe Ben a dosage that is half the adult dosage, what is Ben's age, in years?

A) 7

B) 9

C) 11

D) 13

19

If $3(x - 2y) - 3z = 0$, which of the following expresses x in terms of y and z?

A) $\dfrac{2y + 3z}{3}$

B) $2y + z$

C) $y + 2z$

D) $6y + 3z$

20

$$xy^2 + x - y^2 - 1 = 0$$

If the equation above is true for all real values of y, what must the value of x be?

Questions 21-22 refer to the following information.

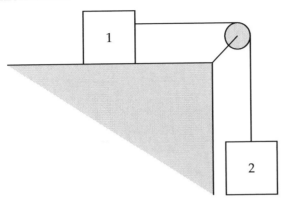

In the figure above, two objects are connected by a string which is threaded through a pulley. Using its weight, object 2 moves object 1 along a flat surface. The acceleration a of the two objects can be determined by the following formula

$$a = \frac{m_2 g - \mu m_1 g}{m_1 + m_2}$$

where m_1 and m_2 are the masses of object 1 and object 2, respectively, in kilograms, g is the acceleration due to Earth's gravity measured in $\frac{m}{\sec^2}$, and μ is a constant known as the coefficient of friction.

21

Which of the following expresses μ in terms of the other variables?

A) $\mu = \dfrac{a(m_1 + m_2)}{m_1 m_2 g^2}$

B) $\mu = \dfrac{a(m_1 + m_2)}{m_2 g - m_1 g}$

C) $\mu = \dfrac{m_2 g - a(m_1 + m_2)}{m_1 g}$

D) $\mu = \dfrac{a(m_1 + m_2) - m_2 g}{m_1 g}$

$d(m_1 + m_2) = m_2 g^m m_1 g$

$\dfrac{a(m_1 + m_2)}{g}$

22

If the masses of both object 1 and object 2 were doubled, how would the acceleration of the two objects be affected?

A) The acceleration would stay the same.

B) The acceleration would be halved.

C) The acceleration would be doubled.

D) The acceleration would be quadrupled (multipled by a factor of 4).

Questions 23-24 refer to the following information.

$$V = P(1 - r)^t$$

The value V of a car depreciates over t years according to the formula above, where P is the original price and r is the annual rate of depreciation.

23

Which of the following expresses r in terms of $V, P,$ and t?

A) $r = 1 - \sqrt[t]{\dfrac{V}{P}}$

B) $r = 1 + \sqrt[t]{\dfrac{V}{P}}$

C) $r = \sqrt[t]{\dfrac{V}{P}} - 1$

D) $r = 1 - \dfrac{\sqrt[t]{V}}{P}$

24

If a car depreciates to a value equal to half its original price after 5 years, then which of the following is closest to the car's annual rate of depreciation?

A) 0.13

B) 0.15

C) 0.16

D) 0.2

9

More Equation Solving Strategies

In this chapter, we'll touch on two equation solving strategies that are necessary for some of the tougher questions.

1. Matching coefficients

EXAMPLE 1: If $(x + a)^2 = x^2 + 8x + b$, what is the value of b?

It's hard to see anything meaningful right away on both sides of the equation. So let's expand the left side first and see if that takes us anywhere.

$$(x + a)^2 = (x + a)(x + a) = x^2 + 2ax + a^2$$

So now we have

$$x^2 + 2ax + a^2 = x^2 + 8x + b$$

We can match up the coefficients.

$$x^2 + \underline{2a}x + \underline{a^2} = x^2 + \underline{8}x + \underline{b}$$

So,

$$2a = 8$$
$$a^2 = b$$

Solving the equations, $a = 4$ and $b = \boxed{16}$.

63

2. Clearing denominators

When you solve an equation like $\frac{1}{2}x + \frac{1}{3}x = 10$, a likely first step is to get rid of the fractions, which are harder to work with. How do we do that? By multiplying both sides by 6. But where did that 6 come from? 2 times 3. So this is what you're actually doing when you multiply by 6:

$$\frac{1}{2}x \cdot (2 \cdot 3) + \frac{1}{3}x \cdot (2 \cdot 3) = 10 \cdot (2 \cdot 3)$$

$$\frac{1}{\cancel{2}}x \cdot (\cancel{2} \cdot 3) + \frac{1}{\cancel{3}}x \cdot (2 \cdot \cancel{3}) = 10 \cdot (2 \cdot 3)$$

$$3x + 2x = 60$$

We got rid of the fractions by clearing the denominators. Here's the takeaway: we can do the same thing even when there are variables in the denominators.

EXAMPLE 2:

$$\frac{3}{x} + \frac{5}{x+2} = 2$$

If x is a solution to the equation above and $x > 0$, what is the value of x?

In the same way we multiplied by $2 \cdot 3$ before, we can multiply by $x(x+2)$ here.

$$\frac{3}{x} \cdot x(x+2) + \frac{5}{x+2} \cdot x(x+2) = 2 \cdot x(x+2)$$

$$\frac{3}{\cancel{x}} \cdot \cancel{x}(x+2) + \frac{5}{\cancel{x+2}} \cdot x\cancel{(x+2)} = 2x(x+2)$$

$$3(x+2) + 5x = 2x^2 + 4x$$

$$3x + 6 + 5x = 2x^2 + 4x$$

$$0 = 2x^2 - 4x - 6$$

$$0 = x^2 - 2x - 3$$

$$0 = (x-3)(x+1)$$

$x = 3$ or $x = -1$ but because $x > 0$, $x = \boxed{3}$.

Here's one final example that showcases both of the strategies in this chapter.

EXAMPLE 3:

$$\frac{3x}{x+1} + \frac{5}{ax+2} = \frac{-6x^2 + 11x + 5}{(x+1)(ax+2)}$$

In the equation above, $x \neq -\dfrac{2}{a}$ and a is a constant. What is the value of a?

A) -6 B) -2 C) 2 D) 6

Let's clear the denominators by multiplying both sides by $(x+1)(ax+2)$:

$$\frac{3x}{x+1} \cdot (x+1)(ax+2) + \frac{5}{ax+2} \cdot (x+1)(ax+2) = \frac{-6x^2 + 11x + 5}{(x+1)(ax+2)} \cdot (x+1)(ax+2)$$

$$\frac{3x}{\cancel{x+1}} \cdot \cancel{(x+1)}(ax+2) + \frac{5}{\cancel{ax+2}} \cdot (x+1)\cancel{(ax+2)} = \frac{-6x^2 + 11x + 5}{\cancel{(x+1)}\cancel{(ax+2)}} \cdot \cancel{(x+1)}\cancel{(ax+2)}$$

$$3x(ax+2) + 5(x+1) = -6x^2 + 11x + 5$$

$$3ax^2 + 6x + 5x + 5 = -6x^2 + 11x + 5$$

Comparing the coefficients of the x^2 term on either side, $3a = -6$. Therefore, $a = -2$. Answer $\boxed{(B)}$.

CHAPTER EXERCISE: Answers for this chapter start on page 272.

A calculator should NOT be used on the
following questions.

1

If $(2x + 3)(ax - 5) = 12x^2 + bx - 15$ for all
values of x, what is the value of b?

A) 6

B) 8

C) 10

D) 12

2

If $(x + 3y)^2 = x^2 + 9y^2 + 42$, what is the value of
x^2y^2?

3

If $\dfrac{ab + a}{b} = \dfrac{a}{b} + 5$ for all values of b, what is the
value of a?

4

If $\dfrac{1}{x} - \dfrac{1}{x - 4} = 1$, what is the value of x?

5

If $n < 0$ and $4x^2 + mx + 9 = (2x + n)^2$, what is
the value of $m + n$?

A) -15

B) -9

C) -3

D) 12

6

If $\dfrac{1}{x} + \dfrac{1}{y} = \dfrac{1}{p}$, what is x in terms of p and y?

A) $p - y$

B) $\dfrac{py}{p + y}$

C) $\dfrac{py}{p - y}$

D) $\dfrac{py}{y - p}$

7

$$(2x + a)(3x + b) = 6x^2 + cx + 7$$

In the equation above, a and b are integers. If the
equation is true for all values of x, what are the
two possible values of c?

A) 8 and 12

B) 14 and 21

C) 15 and 18

D) 17 and 23

8

$$\frac{12x^2 + mx + 23}{2x + 1} = 6x - 18 + \frac{41}{2x + 1}$$

In the equation above, m is a constant and $x \neq -\frac{1}{2}$. What is the value of m?

A) -42

B) -36

C) -30

D) 42

9

$$(x^3 + kx^2 - 3)(x - 2) = x^4 + 7x^3 - 18x^2 - 3x + 6$$

In the equation above, k is a constant. If the equation is true for all values of x, what is the value of k?

A) -9

B) 5

C) 7

D) 9

10

$$\frac{3}{n - 1} + \frac{2n}{n + 1} = 3$$

If $n > 0$, for what value of n is the equation above true?

11

What is one possible solution to the equation $\frac{12}{x + 2} - \frac{2}{x - 2} = 1$?

12

$$\frac{4}{x - 1} + \frac{2}{x + 1} = \frac{35}{x^2 - 1}$$

If $x > 1$, what is the solution to the equation above?

10
Systems of Equations

A system of equations refers to 2 or more equations that deal with the same set of variables.

$$-5x + y = -7$$
$$-3x - 2y = -12$$

There are two main ways of solving systems of 2 equations: substitution and elimination.

Substitution

Substitution is all about isolating one variable, either x or y, in the fastest way possible.

Taking the example above, we can see that it's easiest to isolate y in the first equation because it has no coefficient. Adding $5x$ to both sides, we get

$$y = 5x - 7$$

We can then substitute the y in the second equation with $5x - 7$ and solve from there.

$$-3x - 2(5x - 7) = -12$$
$$-3x - 10x + 14 = -12$$
$$-13x = -26$$
$$x = 2$$

Substituting $x = 2$ back into $y = 5x - 7$, $y = 5(2) - 7 = 3$.

The solution is $x = 2, y = 3$, which can be denoted as $(2, 3)$.

Elimination

Elimination is about getting the same coefficients for one variable across the two equations so that you can add or subtract the equations, thereby eliminating that variable.

Using the same example, we can multiply the first equation by 2 so that the y's have the same coefficient (we don't worry about the sign because we can add or subtract the equations).

$$-10x + 2y = -14$$
$$-3x - 2y = -12$$

To eliminate y, we add the equations.

$$
\begin{array}{r}
-10x + 2y = -14 \\
-3x - 2y = -12 \\
\hline
-13x = -26
\end{array}
$$

Now, we can see that $x = 2$. This result can be used in either of the original equations to solve for y. We'll pick the first equation.

$$
\begin{aligned}
-10(2) + 2y &= -14 \\
-20 + 2y &= -14 \\
2y &= 6 \\
y &= 3
\end{aligned}
$$

And finally, we get the same solution as we got using substitution: $x = 2, y = 3$.

When solving systems of equations, you can use either method, but one of them will typically be faster. If you see a variable with no coefficient, like in $-5x + y = -7$ above, substitution is likely the best route. If you see matching coefficients or you see that it's easy to get matching coefficients, elimination is likely the best route. The example above was simple enough for both methods to work well (though substitution was slightly faster). In these cases, it comes down to your personal preference.

No solutions

A system of equations has no solutions when the same equation is set to a different constant:

$$
\begin{aligned}
3x + 2y &= 5 \\
3x + 2y &= -4
\end{aligned}
$$

The equations above contradict each other. There is no x and y that will make both of them true at the same time. The system has no solution. Note that

$$
\begin{aligned}
3x + 2y &= 5 \\
6x + 4y &= -8
\end{aligned}
$$

also has no solution. Why? Because the second equation can be divided by 2 to get the original equation.

EXAMPLE 1:

$$-ax - 12y = 15$$
$$4x + 3y = -2$$

If the system of equations above has no solution, what is the value of a?

We must get the coefficients to match so that we can compare the two equations. To do that, we multiply the second equation by -4:

$$-ax - 12y = 15$$
$$-16x - 12y = 8$$

See how the -12's match now? Now let's compare. If $\boxed{a = 16}$, then we get our two contradicting equations with no solution. One is set to 15 and the other is set to 8.

Infinite solutions

A system of equations has infinite solutions when both equations are essentially the same:

$$3x + 2y = 5$$
$$3x + 2y = 5$$

$(1, 1), (3, -2), (5, -5)$ are all solutions to the system above, to name just a few. Note that

$$6x + 4y = 10$$
$$3x + 2y = 5$$

also has an infinite number of solutions. The first equation can be divided by 2 to get the same equation as the second.

EXAMPLE 2:

$$3x - 5y = 8$$
$$mx - ny = 32$$

In the system of equations above, m and n are constants. If the system has infinitely many solutions, what is the value of $m + n$?

Both equations need to be the same for there to be an infinite number of solutions. We multiply the first equation by 4 to get the right hand sides to match:

$$12x - 20y = 32$$
$$mx - ny = 32$$

Now we can clearly see that $m = 12$ and $n = 20$. Therefore, $m + n = \boxed{32}$.

Word problems

You will most definitely run into a question that asks you to translate a situation into a system of equations. Here's a classic example:

EXAMPLE 3: A group of 30 students order lunch from a restaurant. Each student gets either a burger or a salad. The price of a burger is $5 and the price of a salad is $6. If the group spent a total of $162, how many students ordered burgers?

Let x be the number of students who ordered burgers and y be the number who ordered salads. We can then make two equations:

$$x + y = 30$$
$$5x + 6y = 162$$

Make sure you completely understand how these equations were made. This type of question is guaranteed to be on the test.

We'll use elimination to solve this system. Multiply the first equation by 6 and subtract:

$$6x + 6y = 180$$
$$5x + 6y = 162$$
$$\overline{ x = \boxed{18}}$$

18 students got burgers.

More complex systems

You might encounter systems of equations that are a bit more complicated than the standard ones you've seen above. For these systems, substitution and some equation manipulation will typically do the trick.

EXAMPLE 4:

$$y + 3x = 0$$
$$x^2 + 2y^2 = 76$$

If (x, y) is a solution to the system of equations above and $y > 0$, what is the value of y?

In the first equation, we isolate y to get $y = -3x$. Plugging this into the second equation,

$$x^2 + 2(-3x)^2 = 76$$
$$x^2 + 2(9x^2) = 76$$
$$x^2 + 18x^2 = 76$$
$$19x^2 = 76$$
$$x^2 = 4$$
$$x = \pm 2$$

If $x = 2$, then $y = -3(2) = -6$. If $x = -2$, then $y = -3(-2) = 6$. Because $y > 0$, $y = \boxed{6}$.

EXAMPLE 5:

$$xy + 2y = 2$$
$$\left(\frac{1}{x+2}\right)^2 + \left(\frac{1}{x+2}\right) - 6 = 0$$

If (x, y) is a solution to the equation above, what is a possible value for $|y|$?

Notice the $(x + 2)$'s lying around in both equations. This is a hint that there might be a clever substitution somewhere, especially for a problem as complicated as this one. Isolating y in the first equation,

$$xy + 2y = 2$$
$$y(x + 2) = 2$$
$$y = \frac{2}{x + 2}$$

From here, $\dfrac{y}{2} = \dfrac{1}{x+2}$. Why would I want this form? So I can substitute $\dfrac{1}{x+2}$ in the second equation with $\dfrac{y}{2}$. As you do these tougher questions, you must keep an eye out for any simplifying manipulations such as this one.

Substituting, we get

$$\left(\frac{1}{x+2}\right)^2 + \left(\frac{1}{x+2}\right) - 6 = 0$$

$$\left(\frac{y}{2}\right)^2 + \left(\frac{y}{2}\right) - 6 = 0$$

$$\frac{y^2}{4} + \frac{y}{2} - 6 = 0$$

$$y^2 + 2y - 24 = 0$$

$$(y+6)(y-4) = 0$$

Finally, $y = -6$ or 4, and $|y|$ can be either $\boxed{6 \text{ or } 4}$.

How will you know whether there's a clever substitution or "trick" you can use? Practice. And even then, you won't always know for sure. Just keep in mind that SAT questions are designed to be done without a crazy number of steps. So if you feel like you're running in circles or hitting a wall, take a step back and try something else. To get a perfect score, you must be comfortable with trial and error.

EXAMPLE 6: If $xy = 8$, $xz = 5$, and $yz = 10$, what is the value of xyz?

Here's the trick. Multiply all three equations. Multiply the left sides, and multiply the right sides. The result is

$$x^2 y^2 z^2 = 400$$

Square root both sides.

$$xyz = \boxed{20}$$

Notice how we were able to get the answer without knowing the values of $x, y,$ or z.

Graphs

Learning a bit about equations and their graphs will inform our understanding of systems of equations.

The solutions to a system of equations are the intersection points of the graphs of the equations. Therefore, the number of solutions to a system of equations is equal to the number of intersection points.

Take, for example, the system of equations at the beginning of this chapter:

$$-5x + y = -7$$
$$-3x - 2y = -12$$

We can put both equations into $y = mx + b$ form (we won't show that here) and graph them to get the following lines.

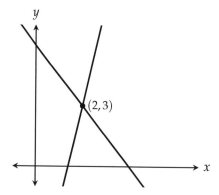

The solution to the system, $(2, 3)$, is the intersection point. There is only one intersection point, so there is only one solution.

What about graphs of systems that have infinite solutions or no solutions?

Graphing the following system, which has no solution because its equations contradict each other,

$$y - 2x = 1$$
$$y - 2x = -3$$

we get

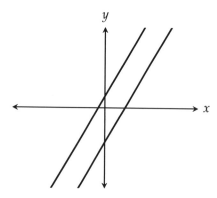

What do you notice about the lines? They have no intersection points. They're parallel. Makes sense, right?

And for a system with infinite solutions?

$$2y - 4x = 2$$
$$y - 2x = 1$$

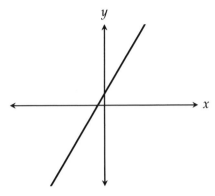

It's just one line! Well, actually it's two lines, but because they're the same line, they overlap and intersect in an infinite number of places. Hence, an infinite number of solutions.

EXAMPLE 7: In the xy-plane, the lines $y = 3x - 5$ and $y = -2x + 10$ intersect at the point (h, k). What is the value of k?

As mentioned earlier, the solutions to a system of equations are the intersection points of the graphs of those equations, and vice versa. **So to find the point(s) where two graphs intersect, solve the system consisting of their equations.** In this problem, that system is

$$y = 3x - 5$$
$$y = -2x + 10$$

Substituting the first equation into the second, we get

$$3x - 5 = -2x + 10$$
$$5x = 15$$
$$x = 3$$

When $x = 3$, $y = 3(3) - 5 = 4$. So the two lines intersect at $(3, 4)$ and $k = \boxed{4}$.

EXAMPLE 8:

$$y = x^2 - 5x + 6$$
$$y = x + 1$$

The system of equations above is graphed in the xy-plane. If the ordered pair (x, y) represents an intersection point of the graphs of the two equations, what is one possible value of y ?

The solutions to the system are the intersection points, so let's solve the system. Substituting the first equation into the second, we get

$$x^2 - 5x + 6 = x + 1$$
$$x^2 - 6x + 5 = 0$$
$$(x - 1)(x - 5) = 0$$
$$x = 1 \text{ or } 5$$

When $x = 1$, $y = 1 + 1 = 2$. When $x = 5$, $y = 5 + 1 = 6$. So the graphs of the two equations intersect at $(1, 2)$ and $(5, 6)$, which means the possible values of y are $\boxed{2}$ and $\boxed{6}$.

EXAMPLE 9:

$$y^2 = x + 3$$
$$y = |x|$$

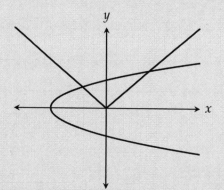

A system of two equations and their graphs in the xy-plane are shown above. How many solutions does the system have?

A) One   B) Two   C) Three   D) Four

Simple. The graphs intersect in two places so there are two solutions. Answer $\boxed{(B)}$.

CHAPTER EXERCISE: Answers for this chapter start on page 275.

A calculator should NOT be used on the following questions.

1

$$3x - 5y = -11$$
$$x = 1 - 3y$$

What is the solution (x, y) to the system of equations above?

A) $(-5, 2)$

B) $(-2, 1)$

C) $(1, 0)$

D) $(4, -1)$

2

$$y + 2x = 20$$
$$6x - 5y = 12$$

What is the solution (x, y) to the system of equations above?

A) $(-7, 6)$

B) $(-6, 7)$

C) $(6, 7)$

D) $(7, 6)$

3

$$3x - 4y = 21$$
$$4x - 3y = 14$$

If (x, y) is a solution to the system of equations above, what is the value of $y - x$?

A) -18

B) -5

C) 5

D) 8

4

$$2x + 5y = 24$$
$$x + 4y = 15$$

If (x, y) satisfies the system of equations above, what is the value of $x + y$?

A) 7

B) 8

C) 9

D) 10

5

$$3x + y = -2x + 8$$
$$-3x + 2y = -10$$

If (x, y) is a solution to the system of equations above, what is the value of xy?

A) -16

B) -8

C) -4

D) 4

6

$$y = ax + b$$
$$y = -bx$$

The equations of two lines in the xy-plane are shown above, where a and b are constants. If the two lines intersect at $(2, 8)$, what is the value of a?

A) 2

B) 4

C) 6

D) 8

7

$$y = x^2 + 1$$
$$y = x - 1$$

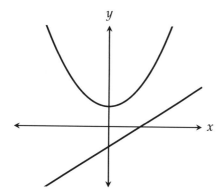

A system of two equations and their graphs in the xy-plane are shown above. How many solutions does the system have?

A) Zero

B) One

C) Two

D) Three

8

$$-5x = y + 2$$
$$2(2x - 1) = 3 - 3y$$

What is the solution (x, y) to the system of equations above?

A) $(-2, 8)$

B) $(-1, 3)$

C) $(1, -7)$

D) $(3, -17)$

9

$$2x - 4y = 8$$
$$x + 2y = 4$$

How many solutions (x, y) are there to the system of equations above?

A) Zero

B) One

C) Two

D) More than two

10

$$2x - 5y = a$$
$$bx + 10y = -8$$

In the system of equations above, a and b are constants. If the system has infinitely many solutions, what is the value of a?

A) -4

B) $\dfrac{1}{4}$

C) 4

D) 16

11

$$ax + 2y = 5$$
$$3x - 6y = 20$$

In the system of equations above, a is a constant. If the system has one solution, which of the following can NOT be the value of a?

A) -1

B) $\dfrac{3}{4}$

C) 1

D) 3

12

$$4x - \frac{1}{3}y = -8$$

$$y = 4x + 16$$

What is the solution (x, y) to the system of equations above?

A) $(-2, 8)$

B) $(-1, 12)$

C) $(1, 20)$

D) $(3, 28)$

13

$$y = 0.5x + 14$$

$$x - y = -18$$

According to the system of equations above, what is the value of y?

14

$$\frac{1}{3}x - \frac{1}{6}y = 4$$

$$6x - ay = 8$$

In the system of equations above, a is a constant. If the system has no solution, what is the value of a?

A) $\frac{1}{3}$

B) 1

C) 3

D) 6

15

$$3x - 6y = 15$$

$$-2x + 4y = -10$$

How many solutions (x, y) are there to the system of equations above?

A) Zero

B) One

C) Two

D) More than two

16

$$mx - 6y = 10$$

$$2x - ny = 5$$

In the system of equations above, m and n are constants. If the system has infinitely many solutions, what is the value of $\frac{m}{n}$?

A) $\frac{1}{12}$

B) $\frac{1}{3}$

C) $\frac{4}{3}$

D) 3

17

$$y = \sqrt{x} + 3$$

$$\sqrt{4x} - y = 3$$

If (x, y) is the solution to the system of equations above, what is the value of y?

A calculator is allowed on the following questions.

18

A local supermarket sells jelly in small, medium, and large jars. Sixteen small jars weigh as much as two medium jars and one large jar. Four small jars and one medium jar have the same weight as one large jar. How many small jars have the weight of one large jar?

A) 7

B) 8

C) 9

D) 10

19

On a math test with 30 questions, 5 points are rewarded for each correct answer and 2 points are deducted for each incorrect answer. If James answered all the questions and scored 59 points, solving which of the following systems of equations gives his number of correct answers, x, and his number of incorrect answers, y, on the math test?

A) $\quad x + y = 59$
$\quad\quad 5x - 2y = 30$

B) $\quad x + y = 30$
$\quad\quad 5x + 2y = 59$

C) $\quad x + y = 30$
$\quad\quad 2x - 5y = 59$

D) $\quad x + y = 30$
$\quad\quad 5x - 2y = 59$

20

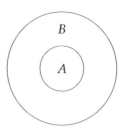

A game of darts rewards points depending on which region is hit. There are two regions, A and B, as shown above. James throws 3 darts, hitting region A once and region B twice, for a total of 18 points. Oleg also throws 3 darts, but hits regions A twice and region B once for a total of 21 points. How many points are rewarded for hitting region B once?

21

A restaurant has two types of tables, rectangular ones that can each seat 4 people and circular tables that can each seat 8 people. If 144 people are enough to fill all 30 tables at the restaurant, how many rectangular tables does the restaurant have?

A) 12

B) 16

C) 20

D) 24

22

In the xy-plane, the graph of $y = x^2 - 7x + 7$ intersects the graph of $y = 2x - 1$ at the points $(1, 1)$ and (p, q). What is the value of p ?

23

$$x^2 - 2x = y - 1$$
$$x = y - 11$$

If (x, y) is a solution to the system of equations above, what is one possible value of y ?

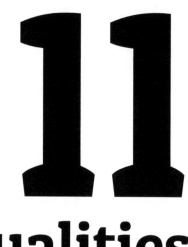

Inequalities

Just as we had equations and systems of equations, we can have inequalities and systems of inequalities.

The only difference is that you must reverse the sign every time you either multiply or divide both sides by a negative number.

For example,

$$2x + 3 < 9$$

Do we have to reverse the sign at any point? Well, we would subtract by 3 to get $2x < 6$ and then divide by 2 to get $x < 3$. Yes, we did a subtraction but at no point did we multiply or divide by a negative number. Therefore, the sign stays the same.

Let's take another example:

$$3x + 5 < 4x + 4$$

The first step is to combine like terms. We subtract both sides by $4x$ to get the x's on the left hand side. We then subtract both sides by 5 to get the constants on the right hand side:

$$3x - 4x < 4 - 5$$
$$-x < -1$$

Notice that the sign hasn't changed yet. Now, to get rid of the negative in front of the x, we need to **multiply** both sides by -1. Doing so means we need to reverse the sign.

$$x > 1$$

This concept is the cause of so many silly mistakes that it's important to reiterate it. Just working with negative numbers does NOT mean you need to change the sign. Some students see that they're dividing a negative number and impulsively reverse the sign. Don't do that. Only reverse the sign when you multiply or divide both sides **by** a negative number.

EXAMPLE 1: Which of the following integers is a solution to the inequality $-3x - 7 \leq -7x - 27$?

A) -6 B) -3 C) 1   D) 4

$$-3x - 7 \leq -7x - 27$$
$$4x \leq -20$$
$$x \leq -5$$

At no point did we multiply or divide by a negative number so there was no need to reverse the sign. We divided a negative number, -20, but we did so by a positive number, 4.

The only answer choice that satisfies $x \leq -5$ is -6, answer $\boxed{(A)}$.

EXAMPLE 2: If $-7 \leq -2x + 3 \leq 15$, which of the following must be true?

A) $5 \leq x \leq 6$ B) $-6 \leq x \leq -5$ C) $-6 \leq x \leq 5$ D) $-5 \leq x \leq 6$

So how do we solve these "two-inequalities-in-one" problems? Well, we can split them up into two inequalities that we can solve separately:

$$-7 \leq -2x + 3$$
$$-2x + 3 \leq 15$$

Solving the first inequality,

$$-7 \leq -2x + 3$$
$$-10 \leq -2x$$
$$5 \geq x$$

Solving the second inequality,

$$-2x + 3 \leq 15$$
$$-2x \leq 12$$
$$x \geq -6$$

Putting the two results together, we get $-6 \leq x \leq 5$. Answer $\boxed{(C)}$.

EXAMPLE 3: To follow his diet plan, James must limit his daily sugar consumption to at most 40 grams. One cookie has 5 grams of sugar and one fruit salad contains 7 grams of sugar. If James ate only cookies and fruit salads, which of the following inequalities represents the possible number of cookies c and fruit salads s that he could eat in one day and remain within his diet's sugar limit?

A) $\dfrac{5}{c} + \dfrac{7}{s} < 40$ B) $\dfrac{5}{c} + \dfrac{7}{s} \leq 40$ C) $5c + 7s < 40$ D) $5c + 7s \leq 40$

The total amount of sugar he gets from cookies is $5c$. The total amount of sugar he gets from fruit salads is $7s$. So his total sugar intake for any given day is $5c + 7s$, and since it can't be more than 40 grams, $5c + 7s \leq 40$.

Answer $\boxed{(D)}$.

From a graphing standpoint, what does an inequality look like? What does it mean for $y > -x - 1$?

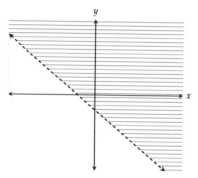

As shown by the shaded region above, the inequality $y > -x - 1$ represents all the points above the line $y = -x - 1$. If you have a hard time keeping track of what's above a line and what's below, just look at the y-axis. The line cuts the y-axis into two parts. The top part of the y-axis is always in the "above" region. The bottom part of the y-axis is always in the "below" region. If the graph doesn't show the intersection with the y-axis, you can always just draw your own vertical line through the graph to determine the "above" and "below" regions.

Also note that the line is dashed. Because $y > -x - 1$ and NOT $y = -x - 1$, the points on the line itself do not satisfy the inequality. If the equation were $y \geq -x - 1$, then the line would be solid, and points on the line would satisfy the inequality.

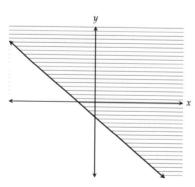

But what about a system of inequalities?

$$y \leq -x + 4$$

$$y \geq \frac{1}{2}x - 3$$

When it comes to graphing, the goal is to find the region with the points that satisfy the system. In this case, we want all the points below $y = -x + 4$ but above $y = \frac{1}{2}x - 3$. We can shade the regions below $y = -x + 4$ and above $y = \frac{1}{2}x - 3$ to see where the shaded regions overlap. The overlapping region will contain all the points that satisfy both inequalities.

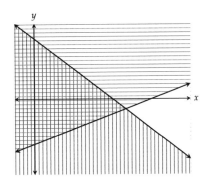

$$y \leq -x + 4$$

$$y \geq \frac{1}{2}x - 3$$

The overlapping region on the left represents all the solutions to the system.

Solving the system as if it were a system of equations instead of a system of inequalities gives the intersection point, which, in this case, happens to be the solution with the highest value of x. Substituting the first "equation" into the second, we get

$$-x + 4 = \frac{1}{2}x - 3$$

$$-2x + 8 = x - 6$$

$$-3x = -14$$

$$x = \frac{-14}{-3} \approx 4.66$$

At $x = 4.66$, $y = -4.66 + 4 = -0.66$ (we get this from the first equation). Therefore, $(4.66, -0.66)$ is the solution with the highest value of x. There are no solutions in which x is 5, 6, or larger.

While finding the intersection point in this example may have seemed a bit pointless (haha!), these points can be very important in the context of a given situation, such as finding the right price to maximize profit or figuring out the right materials for a construction project.

EXAMPLE 4:

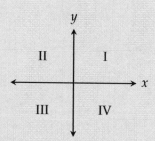

The following system of inequalities is graphed in the xy-plane above.

$$y \geq -3x + 1$$
$$y \geq 2x - 3$$

Which quadrants contain solutions to the system?

A) Quadrants I and II   B) Quadrants I and IV   C) Quadrants III and IV   D) Quadrants I, II, and IV

First, graph the equations, preferably with your graphing calculator. Then shade the regions and find the overlapping region.

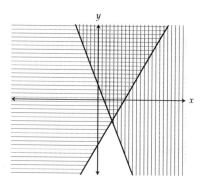

As you can see, the overlapping region, which contains all the solutions, is the top region. It has points in quadrants I, II, and IV. Answer $\boxed{(D)}$.

EXAMPLE 5: Ecologists have determined that the number of frogs y must be greater than or equal to three times the number of snakes x for a healthy ecosystem to be maintained in a particular forest. In addition, the number of frogs and the number of snakes must sum to at least 400.

PART 1: Which of the following systems of inequalities expresses these conditions for a healthy ecosystem?

A) $y \geq 3x$
     $y - x > 400$

B) $y \geq 3x$
     $y - x \geq 400$

C) $y \geq 3x$
     $y + x \geq 400$

D) $y \leq 3x$
     $y + x \leq 400$

PART 2: What is the minimum possible number of frogs in a healthy ecosystem?

Part 1 Solution: The number of frogs, y, must be at least three times the number of snakes, x. So, $y \geq 3x$. The number of frogs and the number of snakes must sum to at least 400, so $y + x \geq 400$. Answer $\boxed{(C)}$.

Part 2 Solution: In these types of questions, the intersection point is typically what we're looking for, but we'll graph the inequalities just to make sure. First, put the second inequality into $y = mx + b$ form.

$$y \geq 3x$$
$$y \geq -x + 400$$

Then graph the inequalities using your calculator.

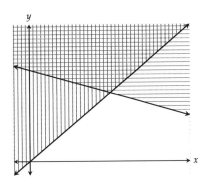

The graph confirms that y, the number of frogs, is at a minimum at the intersection point. After all, the overlapping region (the top region) represents all possible solutions and the intersection point is at the bottom of this region, representing the solution with the minimum number of frogs.

We can find the coordinates of that intersection point by solving a system of equations based on the two lines.

$$y = 3x$$
$$y = -x + 400$$

Substituting the first equation into the second,

$$3x = -x + 400$$
$$4x = 400$$
$$x = 100$$

100 is the x-coordinate. The y-coordinate is $y = 3x = 3(100) = 300$. The intersection point is at $(100, 300)$ and the minimum number of frogs is $\boxed{300}$ in a healthy ecosystem.

CHAPTER EXERCISE: Answers for this chapter start on page 279.

A calculator is allowed on the following questions.

1

Which of the following is a solution to the inequality $-x - 4 > 4x - 14$?

A) -1

B) 2

C) 5

D) 8

2

If $\frac{3}{4}x - 4 > \frac{1}{2}x - 10$, which of the following must be true?

A) $x < 24$

B) $x > 24$

C) $x < -24$

D) $x > -24$

3

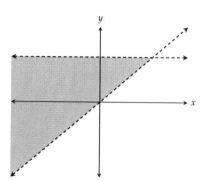

Which of the following systems of inequalities could be the one graphed in the xy-plane above?

A) $y > 3$
   $y > x$

B) $y < 3$
   $y < x$

C) $y < 3$
   $y > x$

D) $y > 3$
   $y < x$

4

Jerry estimates that there are m marbles in a jar. Harry, who knows the actual number of marbles in the jar, notes that the actual number, n, is within 10 marbles (inclusive) of Jerry's estimate. Which of the following inequalities represents the relationship between Jerry's estimate and the actual number of marbles in the jar?

A) $n + 10 \leq m \leq n - 10$

B) $m - 10 \leq n \leq m + 10$

C) $n \leq m \leq 10n$

D) $\frac{m}{10} \leq n \leq 10m$

5

A manufacturer produces chairs for a retail store according to the formula, $M = 12P + 100$, where M is the number of units produced and P is the retail price of each chair. The number of units sold by the retail store is given by $N = -3P + 970$, where N is the number of units sold and P is the retail price of each chair. What are all the values of P for which the number of units produced is greater than or equal to the number of units sold?

A) $P \geq 58$

B) $P \leq 58$

C) $P \geq 55$

D) $P \leq 55$

6

If n is an integer and $3(n - 2) > -4(n - 9)$, what is the least possible value of n?

7

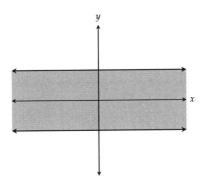

The graph in the xy-plane above could represent which of the following systems of inequalities?

A) $y \geq 3$
   $y \leq -3$

B) $y \leq 3$
   $y \geq -3$

C) $x \geq 3$
   $x \leq -3$

D) $x \leq 3$
   $x \geq -3$

8

To get to work, Harry must travel 8 miles by bus and 16 miles by train everyday. The bus travels at an average speed of x miles per hour and the train travels at an average speed of y miles per hour. If Harry's daily commute never takes more than 1 hour, which of the following inequalities represents the possible average speeds of the bus and train during the commute?

A) $\dfrac{8}{x} + \dfrac{16}{y} \leq 1$

B) $\dfrac{16}{x} + \dfrac{8}{y} \leq 1$

C) $\dfrac{x}{8} + \dfrac{y}{16} \leq 1$

D) $8x + 16y \leq 1$

9

An ice cream distributor contracts out to two different companies to manufacture cartons of ice cream. Company A can produce 80 cartons each hour and Company B can produce 140 cartons each hour. The distributor needs to fulfill an order of over 1,100 cartons in 10 hours of contract time. It contracts out x hours to Company A and the remaining hours to Company B. Which of the following inequalities gives all possible values of x in the context of this problem?

A) $\dfrac{80}{x} + \dfrac{140}{10-x} > 1,100$

B) $140x + 80(10 - x) > 1,100$

C) $80x + 140(10 - x) > 1,100$

D) $80x + 140(x - 10) > 1,100$

10

$$y \geq \frac{3}{2}x + 2$$

$$y \leq -2x - 5$$

Which of the following graphs in the xy-plane could represent the system of inequalities above?

A)

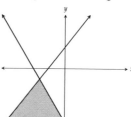

B)

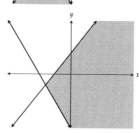

C)

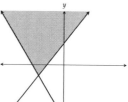

D)

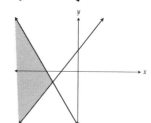

11

$$y > 15x + a$$
$$y < 5x + b$$

In the system of inequalities above, a and b are constants. If $(1, 20)$ is a solution to the system, which of the following could be the value of $b - a$?

A) 6

B) 8

C) 10

D) 12

12

Tina works no more than 30 hours at a nail salon each week. She can do a manicure in 20 minutes and a pedicure in 30 minutes. Each manicure earns her $25 and each pedicure earns her $40, and she must earn at least $900 to cover her expenses. If during one week, she does enough manicures m and pedicures p to cover her expenses, which of the following systems of inequalities describes her working hours and her earnings?

A) $3m + 2p \leq 30$
$25m + 40p \geq 900$

B) $2m + 3p \leq 30$
$25m + 40p \geq 900$

C) $\dfrac{m}{3} + \dfrac{p}{2} \leq 30$
$25m + 40p \geq 900$

D) $\dfrac{m}{3} + \dfrac{p}{2} \geq 900$
$25m + 40p \leq 30$

13

If $k \leq x \leq 3k + 12$, which of the following must be true?

  I. $x - 12 \leq 3k$
 II. $k \geq -6$
III. $x - k \geq 0$

A) I only

B) I and II only

C) II and III only

D) I, II, and III

14

If $-\dfrac{20}{3} < -2x + 4 < -\dfrac{9}{2}$, what is one possible value of $x - 2$?

15

Joyce wants to create a rectangular garden that has an area of at least 300 square meters and a perimeter of at least 70 meters. If the length of the garden is x meters long and the width is y meters long, which of the following systems of inequalities represents Joyce's requirements?

A) $xy \geq 70$
$x + y \geq 300$

B) $xy \geq 150$
$x + y \geq 70$

C) $xy \geq 300$
$x + y \geq 70$

D) $xy \geq 300$
$x + y \geq 35$

16

If $a < b$, which of the following must be true?

    I. $a^2 < b^2$

   II. $2a < 2b$

  III. $-b < -a$

A) II only

B) I and II only

C) II and III only

D) I, II, and III

12

Word Problems

For many students, solving word problems is a frustrating experience. They require you to translate the question before you can even do the math. The examples and the exercises in this chapter will show you how to handle the full range of word problems that are tested. You will develop an instinct for translating words into math, setting the right variables, and finally solving for the answer. Experience is the best guide.

EXAMPLE 1: The sum of three consecutive integers is 72. What is the largest of these three integers?

The most important technique in solving word problems is to let a variable be one of the things you don't know. In this problem, we don't know any of the three integers, so we let the smallest one be x. It doesn't matter which number we set as x, as long as we're consistent throughout the problem.

So if x is the smallest, then our consecutive integers are

$$x, x+1, x+2$$

Because they sum to 72, we can make an equation:

$$
\begin{aligned}
x + (x+1) + (x+2) &= 72 \\
3x + 3 &= 72 \\
3x &= 69 \\
x &= 23
\end{aligned}
$$

And because x is the smallest, our three consecutive integers must be

$$23, 24, 25$$

The largest one is $\boxed{25}$.

What if we had let x be the largest integer? Our three integers would've been

$$x - 2, x - 1, x$$

And our solution would've looked like this:

$$(x - 2) + (x - 1) + x = 72$$
$$3x - 3 = 72$$
$$3x = 75$$
$$x = 25$$

And because x was set to be the largest of the three integers this time, we're already at the answer!

On SAT word problems, think about which unknown you want to set as a variable. Often times, that unknown will be what the question is asking for. Other times, it will be an unknown you specifically choose to make the problem easier to set up and solve. And sometimes, as was the case in Example 1, it doesn't matter which unknown you pick; you'll end up with the same answer with the same effort.

> **EXAMPLE 2:** One number is 3 times another number. If they sum to 44, what is the larger of the two numbers?

In this problem, we want to set x to be the smaller of the two numbers. That way, the two numbers can be expressed as

$$x \text{ and } 3x$$

If we let x be the larger of the two, we would have to work with

$$x \text{ and } \frac{x}{3}$$

and fractions are yucky.

Setting up our equation,

$$x + 3x = 44$$
$$4x = 44$$
$$x = 11$$

Be careful—we're not done yet! The question asks for the larger of the two, so we have to multiply x by 3 to get $\boxed{33}$.

> **EXAMPLE 3:** What is a number such that the square of the number is equal to 2.7% of its reciprocal?

Let the number we're looking for be x.

$$x^2 = .027 \times \frac{1}{x}$$

Multiply both sides by x to isolate it.

$$x^3 = .027$$

Cube root both sides.

$$x = \boxed{.3}$$

EXAMPLE 4: Albert is 7 years older than Henry. In 5 years, Albert will be twice as old as Henry. How old is Albert now?

Let x be Albert's age now. We could've assigned x to be Henry's age, but as we mentioned earlier, assigning the variable to be what the question is asking for is typically the faster route. Now at this point, some of you might be thinking of assigning another variable to Henry's age. While that would certainly work, it would only add more steps to the solution. Try to stick to one variable unless the question clearly calls for more.

If Albert is x years old now, then Henry must be $x - 7$ years old.
Five years from now, Albert will be $x + 5$ and Henry will be $x - 2$ years old.

$$x + 5 = 2(x - 2)$$
$$x + 5 = 2x - 4$$
$$x = \boxed{9}$$

EXAMPLE 5: Jake can run 60 yards per minute. Amy can run 120 yards per minute for the first 10 minutes but then slows down to 20 yards per minute thereafter. If they start running at the same time, after how many minutes t will both Jake and Amy have run the same distance, assuming $t > 10$?

The problem already gives us a variable t to work with. We want to equate Jake's distance run with Amy's.

Jake's distance: $60t$
Amy's distance: $120(10) + 20(t - 10)$

$$60t = 120(10) + 20(t - 10)$$
$$60t = 1,200 + 20t - 200$$
$$40t = 1,000$$
$$t = 25$$

After $\boxed{25}$ minutes, they will have run the same distance.

EXAMPLE 6: At a pharmaceutical company, research equipment must be shared among the scientists. There is one microscope for every 4 scientists, one centrifuge for every 3 scientists, and one freezer for every 2 scientists. If there is a total of 52 pieces of research equipment at this company, how many scientists are there?

Let x be the number of scientists. Then the number of microscopes is $\frac{x}{4}$, the number of centrifuges is $\frac{x}{3}$, and the number of freezers is $\frac{x}{2}$.

$$\frac{x}{4} + \frac{x}{3} + \frac{x}{2} = 52$$

Multiply both sides by 12 to get rid of the fractions,

$$3x + 4x + 6x = 52 \cdot 12$$
$$13x = 624$$
$$x = \boxed{48}$$

EXAMPLE 7: Mark and Kevin own $\frac{1}{4}$ and $\frac{1}{3}$ of the books on a shelf, respectively. Lori owns the rest of the books. If Kevin owns 9 more books than Mark, how many books does Lori own?

Let x be the total number of books. Mark then has $\frac{1}{4}x$ books and Kevin has $\frac{1}{3}x$ books. Kevin owns 9 more than Mark, so

$$\frac{1}{3}x - \frac{1}{4}x = 9$$

Multiplying both sides by 12,

$$4x - 3x = 108$$
$$x = 108$$

The total number of books is 108. Mark owns $\frac{1}{4} \times 108 = 27$ books and Kevin owns $\frac{1}{3} \times 108 = 36$ books. Lori must then own $108 - 27 - 36 = \boxed{45}$ books.

EXAMPLE 8: A group of friends wants to split the cost of renting a cabin equally. If each friend pays \$130, they will have \$10 too much. If each friend pays \$120, they will have \$50 too little. How much does it cost to rent the cabin?

We have two unknowns in this problem. We'll let the number of people in the group be n and the cost of renting a cabin be c. From the information given, we can come up with two equations (make sure you see the reasoning behind them):

$$130n - 10 = c$$
$$120n + 50 = c$$

In the first equation, $130n$ represents the total amount the group pays, but because that's 10 dollars too much, we need to subtract 10 to arrive at the cost of rent, c. In the second equation, $120n$ represents the total amount the group pays, but this time it's 50 dollars too little, so we need to add 50 to arrive at c. Substituting c from the first equation into the second, we get

$$120n + 50 = 130n - 10$$
$$-10n = -60$$
$$n = 6$$

So there are 6 friends in the group. And

$$c = 130n - 10 = 130 \cdot 6 - 10 = 770$$

The cost of renting the cabin is $\boxed{770}$.

EXAMPLE 9: Of the 200 jellybeans in a jar, 70% are green and the rest are red. How many green jellybeans must be removed so that 60% of the remaining jellybeans are green?

The answer is NOT 20. You can't just take 10% of the green jellybeans away because as you do that, the total number of jellybeans also goes down. We first find that there are $\frac{7}{10} \times 200 = 140$ green jellybeans. We need to remove x of them so that 60% of what's left is green:

$$\frac{\text{green jellybeans left}}{\text{total jellybeans left}} = 60\%$$

$$\frac{140 - x}{200 - x} = \frac{6}{10}$$

Cross multiplying,

$$10(140 - x) = 6(200 - x)$$
$$1,400 - 10x = 1,200 - 6x$$
$$200 = 4x$$
$$x = 50$$

$\boxed{50}$ green jellybeans need to be removed. This type of word problem with percentages is very common in chemistry and is typically known as a "mixture" problem.

Last but not least is the quintessential area/perimeter word problem.

EXAMPLE 10: A rectangle has a width that is 3 inches shorter than its length. If the area of the rectangle is 108 square inches, what is the perimeter, in inches, of the rectangle?

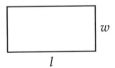

If we let the length be l, then the width w is $l - 3$. Since a rectangle's area is equal to the length times the width, we can set up the following equation:

$$lw = 108$$
$$l(l - 3) = 108$$
$$l^2 - 3l - 108 = 0$$
$$(l - 12)(l + 9) = 0$$

Since the length of a rectangle has to be positive, $l = 12$. The width is then $l - 3 = 12 - 3 = 9$. Finally, the perimeter is $2l + 2w = 2(12) + 2(9) = \boxed{42}$.

Never forget that the perimeter of a rectangle is **twice** the length plus **twice** the width. I've seen too many students just add the length and the width without thinking it through.

CHAPTER EXERCISE: Answers for this chapter start on page 281.

A calculator should NOT be used on the following questions.

1

Which of the following represents the square of the sum of x and y, decreased by the product of x and y?

A) $x^2 + y^2 - xy$

B) $x^2y^2 - xy$

C) $(x+y)^2 - (x+y)$

D) $(x+y)^2 - xy$

2

On a 100 cm ruler, lines are drawn at 10, X, and 98 cm. The distance between the lines at X and 98 cm is three times the distance between the lines at X and 10 cm. What is the value of X?

3

If 5 is added to the square root of x, the result is 9. What is the value of $x + 2$?

$5 + \sqrt{x} = 9$

$\sqrt{x} = 4$ $16 + 2 = 18$

$x = 16$

4

A grocery store sells tomatoes in boxes of 4 or 10. If Melanie buys x boxes of 4 and y boxes of 10, where $x \geq 1$ and $y \geq 1$, for a total of 60 tomatoes, what is one possible value of x?

5

A rectangular monitor has a length of x inches and a width that is one-third of its length. If the perimeter of the monitor is 48 inches, what is the value of x?

6

Susie buys 2 pieces of salmon, each weighing x pounds, and 1 piece of trout, weighing y pounds, where x and y are integers. The salmon cost $3.50 per pound and the trout cost $5 per pound. If the total cost of the fish was $77, which of the following could be the value of y?

A) 4

B) 5

C) 6

D) 7

$2x + y$ $7x + 5y = 77$

7

A 20% nickel alloy was made by combining 2 grams of a 35% nickel alloy with 6 grams of an x% nickel alloy. What is the value of x?

98

A calculator is allowed on the following questions.

8

If $8 + 5x$ is twice $x - 5$, what is the value of x?

A) -6

B) -3

C) $-\dfrac{7}{3}$

D) -2

9

If 75% of 68 is the same as 85% of n, what is the value of n?

10

The Pirates won exactly 4 of their first 15 games. They then played N remaining games and won all of them. If they won exactly half of all the games they played, what is the value of N?

11

Alice and Julie start with the same number of pens. After Alice gives 16 of her pens to Julie, Julie then has two times as many pens as Alice does. How many pens did Alice have at the start?

12

At a Hong Kong learning center, $\dfrac{1}{4}$ of the students take debate, $\dfrac{1}{6}$ of the students take writing, and $\dfrac{1}{8}$ of the students take science. The rest take math. If 33 students take math, what is the total number of students at the learning center?

A) 60

B) 66

C) 72

D) 78

13

Ian has 20 football cards, and Jason has 44 baseball cards. They agree to trade such that Jason gives Ian 2 baseball cards for every card Ian gives to Jason. After how many such trades will Ian and Jason each have an equal number of cards?

A) 9

B) 10

C) 11

D) 12

14

If 3 is subtracted from 3 times the number x, the result is 21. What is the result when 8 is added to half of x?

A) 1

B) 5

C) 8

D) 12

15

At a store, the price of a tie is k dollars less than three times the price of a shirt. If a shirt costs $40 and a tie costs $30, what is the value of k?

16

A wooden board in the shape of a rectangle has a length that is twice its width. If the area of the board is 128 square feet, what is the length, in feet, of the board?

$l = 2w$ $w \cdot 8$

$w \cdot 2w = 128$

$2w^2 \quad w = 64$

17

A bakery gave out coupons to celebrate its grand opening. Each coupon was worth either $1, $3, or $5. Twice as many $1 coupons were given out as $3 coupons, and 3 times as many $3 coupons were given out as $5 coupons. The total value of all the coupons given out was $360. How many $3 coupons were given out?

A) 40
B) 45
C) 48
D) 54

$2t + t$

$3 \times t$

$5x + 15x +$

$t + 9x + 6x = 360$

$20x = 360$

18

Alex, Bob, and Carl all collect seashells. Bob has half as many seashells as Carl. Alex has three times as many seashells as Bob. If Alex and Bob together have 60 seashells, how many seashells does Carl have?

A) 15
B) 20
C) 30
D) 40

$B = \dfrac{C}{2}$

$A = 3B$

$A = \dfrac{3C}{2}$

19

Yoona runs at a steady rate of 1 yard per second. Jessica runs 4 times as fast. If Jessica gives Yoona a head start of 30 yards in a race, how many yards must Jessica run to catch up to Yoona?

31   4   36   24
32   8   37   28
33   12   38   32
34   16   39   36
35   20   40   40

20

Nicky owns a house that has a patio in the shape of a square. She decides to renovate the patio by increasing its length by 4 feet and decreasing its width by 5 feet. If the area of the renovated patio is 90 square feet, what was the original area of the patio, in square feet?

$(s+4)(s-5) = 90$

$s^2 - s - 20 = 90$

$s^2 - s - 110 = 0$

$(s - 11)(s + 10) = 0$

121

13 Lines

Lines are just functions in the form of $f(x) = mx + b$, which is why they are often referred to as linear functions. We'll cover functions as a whole in a future chapter; we're covering lines first because they present some concepts that don't apply to other functions. The SAT tests these concepts so frequently that they deserve their own chapter. Let's dive in!

Given any two points (x_1, y_1) and (x_2, y_2) on a line,

$$\text{Slope of line} = \frac{\text{rise}}{\text{run}} = \frac{y_2 - y_1}{x_2 - x_1}$$

The slope is a measure of the steepness of a line—the bigger the slope, the more steep the line is. The rise is the distance between the y coordinates and the run is the distance between the x coordinates. A slope of 2 means the line goes 2 units up for every 1 unit to the right, or 2 units down for every 1 unit to the left. A slope of $-\frac{2}{3}$ means the line goes 2 units down for every 3 units to the right, or 2 units up for every 3 units to the left.

Lines with positive slope always go up and to the right as in the graph above.

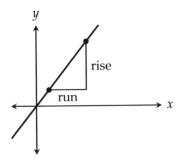

Lines with negative slope go down and to the right:

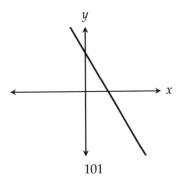

EXAMPLE 1:

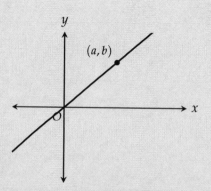

The line shown in the xy-plane above passes through the origin and point (a, b), where $a > b$. Which of the following could be the slope of the line?

A) $-\dfrac{1}{2}$ B) $\dfrac{3}{4}$ C) 1   D) $\dfrac{3}{2}$

First, notice that the slope is positive. The slope, $\dfrac{\text{rise}}{\text{run}}$, is also equal to $\dfrac{b}{a}$.

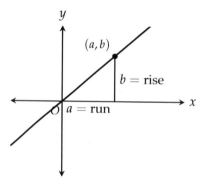

Since $a > b$, $\dfrac{b}{a}$ is always less than 1. For example, if $a = 5$ and $b = 3$, the slope would be $\dfrac{3}{5}$. The only choice that's both positive and less than 1 is answer $\boxed{(B)}$.

EXAMPLE 2: Line m passes through points $(k, 7)$ and $(3, k - 4)$. If the slope of line m is 3, what is the value of k?

$$\text{Slope} = \frac{(k - 4) - 7}{3 - k} = 3$$
$$k - 11 = 3(3 - k)$$
$$k - 11 = 9 - 3k$$
$$4k = 20$$
$$k = \boxed{5}$$

EXAMPLE 3: If a line has a slope of $\frac{1}{3}$ and passes through the point $(1, -2)$, which of the following points also lies on the line?

A) $(-2, -5)$ B) $(-2, -1)$ C) $(4, -1)$ D) $(4, 10)$

A slope of $\frac{1}{3}$ means 1 up for every 3 to the right, or 1 down for every 3 to the left. If we go 3 to the left, the point we get to on the line is $(-2, -3)$. If we go 3 to the right, the point we get to on the line is $(4, -1)$, answer $\boxed{(C)}$.

In this case, we got to the answer pretty quickly, but if we hadn't, we would have continued moving right or left until we found an answer choice that matched. On the SAT, it shouldn't ever take too long to arrive at the answer for a question like this.

In addition to slope, you also need to know what x and y intercepts are. The x-intercept is where the graph crosses the x-axis. Likewise, the y-intercept is where the graph crosses the y-axis.

Let's say we have the line
$$2x + 3y = 12$$

To find the x-intercept, set y equal to 0.

$$2x + 3(0) = 12$$
$$2x = 12$$
$$x = 6$$

The x-intercept is 6.

To find the y-intercept, set x equal to 0.

$$2(0) + 3y = 12$$
$$3y = 12$$
$$y = 4$$

The y-intercept is 4.

EXAMPLE 4: If the line $ax + 3y = 15$, where a is a constant, has an x-intercept that is twice the value of the y-intercept, what is the value of a?

First, set $x = 0$ to find the y-intercept:

$$a(0) + 3y = 15$$
$$3y = 15$$
$$y = 5$$

The y-intercept is 5, which means the x-intercept must be $5 \times 2 = 10$. Plugging in $x = 10, y = 0$,

$$a(10) + 3(0) = 15$$
$$10a = 15$$
$$a = \boxed{1.5}$$

All lines can be expressed in **slope-intercept form**:

$$y = mx + b$$

where m is the slope and b is the y-intercept. So for the line $y = 2x - 3$, the slope is 2 and the y-intercept is -3:

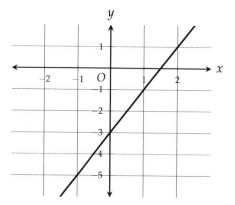

While all lines can be expressed in slope-intercept form, sometimes it'll take some work to get there. If you're given a slope and a y-intercept, then of course it's really easy to get the equation of the line. But what if we're handed a slope and a point instead of a slope and a y-intercept? Then it'll be more convenient to use **point-slope form**:

$$y - y_1 = m(x - x_1)$$

where (x_1, y_1) is the given point. For example, let's say we want to find the equation of a line that has a slope of 3 and passes through the point $(1, -2)$. The equation of the line is then

$$y - (-2) = 3(x - 1)$$

Once it's in point-slope form, we can then expand and shift things around to get to slope-intercept form if we need to.

$$y - (-2) = 3(x - 1)$$
$$y + 2 = 3x - 3$$
$$y = 3x - 5$$

EXAMPLE 5:

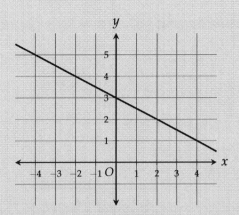

Which of the following could be the equation of the line shown in the *xy*-plane above?

A) $y = -2x + 3$ B) $y = \dfrac{1}{2}x + 3$ C) $y = -\dfrac{1}{2}x + 3$ D) $y = 2x - 3$

To get the equation of the line $y = mx + b$, we need to find the slope m and the y-intercept b. The line crosses the y-axis at 3, so $b = 3$. The line goes downward from left to right, down 1 for every 2 to the right, so the slope m is $-\dfrac{1}{2}$. Therefore, the equation of the line is $y = -\dfrac{1}{2}x + 3$. Answer $\boxed{(C)}$.

EXAMPLE 6: A line l passes through the points $(-2, 3)$ and $(3, 13)$. What is the y-intercept of line l?

$$\text{Slope} = \frac{y_2 - y_1}{x_2 - x_1} = \frac{13 - 3}{3 - (-2)} = 2$$

Using point-slope form, our line is

$$y - 13 = 2(x - 3)$$

Note that we could've used the other point $(-2, 3)$. The result will turn out to be the same.

$$y - 13 = 2(x - 3)$$
$$y = 2x - 6 + 13$$
$$y = 2x + 7$$

After putting the equation into slope-intercept form, we can easily see that the y-intercept is $\boxed{7}$.

There are a few more things you need to know about lines.

Two lines are parallel if they have the same slope.

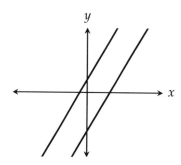

Two lines are perpendicular if the product of their slopes is -1. In other words, if one slope is the negative reciprocal of the other (e.g. 2 and $-\frac{1}{2}$).

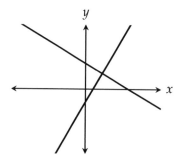

EXAMPLE 7: Line m has a slope of $\frac{2}{3}$ and passes through the point $(4,3)$. If line n is perpendicular to line m and passes through the same point $(4,3)$, which of the following could be the equation of line n?

A) $y = -\frac{2}{3}x + 9$ B) $y = -\frac{3}{2}x - 3$ C) $y = -\frac{3}{2}x + 6$ D) $y = -\frac{3}{2}x + 9$

Because it's perpendicular to line m, line n must have a slope of $-\frac{3}{2}$. Using point-slope form,

$$y - 3 = -\frac{3}{2}(x - 4)$$

$$y = -\frac{3}{2}x + 6 + 3$$

$$y = -\frac{3}{2}x + 9$$

We get the equation into slope-intercept form to see that the answer is $\boxed{(D)}$.

Finally, you'll need to know the equations of horizontal and vertical lines. The equation of the vertical line that passes through $x = 3$ is, well, $x = 3$.

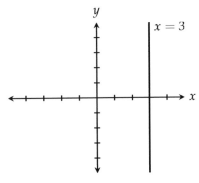

The equation of the horizontal line that passes through $(0,3)$ is $y = 3$.

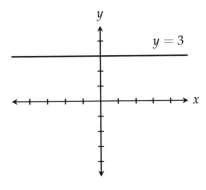

CHAPTER EXERCISE: Answers for this chapter start on page 284.

A calculator should NOT be used on the following questions.

1

What is the equation of the line parallel to the y-axis and 3 units to the right of the y-axis?

A) $x = -3$

B) $x = 3$

C) $y = -3$

D) $y = 3$

2

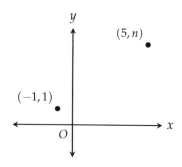

Note: Figure not drawn to scale.

In the figure above, the slope of the line through the two plotted points is $\dfrac{1}{3}$. What is the value of n?

A) 9

B) 4

C) 3

D) $\dfrac{7}{3}$

3

In the xy-plane, points $(-3, 5)$ and $(6, 8)$ lie on line l. Which of the following points is also on line l?

A) $(0, 6)$

B) $(3, 8)$

C) $(9, 10)$

D) $(12, 11)$

4

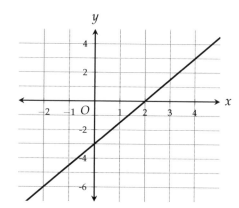

The graph of line l is shown in the xy-plane above. Which of the following is an equation of a line that is parallel to line l?

A) $y = -\dfrac{2}{3}x + 2$

B) $y = \dfrac{2}{3}x + 10$

C) $y = \dfrac{3}{2}x - 4$

D) $y = 3x - 1$

5

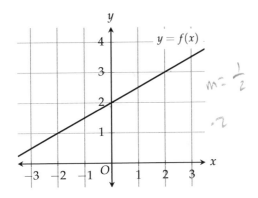

In the xy-plane above, the graph of the linear function f is perpendicular to the graph of the linear function g (not shown). If the graphs of f and g intersect at the point $\left(1, \dfrac{5}{2}\right)$, what is the value of $g(-1)$?

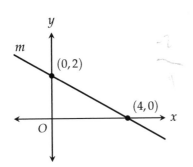

A calculator is allowed on the following questions.

6

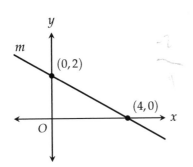

What is the slope of the line m in the figure above?

A) -2

B) $-\dfrac{1}{2}$

C) $\dfrac{1}{4}$

D) $\dfrac{1}{2}$

7

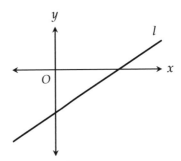

Line l in the xy-coordinate system above can be represented by the equation $y = mx + b$. Which of the following must be true?

A) $mb > 0$

B) $mb < 0$

C) $mb = 0$

D) $mb = 1$

8

The line $y = -2x - 2$ is perpendicular to line l. If these two lines have the same y-intercept, which of the following could be the equation of line l?

A) $y = -2x - 2$

B) $y = 2x - 2$

C) $y = -\dfrac{1}{2}x - 2$

D) $y = \dfrac{1}{2}x - 2$

9

The slope of line l is $\dfrac{1}{2}$ and its y-intercept is 3. What is the equation of the line perpendicular to line l that goes through $(1, 5)$?

A) $y = -2x + 3$

B) $y = -2x + 7$

C) $y = -\dfrac{1}{2}x + \dfrac{11}{2}$

D) $y = \dfrac{1}{2}x + \dfrac{9}{2}$

10

A line with a slope of $\dfrac{2}{3}$ passes through the points $(1, 4)$ and $(x, 10)$. What is the value of x?

A) 4

B) 6

C) 8

D) 10

11

In the xy-plane, the line with equation $ax - \dfrac{1}{3}y = 8$, where a is a constant, passes through the point $(2, 6)$. What is the x-coordinate of the x-intercept of the line?

12

$$y = \dfrac{a}{b}x + c$$

$$y = \dfrac{d}{e}x + c$$

The equations of two perpendicular lines in the xy-plane are shown above, where $a, b, c, d,$ and e are constants. If $0 < \dfrac{a}{b} < 1$, which of the following must be true?

A) $\dfrac{d}{e} < -1$

B) $-1 < \dfrac{d}{e} < 0$

C) $0 < \dfrac{d}{e} < 1$

D) $\dfrac{d}{e} > 1$

110

14

Interpreting Linear Models

On the SAT, you will encounter linear model questions that are a direct extension of the previous chapter about lines. You'll have to interpret the meaning of the numbers in these models within a real world context, applying your understanding of slope and y-intercept to do so.

> **EXAMPLE 1:** The value V, in dollars, of a home from 2006 to 2015 can be estimated by the equation $V = 240,000 - 5,000T$, where T is the number of years since 2006.
>
> **PART 1:** Which of the following best describes the meaning of the number 240,000 in the equation?
>
> A) The value of the home in 2006
>
> B) The value of the home in 2015
>
> C) The average value of the home from 2006 to 2015
>
> D) The increase in the value of the home from 2006 to 2015
>
> **PART 2:** Which of the following best describes the meaning of the number 5,000 in the equation?
>
> A) The number of homes sold each year
>
> B) The yearly decrease in the value of the home
>
> C) The difference between the value of the home in 2006 and in 2015
>
> D) The yearly decrease in the value of the home per square foot

Part 1 Solution: Many of these questions will give you an equation in $y = mx + b$ form. The y-intercept b will typically designate an initial value, the value when $x = 0$. In this case, the y-intercept is 240,000 and it describes the value of the home when $T = 0$, zero years after 2006, which, of course, is 2006. Answer $\boxed{(A)}$.

Part 2 Solution: Again, we're dealing with an equation of the form $y = mx + b$. The slope m always designates a rate, the increase or decrease in y for each increase in x. In this case, the slope is $-5,000$, which means the value of the home decreases by 5,000 for each year that goes by. Answer $\boxed{(B)}$.

It's important that you don't get tricked into choosing a rate that looks right but ultimately doesn't fit the context set by the variables x and y (in this case, T and V). Answer (A) is wrong because we're not dealing with the number of homes sold; we're dealing with the value of a home. Answer (D) is wrong because the numbers in the equation aren't on a per-square-foot basis. Always be aware of the variables you're working with.

EXAMPLE 2: The maximum height of a plant h, in inches, can be determined by the equation $h = \dfrac{4x + 6}{5}$, where x is the amount of fertilizer, in grams, used to grow the plant.

PART 1: According to the equation, one more gram of fertilizer would increase the maximum height of a plant by how many inches?

PART 2: To raise the maximum height of a plant by exactly one inch, how many more grams of fertilizer should be used in growing the plant?

Part 1 Solution: This question is essentially asking for the change in h for every 1 unit increase in x. This is the slope. From the equation, we can see that the slope is $\dfrac{4}{5}$, or $\boxed{0.8}$. To make this even clearer, we can put the equation into $y = mx + b$ form by splitting up the fraction: $h = \dfrac{4}{5}x + \dfrac{6}{5}$. Note that when we're dealing with changes in x and y, the y-intercept b is irrelevant because it's a constant that's always there.

Part 2 Solution: Because this question is asking for the change in x for every 1 unit increase in h, the reverse of Part 1, we need to rearrange the equation so that we have x in terms of h.

$$h = \frac{4x + 6}{5}$$

$$5h = 4x + 6$$

$$5h - 6 = 4x$$

$$x = \frac{5}{4}h - \frac{3}{2}$$

Now we can see that x increases by $\dfrac{5}{4}$, or $\boxed{1.25}$, when h increases by 1. The answer is just the slope of our new equation. A shortcut for this type of question is to take the reciprocal of the slope of the original equation. The reciprocal of $\dfrac{4}{5}$ is $\dfrac{5}{4}$.

EXAMPLE 3:

$$T = 65 - 6m$$

A can of soda is put into a freezer. The temperature T of the soda, in degrees Fahrenheit, can be found by using the equation above, where m is the number of minutes the can has been in the freezer. What is the decrease in the temperature of the soda, in degrees Fahrenheit, for every 5 minutes the can is left in the freezer?

The slope of -6 represents the change in the temperature for every 1 minute the can is left in the freezer. So for every 5 minutes, the temperature of the soda decreases by $5 \times 6 = \boxed{30}$ degrees Fahrenheit.

CHAPTER EXERCISE: Answers for this chapter start on page 286.

A calculator should NOT be used on the following questions.

1

The water level h, in feet, in a large aquarium can be modeled by $h = 100 - 3d$, where d is the number of days that have passed since the aquarium was last refilled. Based on the model, how does the water level change each day?

A) Decreases by 3 feet

B) Increases by 3 feet

C) Decreases by 100 feet

D) Increases by 100 feet

2

The number of loaves of bread b remaining in a bakery each day can be estimated by the equation $b = 200 - 18h$, where h is the number of hours that have passed since the store's opening. What is the meaning of the value 18 in this equation?

A) The bakery sells all its loaves of bread in 18 hours.

B) The bakery sells 18 loaves of bread each hour.

C) The bakery sells a total of 18 loaves of bread each day.

D) There are 18 loaves of bread left in the bakery at the end of each day.

3

A membership website offers video tutorials on programming. The number of members, m, subscribed to the site can be estimated by the equation $m = 500 + 200n$, where n is the number of videos available on the site. Based on the equation, which of the following statements is true?

A) For every one additional video, the site gains 500 new members.

B) The site initially made 200 videos available to members.

C) The site was able to get 500 members without any available videos.

D) The site gains 500 new members for every 200 additional videos available on the site.

4

$$s = 10 - 2h$$

A recipe suggests sweetening honey tea with sugar. The equation above can be used to determine the amount of sugar s, in teaspoons, that should be added to a tea beverage with h teaspoons of honey. What is the meaning of the 2 in the equation?

A) For every teaspoon of honey in the beverage, two more teaspoons of sugar should be added.

B) For every teaspoon of honey in the beverage, two fewer teaspoons of sugar should be added.

C) For every two teaspoons of honey in the beverage, one more teaspoon of sugar should be added.

D) For every two teaspoons of honey in the beverage, one fewer teaspoon of sugar should be added.

5

The monthly salary of a salesperson at a used car dealership is determined by the expression $1,000 + 2,000xc$, where x is the salesperson's commission rate and c is the number of cars sold by the salesperson. Which of the following statements is the best interpretation of the number 2,000 in the context of this problem?

A) The average price of a used car at the dealership

B) The base monthly salary of a salesperson at the dealership

C) The average monthly commission earned by each salesperson at the dealership

D) The average number of cars sold by the dealership each month

6

$$p = 2,000s + 15,000$$

A state government uses the equation above to estimate the average population p for a town with s schools. Which of the following best describes the meaning of the number 2,000 in the equation?

A) The average number of students at each school in a town

B) The average number of schools in each town

C) The estimated increase in a town's population for each additional school

D) The estimated population of a town without any schools

7

$$h = 100 - 4t$$

The equation above can be used to model the number of hours h until a gallon of milk held at a temperature of t, in degrees Celsius, goes sour. Based on the model, which of the following is the best interpretation of the number 4 in the equation?

A) An increase of $1°C$ will make a gallon of milk go sour 4 hours faster.

B) An increase of $1°C$ will make 4 gallons of milk go sour 1 hour faster.

C) An increase of $4°C$ will make a gallon of milk go sour 1 hour faster.

D) An increase of $4°C$ will make a gallon of milk go sour 4 hours faster.

8

An antique lamp was sold at an auction. The price p of the lamp, in dollars, during the auction can be modeled by the equation $p = 900 - 10t$, where t is the number of seconds left in the auction. According to the model, what is the meaning of the 900 in the equation?

A) The starting auction price of the lamp

B) The final auction price of the lamp

C) The increase in the price of the lamp per second

D) The time it took to auction off the lamp, in seconds

9

$$y = 1.30x - 1.50$$

A bank teller uses the equation above to exchange U.S. dollars into euros, where y is the euro amount and x is the U.S. dollar amount. Which of the following is the best interpretation of the 1.50 in the equation?

A) The bank charges 1.50 euros to do the currency exchange.

B) The bank charges 1.50 U.S. dollars to do the currency exchange.

C) One U.S. dollar is worth 1.50 euros.

D) One euro is worth 1.50 U.S. dollars.

A calculator is allowed on the following questions.

10

$$t = \frac{2x + 9}{5}$$

The equation above models the time t, in seconds, it takes to load a web page with x images. Based on the model, by how many seconds does each image increase the load time of a web page?

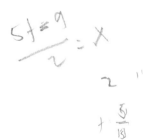

Questions 11-13 refer to the following information.

Daily Profit (y)

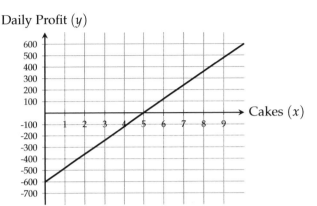

The relationship between the daily profit y, in dollars, of a bakery and the number of cakes sold by the bakery is graphed in the xy-plane above.

11

What does the slope of the line represent?

A) The price of each cake

B) The profit generated from each cake sold

C) The daily profit generated from all the cakes that were sold

D) The number of cakes that need to be sold to make a daily profit of 100 dollars

12

Which of the following is the best interpretation of the y-intercept in the context of this problem?

A) The price of each cake

B) The cost of making each cake

C) The daily costs of running a bakery

D) The daily cost of making the cakes that weren't able to be sold

13

What does it mean that $(5,0)$ is a solution to the equation of the line?

A) The bakery needs to sell 5 cakes per day to cover its daily expenses.

B) Each cake must be sold for at least 5 dollars to cover the cost of making it.

C) It costs 5 dollars to make each cake.

D) Each day, the bakery gives the first 5 cakes away for free.

▲

14

$$T = 56 + 5h$$

To warm up his room, Patrick turns on the heater. The temperature T of his room, in degrees Fahrenheit, can be modeled by the equation above, where h is the number of hours since the heater started running. Based on the model, what is the temperature increase, in degrees Fahrenheit, for every 30 minutes the heater is turned on?

15

$$2y - x = 14$$

Alice owns a pet frog but would like to add turtles to the same tank. The local veterinarian uses the equation above to determine the total amount of water y, in gallons, that should be held in the tank for x turtles to thrive alongside Alice's frog. Based on the equation, which of the following must be true?

I. One additional gallon of water can support two more turtles.

II. One additional turtle requires two more gallons of water.

III. One more turtle requires an additional half a gallon of water.

A) II only

B) III only

C) I and II only

D) I and III only

16

$$C = 1.5 + 2.5x$$

A local post office uses the equation above to determine the cost C, in dollars, of mailing a shipment weighing x pounds. An increase of 10 dollars in the mailing cost is equivalent to an increase of how many pounds in the weight of the shipment?

A) 2

B) 2.5

C) 4

D) 5

15
Functions

A function is a machine that takes an input, transforms it, and spits out an output. In math, functions are denoted by $f(x)$, with x being the input. So for the function

$$f(x) = x^2 + 1$$

every input is squared and then added to one to get the output. It's important to understand that x is a completely arbitrary label—it's just a placeholder for the input. In fact, I can put in whatever I want as the input, including values with x in them:

$$f(2x) = (2x)^2 + 1$$

$$f(a) = a^2 + 1$$

$$f(b+1) = (b+1)^2 + 1$$

$$f(\star) = (\star)^2 + 1$$

$$f(\text{Panda}) = (\text{Panda})^2 + 1$$

Notice the careful use of parentheses. In the first equation, for example, $(2x)^2$ is not the same as $2x^2$. Wrap the input in parentheses and you'll never go wrong.

EXAMPLE 1: If $f(x) = (x+1)^x$, then what is the value of $f(0) + f(1) + f(2) + f(3)$?

Just plug in the inputs.

$$f(0) + f(1) + f(2) + f(3) = (0+1)^0 + (1+1)^1 + (2+1)^2 + (3+1)^3$$

$$= 1^0 + 2^1 + 3^2 + 4^3$$

$$= 1 + 2 + 9 + 64$$

$$= \boxed{76}$$

EXAMPLE 2:

$$f(x) = \frac{4}{x^2 - 10x + 25}$$

For what value of x is the function f above undefined?

Because we can't divide by 0, **a function is undefined when the denominator is zero.** Setting the denominator to zero,

$$x^2 - 10x + 25 = 0$$
$$(x - 5)^2 = 0$$
$$x = \boxed{5}$$

The function f is undefined when $x = 5$.

This would be a good time to talk about domain and range:

- **Domain:** The set of all possible input values (x) to a function (values that don't lead to an invalid operation or an undefined output).

- **Range:** The set of all possible output values (y) from a function.

In Example 2, $x = 5$ leads to $f(x)$ being undefined. However, all other values of x give real number outputs. Therefore, the domain of f is all real numbers except 5. To verify, we can take a look at the graph of f:

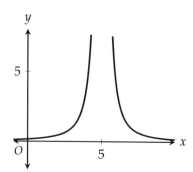

As you can see, the graph has no y-value when $x = 5$. In fact, $x = 5$ is like an invisible line that the graph approaches but never crosses. We call these lines **vertical asymptotes**. To summarize, the function f has one vertical asymptote with equation $x = 5$.

You might've also noticed that the graph never goes below the x-axis. It's another line that the graph approaches but never crosses. The x-axis, in this case, is a **horizontal asymptote**. The function f has one horizontal asymptote with equation $y = 0$.

Because there are no points on the graph that have a y-value of 0 or below, the range of f is all positive real numbers. Put mathematically, $f(x) > 0$. By the way, this makes sense. Because of the square in the denominator of $f(x) = \dfrac{4}{x^2 - 10x + 25} = \dfrac{4}{(x - 5)^2}$, you always get a positive output for any value of x in the domain.

Let's summarize. To find the domain, start with all real numbers and then exclude the values of x for which the function is invalid or undefined. For example, the domain of $y = \sqrt{x}$ is $x \geq 0$ because we can't take the square root of negative numbers.

To find the range, graph the function on your calculator and figure out the possible values of y, taking note of any horizontal asymptotes.

EXAMPLE 3: If $f(x-1) = 6x$ and $g(x) = x+3$, what is the value of $f(g(2))$?

Whenever you see composite functions (functions of other functions), start from the inside and work your way out. First,
$$g(2) = 2+3 = 5$$

Now we have to figure out the value of $f(5)$.

Well, we can plug in $x = 6$ into $f(x-1) = 6x$ to get $f(5) = 6(6) = \boxed{36}$.

EXAMPLE 4: Functions f and g are defined by $f(x) = x+1$ and $g(x) = \dfrac{x}{2}$. If $f(g(f(k))) = 10$, what is the value of k?

Again, we start from the inside and work our way out:
$$f(k) = k+1$$
$$g(k+1) = \frac{k+1}{2}$$
$$f\left(\frac{k+1}{2}\right) = \frac{k+1}{2}+1$$

Finally,
$$\frac{k+1}{2}+1 = 10$$
$$\frac{k+1}{2} = 9$$
$$k+1 = 18$$
$$k = \boxed{17}$$

As we've mentioned, a function takes an input and returns an output. Well, these input and output pairs allow us to graph any function as a set of points in the xy-plane, with the input as x and the output as y. In fact, $y = x^2 + 1$ is the same as $f(x) = x^2 + 1$. Both $f(x)$ and y are the same thing—they're used to denote the output. The only reason we use y is that it's consistent with the y-axis being the y-axis.

Anytime $f(x)$ is used in a graphing question, think of it as the y. So if a question states that $f(x) > 0$, all y values are positive and the graph is always above the x-axis. It's extremely important that you learn to think of points on a graph as the inputs and outputs of a function.

EXAMPLE 5:

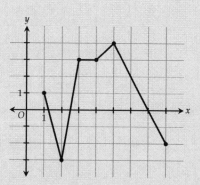

The graph of $f(x)$ is shown in the xy-plane above. For what value of x is $f(x)$ at its maximum?

Again, when it comes to graphs, interpret $f(x)$ as the y. This question is asking for the point on the graph with the highest y-value. That point is $(5, 4)$. The x-value there is $\boxed{5}$.

EXAMPLE 6: If the function with equation $y = ax^2 + 3$ crosses the point $(1, 2)$, what is the value of a?

Remember—a point is just an input and an output, an x and a y. Because $(1, 2)$ is a point on the graph of the function, we can plug in 1 for x and 2 for y.

$$2 = a(1)^2 + 3$$
$$2 = a + 3$$
$$a = \boxed{-1}$$

EXAMPLE 7: If the function $y = x^2 + 2x - 4$ contains the point $(m, 2m)$ and $m > 0$, what is the value of m?

It's important not to get intimidated by all the variables. The question gives us a point on the graph, so let's plug it in.

$$y = x^2 + 2x - 4$$
$$2m = m^2 + 2m - 4$$
$$0 = m^2 - 4$$

From here we can see that $m = \pm 2$. The question states that $m > 0$, so $\boxed{m = 2}$.

The **zeros, roots, and x-intercepts** of a function are all just different terms for the same thing—the values of x that make $f(x) = 0$. Graphically, they refer to the values of x where the function crosses the x-axis.

EXAMPLE 8:

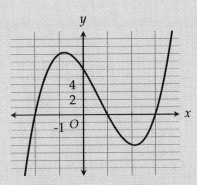

The graph of $f(x) = x^3 - 2x^2 - 5x + 6$ is shown in the xy-plane above.

PART 1: How many distinct zeros does the function f have?

PART 2: If k is a constant such that $f(x) = k$ has 1 solution, which of the following could be the value of k?

A) -3 B) 1 C) 5 D) 9

Part 1 Solution: The graph crosses the x-axis three times, so f has $\boxed{3}$ distinct zeros. From the graph, we can see that these zeros are $-2, 1$, and 3.

Part 2 Solution: This question is quite involved, so don't panic if you feel lost during the explanation. Read all the way through and then go back to the bits that were confusing. I promise you'll be able to make sense of everything.

To truly understand this question, first realize that a constant is just a function. No matter the input, we always get the same output. In this question, we can write it as $y = k$ or $g(x) = k$. So let's say $k = -3$. What does $y = -3$ look like? A horizontal line at -3!

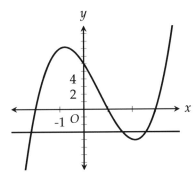

Now when a question asks for the **solutions** to $f(x) = k$, it's merely referring to the intersection points of $f(x)$ and the horizontal line $y = k$. In general, if a question sets two functions equal to each other, $f(x) = g(x)$, and asks you about the solutions, it's referring to the intersection points. After all, it's only at the intersection points that the value of y is the same for both functions. In this particular case, $g(x)$ just happens to be a constant function, $g(x) = k$.

The number of solutions is equivalent to the number of intersection points. So if $k = -3$ as shown above, there must be 3 solutions to $f(x) = -3$, as represented by the 3 intersection points. The solutions themselves are the x-values of those points. We can estimate them to be $-2.2, 1.6$, and 2.6.

Getting back to the original problem, we have to choose a k such that there is only one solution. Now we're thinking backwards. Instead of being given the constant, we have to choose it. Where might we place a horizontal line so that there's only one intersection point? Certainly not at -3 because we just showed how that would result in 3 solutions.

Well, looking back at the graph, we could place one just above 8 or just below -4. Horizontal lines at these values would intersect with $f(x)$ just once. Looking at the answer choices, 9 is the only one that meets our condition. Answer $\boxed{(D)}$.

Let's take a moment to revisit part 1. In part 1, we found the number of intersection points between $f(x)$ and the x-axis. But realize that the x-axis is just the horizontal line $y = 0$. In counting the number of intersection points between $f(x)$ and the horizontal line $y = 0$, what you were really doing is finding the number of solutions to $f(x) = 0$.

If you didn't grasp everything in this example the first time through, it's ok. Take your time and go through it again, making sure you fully understand each of the concepts. The SAT will throw quite a few questions at you related to the zeros of functions as well as the solutions to $f(x) = g(x)$.

Hopefully by now, you're starting to see constants as horizontal lines. So for instance, if $f(x) > 5$, that means the entire graph of f is above the horizontal line $y = 5$. Thinking of constants in this way will help you on a lot of SAT graph questions.

EXAMPLE 9: Which of the following could be the graph of $y = x^3 + 2x^2 + x + 1$?

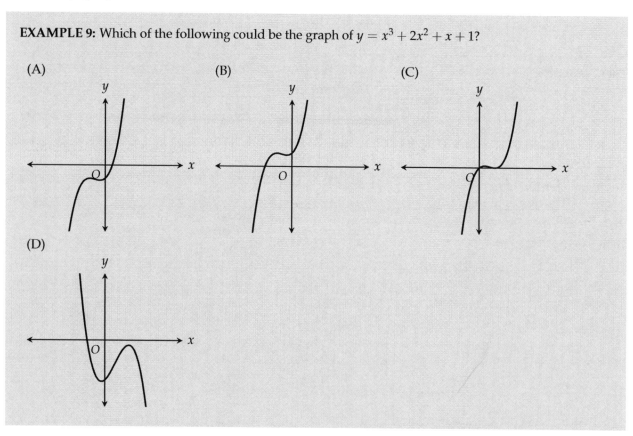

Although the given function looks complicated and you might be tempted to graph it on your calculator, this is the easiest question ever! All you have to do is find a point that's certain to be on the graph and eliminate the graphs that don't have that point. So what's an easy point to find and test?

Plug in $x = 0$ to get $y = 1$. Now which graphs contain the coordinate $(0, 1)$? Only graph $\boxed{(B)}$.

By the way, numbers like 0 and 1 are particularly good for finding "easy" points to use for this strategy.

CHAPTER EXERCISE: Answers for this chapter start on page 288.

A calculator should NOT be used on the following questions.

1

x	y
0	20
1	21
3	29

The table above displays several points on the graph of the function f in the xy-plane. Which of the following could be $f(x)$?

A) $f(x) = 20x$

B) $f(x) = x + 20$

C) $f(x) = x - 20$

D) $f(x) = x^2 + 20$

2

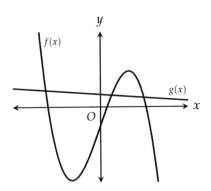

In the portion of the xy-plane shown above, for how many values of x does $f(x) = g(x)$?

A) None

B) One

C) Two

D) Three

3

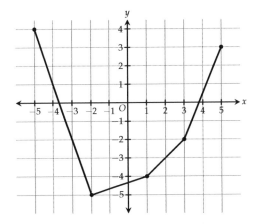

The graph of the function f is shown in the xy-plane above. If $f(a) = f(3)$, which of the following could be the value of a?

A) -4

B) -3

C) -2

D) 1

4

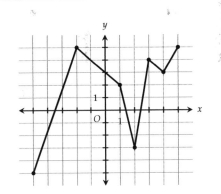

The function f is graphed in the xy-plane above. For how many values of x does $f(x) = 3$?

A) Two

B) Three

C) Four

D) Five

5

For which of the following functions is it true that $f(-3) = f(3)$?

A) $f(x) = \dfrac{2}{x}$

B) $f(x) = \dfrac{x^3}{3}$

C) $f(x) = 3x^2 + 1$

D) $f(x) = x + 2$

6

The function f is defined by $f(x) = 3x + 2$ and the function g is defined by $g(x) = f(2x) - 1$. What is the value of $g(10)$?

7

If $f(x) = \dfrac{16 + x^2}{2x}$ for all $x \neq 0$, what is the value of $f(-4)$?

A) -8

B) -4

C) 4

D) 8

8

x	0	1	2
$f(x)$	-2	3	18

Several values of the function f are given in the table above. If $f(x) = ax^2 + b$ where a and b are constants, what is the value of $f(3)$?

A) 23

B) 39

C) 43

D) 56

9

If $f(x) = x^2$, for which of the following values of c is $f(c) < c$?

A) $\dfrac{1}{2}$

B) 1

C) $\dfrac{3}{2}$

D) 2

10

If the graph of the function f has x-intercepts at -3 and 2, and a y-intercept at 12, which of the following could define f?

A) $f(x) = (x + 3)^2(x - 2)$

B) $f(x) = (x + 3)(x - 2)^2$

C) $f(x) = (x - 3)^2(x + 2)$

D) $f(x) = (x - 3)(x + 2)^2$

11

$$f(x) = x^2 + 1$$

$$g(x) = x^2 - 1$$

The functions f and g are defined above. What is the value of $f(g(2))$?

A) 3

B) 5

C) 10

D) 17

12

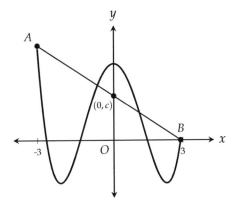

The graph of the function f and line segment $\overline{AB}$ are shown in the xy-plane above. For how many values of x between -3 and 3 does $f(x) = c$?

13

x	$f(x)$
-4	3
-2	5
0	2
2	16
3	4
4	8

The table above gives some values for the function f. If $g(x) = 2f(x)$, what is the value of k if $g(k) = 8$?

A) 2

B) 3

C) 4

D) 8

14

$$f(x) = \sqrt{x - 2}$$

The function f is defined above for all $x \geq 2$. Which of the following is equal to $f(18) - f(11)$?

A) $f(3)$

B) $f(5)$

C) $f(6)$

D) $f(7)$

A calculator is allowed on the following questions.

15

$$y = \frac{x + 1}{x - 1}$$

Which of the following points in the xy-plane is NOT on the graph of y?

A) $\left(-2, \dfrac{1}{3}\right)$

B) $(-1, 0)$

C) $(0, -1)$

D) $(1, 2)$

16

Let the function g be defined by $g(x) = \sqrt{3x}$. If $g(a) = 6$, what is the value of a?

A) 3

B) 6

C) 9

D) 12

Questions 17-18 refer to the following information.

x	$f(x)$	$g(x)$
-2	3	4
-1	5	2
0	-2	-3
1	3	5
2	6	7
3	7	1

The functions f and g are defined for the six values of x shown in the table above.

17

What is the value of $f(g(-1))$?

A) -2

B) 3

C) 5

D) 6

18

If $g(c) = 5$, what is the value of $f(c)$?

A) -2

B) 3

C) 5

D) 6

19

If $f(x) = -3x + 5$ and $\frac{1}{2}f(a) = 10$, what is the value of a?

A) -8

B) -5

C) 5

D) 8

20

x	$f(x)$
0	-4
1	-8
2	3
3	6
4	7
5	2
6	4
7	5

Several values of the function f are given in the table above. If the function g is defined by $g(x) = f(2x - 1)$, what is the value of $g(3)$?

A) 2

B) 6

C) 5

D) 7

21

$$f(x) = 4x - 3$$
$$g(x) = 3x + 5$$

The functions f and g are defined above. Which of the following is equal to $f(8)$?

A) $g(1)$

B) $g(3)$

C) $g(5)$

D) $g(8)$

22

If $f(x)$ is a linear function such that $f(2) \leq f(3)$, $f(4) \geq f(5)$, and $f(6) = 10$, which of the following must be true?

A) $f(3) < f(0) < f(4)$

B) $f(0) = 0$

C) $f(0) > 10$

D) $f(0) = 10$

23

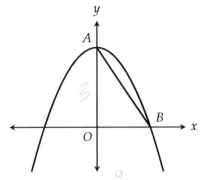

The graph of the function $y = 9 - x^2$ is shown in the xy-plane above. What is the length of $\overline{AB}$?

A) $3\sqrt{2}$

B) $3\sqrt{10}$

C) 9

D) $9\sqrt{10}$

24

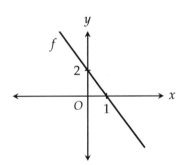

The function f is graphed in the xy-plane above. If the function g is defined by $g(x) = f(x) + 4$, what is the x-intercept of $g(x)$?

A) -3

B) -1

C) 3

D) 4

25

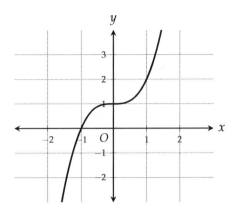

The function $f(x) = x^3 + 1$ is graphed in the xy-plane above. If the function g is defined by $g(x) = x + k$, where k is a constant, and $f(x) = g(x)$ has 3 solutions, which of the following could be the value of k?

A) -1

B) 0

C) 1

D) 2

26

In the xy-plane, the function $y = ax + 12$, where a is a constant, passes through the point $(-a, a)$. If $a > 0$, what is the value of a?

127

16
Quadratics

Just as lines were one group of functions that have their own properties, quadratics are another. A quadratic is a function in the form

$$f(x) = ax^2 + bx + c$$

in which the highest power of x is 2. The graph of a quadratic is a parabola.

To review quadratics, we'll walk through a few examples to demonstrate the various properties you need to know.

QUADRATIC 1:

$$f(x) = x^2 - 4x - 21$$

The Roots

The roots refer to the values of x that make $f(x) = 0$. They're also called x-intercepts and solutions. We'll mainly use the term "root" in this chapter, but the other terms are just as common. Don't forget that they all mean the same thing. Here, we can just factor to find the roots:

$$x^2 - 4x - 21 = 0$$
$$(x - 7)(x + 3) = 0$$
$$x = 7, -3$$

The roots are 7 and -3. Graphically, this means the quadratic crosses the x-axis at $x = 7$ and $x = -3$.

The Sum and Product of the Roots

We already found the roots, so their sum is just $7 + (-3) = 4$ and their product is just $7 \times -3 = -21$. This was really easy, so why do we care about these values? Because sometimes you'll have to find the sum or the product of the roots **without** knowing the roots themselves. How do we do that?

Given a quadratic of the form $y = ax^2 + bx + c$, the sum of the roots is equal to $-\dfrac{b}{a}$ and the product of the roots is equal to $\dfrac{c}{a}$. In our example, $a = 1, b = -4, c = -21$. So,

$$\text{Sum} = -\frac{b}{a} = -\frac{-4}{1} = 4$$

$$\text{Product} = \frac{c}{a} = -\frac{-21}{1} = -21$$

See how we were able to determine these values without knowing the roots themselves? The roots that we found earlier just confirm our values.

The Vertex

The vertex is the midpoint of a parabola.

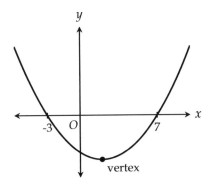

The x-coordinate of the vertex is always the midpoint of the two roots, which can be found by averaging them. Because the roots are 7 and -3, the vertex is at $x = \dfrac{7 + (-3)}{2} = 2$. When $x = 2, f(x) = (2)^2 - 4(2) - 21 = -25$. Therefore, the vertex is at $(2, -25)$. Note that the maximum or minimum of a quadratic is always at the vertex. In this case, it's a minimum of -25.

Vertex Form

Just as slope-intercept form ($y = mx + b$) is one way of representing a line, vertex form is one way of representing a quadratic function. We've already seen two different ways quadratics can be represented, namely standard form ($y = ax^2 + bx + c$) and factored form ($y = (x - a)(x - b)$). Vertex form looks like $y = a(x - h)^2 + k$.

To get a quadratic function into vertex form, we have to do something called completing the square. Let's walk through it step-by-step:

$$y = x^2 - 4x - 21$$

See the middle term? The -4. That's the key. The first step is to divide it by 2 to get -2. Then write the following:

$$y = (x - 2)^2 - 21$$

See where we put the -2? The first part is done. Now the second step is to take that -2 and square it. We get 4.

$$y = (x - 2)^2 - 21 - 4$$

See where we put the 4? We subtracted it at the end. The vertex form is then

$$y = (x - 2)^2 - 25$$

To recap, divide the middle coefficient by 2 to get the number inside the parentheses. Subtract the square of that number at the end. Completing the square takes some time and practice, so if you didn't catch all of this, first prove to yourself that it is indeed the same quadratic by expanding the result. Then repeat the process of completing the square yourself. If you've been taught a slightly different way, feel free to use it. We'll do many more examples in this chapter.

Now why do we care about vertex form? Well, look at the numbers! It's called vertex form for a reason. The vertex $(2, -25)$ can be found just by looking at the numbers in the equation. But we already found the vertex, you say! Yes, that's true, but we had to find the roots to do so earlier, and finding the roots is not always so easy. Vertex form allows us to find the vertex without knowing the roots of a quadratic. It's also very much tested on the SAT!

One final note—one of the most common mistakes students make is to look at $y = (x - 2)^2 - 25$ and think the vertex is at $(-2, -25)$ instead of $(2, -25)$. One pattern of thinking I use to avoid this mistake is to ask, *What value of x would make the thing inside the parentheses zero?* Well, $x = 2$ *would make* $x - 2$ *equal to 0. Therefore, the vertex is at* $x = 2$. This is the same type of thinking you would use to get the solutions from the factored form $y = (x - a)(x - b)$.

The Discriminant

If a quadratic is in the form $ax^2 + bx + c$, then the discriminant is equal to $b^2 - 4ac$. As we'll explain later, the discriminant is a component of the quadratic formula. Before we explain its significance, let's calculate the discriminant for our first example,

$$f(x) = x^2 - 4x - 21$$

$$\text{Discriminant} = b^2 - 4ac = (-4)^2 - 4(1)(-21) = 100$$

Now, what does the discriminant mean? Well, the value of the discriminant does not matter. What matters is the **sign** of the discriminant—whether it's positive, negative, or zero. In other words, we don't care that it's 100, we just care that it's positive. Letting D be short for discriminant,

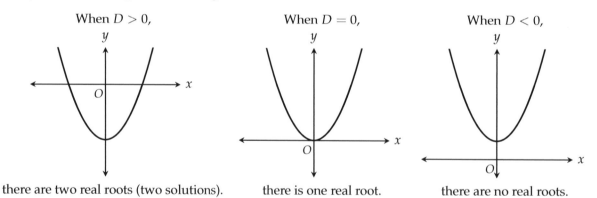

When $D > 0$,	When $D = 0$,	When $D < 0$,
there are two real roots (two solutions).	there is one real root.	there are no real roots.

The Quadratic Formula

As we've seen, the roots are the most important aspect of a quadratic. Once you have the roots, things like vertex form and the discriminant are not as helpful. Unfortunately, the roots aren't always easy to find or work with. That's when vertex form, the discriminant, and the sum/product of the roots can get us to the answer faster.

But if we must find the roots, there is always one surefire way to do so—the quadratic formula.

$$x = \frac{-b \pm \sqrt{b^2 - 4ac}}{2a}$$

for $ax^2 + bx + c = 0$. For learning purposes, let's apply it to our example.

$$f(x) = x^2 - 4x - 21$$

The roots or solutions are

$$x = \frac{-(-4) \pm \sqrt{(-4)^2 - 4(1)(-21)}}{2(1)} = \frac{4 \pm \sqrt{100}}{2} = \frac{4 \pm 10}{2} = 7 \text{ or } -3$$

And we get the same values as we did through factoring.

Notice that the discriminant, $b^2 - 4ac$, is tucked under the square root in the quadratic formula. How does this help us to understand what we know about the discriminant?

Well, when $b^2 - 4ac > 0$, the "$\pm$" takes effect and we end up with two different roots. When $b^2 - 4ac = 0$, the "$\pm$" does not have an effect since we're essentially adding and subtracting 0, both of which give us the same root. When $b^2 - 4ac < 0$, we're taking the square root of a negative number, which is undefined and gives us no real roots (we'll talk about imaginary number in a later chapter).

Hopefully, the quadratic formula helps you understand where the discriminant and its various meanings come from. Understanding this connection will help you remember the concepts.

Now that we've taken you on a thorough tour through the properties of quadratics, we'll go through a few more examples to illustrate some important variations, but we'll do so at a much faster pace.

QUADRATIC 2:
$$f(x) = -x^2 + 6x - 10$$

The Roots

This quadratic cannot be factored. And in fact, if we look at the discriminant,

$$b^2 - 4ac = (6)^2 - 4(-1)(-10) = -4$$

it's negative, which means there are no real roots or solutions. The graph of the quadratic makes this even more clear:

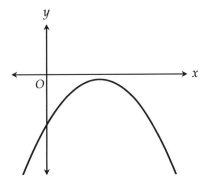

When the coefficient of the x^2 term is negative, the parabola is in the shape of an upside-down "U."

The Sum and Product of the Roots

$$f(x) = -x^2 + 6x - 10$$

$$\text{Sum} = -\frac{b}{a} = -\frac{6}{-1} = 6$$

$$\text{Product} = \frac{c}{a} = \frac{-10}{-1} = 10$$

Wait, what!? We already determined that there were no roots. How can there be a sum and a product of roots that don't exist? Well, the quadratic doesn't have any *real* roots, but it does have *imaginary* roots. The values above are the sum and product of these imaginary roots. We'll cover imaginary numbers in a later chapter.

Vertex Form

Because the roots are imaginary, we can't use their midpoint to find the vertex. In these cases, we must get the quadratic in vertex form. We'll have to complete the square.

$$y = -x^2 + 6x - 10$$

First, multiply everything by negative 1 to get the negative out of the x^2 term. Having the negative there makes things needlessly complicated. We'll multiply everything back by -1 later.

$$-y = x^2 - 6x + 10$$

Divide the middle term by 2 to get -3 and square this result to get 9. Remember that we put the -3 inside the parentheses with x and subtract the 9 at the end. Putting these pieces in place,

$$-y = (x - 3)^2 + 10 - 9$$

$$-y = (x - 3)^2 + 1$$

Now multiply everything by -1 again,

$$y = -(x - 3)^2 - 1$$

Now it's easy to see that the vertex is at $(3, -1)$. And because the graph is an upside-down "U," -1 is the maximum value of $f(x)$.

QUADRATIC 3:

$$f(x) = 2x^2 + 5x - 3$$

The Roots

We can factor this quadratic to get

$$2x^2 + 5x - 3 = 0$$
$$(2x - 1)(x + 3) = 0$$
$$x = 0.5, -3$$

The roots are 0.5 and -3. If you don't know how we factored this, unfortunately teaching factoring from the ground up is not within the scope of this book. Don't be afraid to look up factoring lessons and drills online and in your textbooks. It's an essential skill to have. Just know that all methods involve a little trial and error.

If you're ever stuck, the quadratic formula is always an option.

The Sum and Product of the Roots

$$\text{Sum} = -\frac{b}{a} = -\frac{5}{2} = -2.5$$

$$\text{Product} = \frac{c}{a} = \frac{-3}{2} = -1.5$$

The Vertex

Averaging the two roots to find the x-coordinate of the vertex,

$$\frac{0.5 + (-3)}{2} = \frac{-2.5}{2} = -1.25$$

Plugging this into $f(x)$ to find the y-coordinate,

$$f(-1.25) = 2(-1.25)^2 + 5(-1.25) - 3 = -6.125$$

The vertex is at $(-1.25, -6.125)$. Because the quadratic opens upward in the shape of a "U," the minimum value of $f(x)$ is -6.125.

Vertex Form

$$y = 2x^2 + 5x - 3$$

First, divide everything by 2. Before completing the square, always make sure the coefficient of x^2 is 1. We'll multiply the 2 back later.

$$\frac{y}{2} = x^2 + \frac{5}{2}x - \frac{3}{2}$$

Divide the middle term by 2 to get $\frac{5}{4}$ and square this result to get $\frac{25}{16}$. We put the $\frac{5}{4}$ inside the parentheses with x and subtract the $\frac{25}{16}$ at the end.

$$\frac{y}{2} = \left(x + \frac{5}{4}\right)^2 - \frac{3}{2} - \frac{25}{16}$$

Combining the constants,

$$\frac{y}{2} = \left(x + \frac{5}{4}\right)^2 - \frac{49}{16}$$

Multiplying by 2,

$$y = 2\left(x + \frac{5}{4}\right)^2 - \frac{49}{8}$$

$$y = 2(x + 1.25)^2 - 6.125$$

This is consistent with the vertex found above.

The Discriminant

For the sake of completeness, let's calculate the discriminant. Hopefully, it will confirm the fact that this quadratic has two distinct real roots.

$$y = 2x^2 + 5x - 3$$

$$\text{Discriminant} = b^2 - 4ac = (5)^2 - 4(2)(-3) = 49$$

The discriminant is positive, which confirms the fact that this quadratic has two real roots.

QUADRATIC 4:

$$f(x) = 4x^2 - 12x + 9$$

The Roots

We could factor this, but let's use the quadratic formula instead.

$$x = \frac{-b \pm \sqrt{b^2 - 4ac}}{2a} = \frac{-(-12) \pm \sqrt{(-12)^2 - 4(4)(9)}}{2(4)} = \frac{12 \pm \sqrt{0}}{8} = \frac{3}{2}$$

As you can see, the discriminant is 0 and the quadratic has just one root, $\frac{3}{2}$.

The Sum and Product of the Roots

$$\text{Sum} = -\frac{b}{a} = -\frac{-12}{4} = 3$$

$$\text{Product} = \frac{c}{a} = \frac{9}{4}$$

If we only have one root, how is it that we can have a sum and a product of two roots? Why are they different from the one root we found?

Here's the thing. While we may say a quadratic has just one root, it really has two roots that are the same. After all, a quadratic, with an x^2 term, is expected to have two roots. When they're the same, we just refer to them as one.

So our "two" roots are $\frac{3}{2}$ and $\frac{3}{2}$. If we add them, we do indeed get 3, and if we multiply them, we do get $\frac{9}{4}$.

The Vertex

When a quadratic has just one root, the x-coordinate of the vertex is the same as the root. That's because a quadratic is tangent to the x-axis when it has one root.

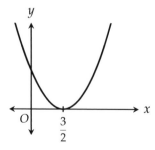

The y-coordinate is, of course, 0. Therefore, the vertex is at $\left(\frac{3}{2}, 0\right)$. The minimum value of $f(x)$ is 0.

Vertex Form

$$y = 4x^2 - 12x + 9$$

First, divide everything by 4. Before completing the square, always make sure the coefficient of x^2 is 1. We'll multiply the 4 back later.

$$\frac{y}{4} = x^2 - 3x + \frac{9}{4}$$

Divide the middle term by 2 to get $-\frac{3}{2}$ and square this result to get $\frac{9}{4}$. We put the $-\frac{3}{2}$ inside the parentheses with x and subtract the $\frac{9}{4}$ at the end.

$$\frac{y}{4} = \left(x - \frac{3}{2}\right)^2 + \frac{9}{4} - \frac{9}{4}$$

The constants cancel out.

$$\frac{y}{4} = \left(x - \frac{3}{2}\right)^2$$

Multiplying by 4,

$$y = 4\left(x - \frac{3}{2}\right)^2$$

This is consistent with the vertex found above.

Wow! We just covered pretty much everything you need to know about quadratics. Unfortunately, we're not quite done yet as there are a few tough question variations that you should be exposed to.

EXAMPLE 1: In the xy-plane, the parabola with equation $y = x^2 - 5x + 6$ intersects the line $y = 3x - 10$ at point (a, b). What is the value of b?

This is a question type that we already covered in the systems of equations chapter, but we're reviewing it again here because it will help you understand the next few examples. The core concept is that whenever you have to find the intersection point(s) of two graphs, solve the system consisting of their equations. The solutions to the system are the intersection points. Here, we have

$$y = x^2 - 5x + 6$$
$$y = 3x - 10$$

Substituting the second equation into the first,

$$3x - 10 = x^2 - 5x + 6$$
$$0 = x^2 - 8x + 16$$
$$0 = (x - 4)^2$$
$$x = 4$$

To find the y, we plug $x = 4$ into either of the original equations: $y = 3(4) - 10 = 2$. Therefore, the point of intersection is at $(4, 2)$ and $b = \boxed{2}$.

EXAMPLE 2: How many times does the graph of $y = -x^2 + 6x + 3$ intersect the line $y = 10$ in the xy-plane?

We're dealing with the intersection of two graphs again. So what do we do? We solve the system consisting of their equations. Substituting the second equation into the first, we get

$$10 = -x^2 + 6x + 3$$

$$0 = -x^2 + 6x - 7$$

Now we *could* go ahead and finish solving this to find the intersection point(s) just like we did in the previous example, but there's a faster way. For the purposes of this question, we don't care where the intersection points are. We just want to know *how many* there are.

Sound familiar? We can use the discriminant to do that.

$$\text{Discriminant} = b^2 - 4ac = (6)^2 - 4(-1)(-7) = 8$$

The discriminant is positive, which means there are 2 solutions to the equation we set up above. If there are 2 solutions to the equation above, there must be $\boxed{2}$ intersection points. To summarize, we didn't bother finding the two values of x. They could've been $x = 2$ and $x = 100$ for all we care, and the intersection points might've been $(2, 5)$ and $(100, 6)$. It doesn't matter. What mattered was that there were two of them, and we used the discriminant to determine that. If the discriminant were 0, there would only be one intersection point. And if the discriminant were less than 0, there would be no intersection points.

Make sure you understand this question. Feel free to go back and figure out where the intersection points actually are (*Hint:* It's not fun. You'll need the quadratic formula. That's why the discriminant was so helpful).

EXAMPLE 3:

$$y - k = 0$$

$$y = x^2 - 3x + 1$$

In the system of equations above, k is a constant. For which of the following values of k does the system of equations have no real solutions?

A) -2 B) -1 C) 0 D) 1

First, we get $y = k$ from the first equation and substitute this into the second equation,

$$k = x^2 - 3x + 1$$

$$0 = x^2 - 3x + (1 - k)$$

If the system of equations has no real solution, then the equation above should have no real solution. The discriminant should be less than 0.

$$\text{Discriminant} = b^2 - 4ac = (-3)^2 - 4(1)(1 - k) = 9 - 4 + 4k = 5 + 4k$$

Now we test each of the answer choices to see which one results in $5 + 4k$ being negative. Only -2, answer $\boxed{(A)}$, produces a negative discriminant.

These questions are some of the toughest you'll see on the SAT, especially when you can't use your calculator. Go back and make sure you understand them.

EXAMPLE 4: A biologist uses the function $p(n) = -100n^2 + 1,000n$ to model the population of seagulls on a beach in year number n, where $1 \leq n \leq 10$. Which of the following equivalent forms of $p(n)$ displays the maximum population of seagulls and the number of the year in which the population reaches that maximum as constants or coefficients?

(A) $p(n) = -4n(25n - 250)$ (B) $p(n) = -10(10n^2 - 100n)$ (C) $p(n) = -100(n-5)^2 + 2,500$

(D) $p(n) = -100(n-7)^2 + 4,900$

Anytime you see a quadratics question that deals with the maximum or minimum of a function output (i.e. the y-value), either figure out the vertex or look for vertex form. After all, the vertex is where the maximum or minimum occurs. In fact, the answer is either (C) or (D) because those are the only ones in vertex form. Furthermore, with a little calculation, it's easy to see that (D) does not expand to be the original equation, so the answer is (C).

However, for learning purposes (and for the tougher questions), I'll show you how to do this question in two different ways. We can find the vertex using the average of the roots and then reverse engineer the vertex form. Or we can transform the equation into vertex form directly.

Solution 1: To find the roots, we set the equation equal to 0 and factor,

$$-100n^2 + 1,000n = 0$$
$$-100n(n - 10) = 0$$
$$n = 0, 10$$

The roots are 0 and 10, which means the x-coordinate of the vertex is 5. Now we can plug 5 into $p(n)$ to find the y-coordinate.
$$p(5) = -100(5)^2 + 1,000(5) = 2,500$$

So the vertex is at $(5, 2500)$. Now remember what vertex form looks like: $y = a(x - h)^2 + k$. Given our values, we have
$$p(n) = a(n - 5)^2 + 2,500$$

We now need to find what a is. To do that, we need another point to work with. Well, it's easy to see that $p(n)$ passes through the point $(0, 0)$. Plugging that in,

$$0 = a(0 - 5)^2 + 2,500$$
$$0 = 25a + 2,500$$
$$-25a = 2,500$$
$$a = -100$$

Finally, $p(n) = -100(n - 5)^2 + 2,500$. Answer $\boxed{(C)}$.

Solution 2: This second method involves completing the square to get the vertex form directly. First, divide everything by -100 to ensure the coefficient of n^2 is 1.

$$p(n) = -100n^2 + 1,000n$$

$$\frac{p(n)}{-100} = n^2 - 10n$$

Do you remember what to do next? If we wrote the constant 0 at the end, the "middle" term would be $-10n$. Divide the -10 by 2 to get -5 and square that to get 25. The -5 belongs inside the parentheses with n and the 25 gets subtracted at the end.

$$\frac{p(n)}{-100} = (n-5)^2 - 25$$

Now we can multiply everything back by -100.

$$p(n) = -100(n-5)^2 + 2,500$$

And again, we prove that the answer is $\boxed{(C)}$.

Review:

Given a quadratic of the form, $y = ax^2 + bx + c$,

The roots, also called solutions and x-intercepts, can be found in the following ways:

- Factoring
- Graph on the calculator (look for the x-intercepts)
- The quadratic formula $x = \dfrac{-b \pm \sqrt{b^2 - 4ac}}{2a}$

Sum of the Roots $= -\dfrac{b}{a}$

Product of the Roots $= \dfrac{c}{a}$

The **discriminant** $D = b^2 - 4ac$

- When $D > 0$, there are two real solutions.
- When $D = 0$, there is one real solution.
- When $D < 0$, there are no real solutions.

To find the **vertex**,

- Take the average of the roots to get the x-coordinate. Then plug that value into the quadratic to get the y-coordinate.
- Put the quadratic in vertex form by **completing the square**.

  1. Ensure the coefficient of x^2 is positive 1 by dividing everything by a.

  $$\frac{y}{a} = x^2 + \frac{b}{a}x + \frac{c}{a}$$

  2. Divide the coefficient of the middle term bx to get $\dfrac{b}{2a}$. Square that result to get $\dfrac{b^2}{4a^2}$. Put $\dfrac{b}{2a}$ inside the parentheses with x and subtract $\dfrac{b^2}{4a^2}$ at the end.

  $$\frac{y}{a} = \left(x + \frac{b}{2a}\right)^2 + \frac{c}{a} - \frac{b^2}{4a^2}$$

  3. Multiply everything by a.

  $$y = a\left(x + \frac{b}{2a}\right)^2 + c - \frac{b^2}{4a}$$

  4. It's unnecessary to memorize these steps with the variables. Practice on quadratics with actual numbers. However, do remember what vertex form looks like: $y = a(x - h)^2 + k$.

Whenever you're asked for the **minimum** or the **maximum** of a quadratic, find the vertex.

CHAPTER EXERCISE: Answers for this chapter start on page 291.

A calculator should NOT be used on the following questions.

1

In the xy-plane, what is the distance between the two x-intercepts of the parabola $y = x^2 - 3x - 10$?

A) 3

B) 5

C) 7

D) 10

2

What are the solutions to $x^2 + 4x + 2 = 0$?

A) $x = -2 \pm \sqrt{2}$

B) $x = 2 \pm 2\sqrt{2}$

C) $x = -2 \pm 2\sqrt{2}$

D) $x = -4 \pm 2\sqrt{2}$

3

If $a < 1$ and $2a^2 - 7a + 3 = 0$, what is the value of a?

4

$$3x^2 + 10x = 8$$

If a and b are the two solutions to the equation above and $a > b$, what is the value of b^2?

A) $\dfrac{4}{9}$

B) $\dfrac{2}{3}$

C) 4

D) 16

5

What is the sum of the solutions of $(2x - 3)^2 = 4x + 5$?

6

$$y = -3$$
$$y = x^2 + cx$$

In the system of equations above, c is a constant. For which of the following values of c does the system of equations have exactly two real solutions?

A) -4

B) 1

C) 2

D) 3

A calculator is allowed on the following questions.

7

At which of the following points does the line with equation $y = 4$ intersect the parabola $y = (x+2)^2 - 5$ in the xy-plane?

A) $(-1, 4)$ and $(-5, 4)$

B) $(1, 4)$ and $(-5, 4)$

C) $(1, 4)$ and $(5, 4)$

D) $(-11, 4)$ and $(7, 4)$

8

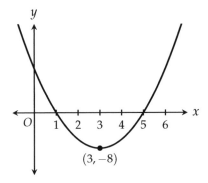

$(3, -8)$

Which of the following equations represents the parabola shown in the xy-plane above?

A) $y = (x-3)^2 - 8$

B) $y = (x+3)^2 + 8$

C) $y = 2(x-3)^2 - 8$

D) $y = 2(x+3)^2 - 8$

9

For what value of t does the equation $v = 5t - t^2$ result in the maximum value of v?

10

$$P = m^2 - 100m - 120,000$$

The monthly profit of a mattress company can be modeled by the equation above, where P is the profit, in dollars, and m is the number of mattresses sold. What is the minimum number of mattresses the company must sell in a given month so that it does not lose money during that month?

11

$$y = -3$$
$$y = ax^2 + 4x - 4$$

In the system of equations above, a is a constant. For which of the following values of a does the system of equations have exactly one real solution?

A) -4

B) -2

C) 2

D) 4

12

$$f(x) = -x^2 + 6x + 20$$

The function f is defined above. Which of the following equivalent forms of $f(x)$ displays the maximum value of f as a constant or coefficient?

A) $f(x) = -(x-3)^2 + 11$

B) $f(x) = -(x-3)^2 + 29$

C) $f(x) = -(x+3)^2 + 11$

D) $f(x) = -(x+3)^2 + 29$

13

$$y = a(x - 3)(x - k)$$

In the quadratic equation above, a and k are constants. If the graph of the equation in the xy-plane is a parabola with vertex $(5, -32)$, what is the value of a?

A) 2

B) 5

C) 6

D) 8

14

In the xy-plane, the line $y = 2x + b$ intersects the parabola $y = x^2 + bx + 5$ at the point $(3, k)$. If b is a constant, what is the value of k?

A) 0

B) 1

C) 2

D) 3

Synthetic Division

Synthetic division involves dividing one polynomial by another in the same way you divided numbers in 3rd grade.

$$\begin{array}{r} 1\ 8\ \text{R}\ 2 \\ 3\overline{\smash{)}5\ 6} \end{array} \qquad \begin{array}{r} x^2\ +\ 3x\ -\ 2 \quad\ \text{R}\ -1 \\ x-1\overline{\smash{)}x^3\ +\ 2x^2\ -\ 5x\ +\ 1} \end{array}$$

I'll teach you the long "mathematical" way first, but then direct you towards several shortcuts that will get you through almost any synthetic division question on the SAT without using the long way. These questions rarely show up, and if they do, they'll show up only once.

Let's retrace the steps of dividing 56 by 3 so you can see how the same logic applies to synthetic division.

First, we see that 3 goes into 5 once. We put a 1 on top and a $1 \times 3 = 3$ below the 5. We then subtract to get 2 and bring the 6 down.

$$\begin{array}{r} 1 \\ 3\overline{\smash{)}5\ 6} \\ \underline{3} \\ 2\ 6 \end{array}$$

Now how many times does 3 go into 26? 8 times. So we put an 8 up top and a $3 \times 8 = 24$ below the 26. Subtracting, we get 2.

$$\begin{array}{r} 1\ 8 \\ 3\overline{\smash{)}5\ 6} \\ \underline{3} \\ 2\ 6 \\ \underline{2\ 4} \\ 2 \end{array}$$

At this point, there are no more digits to bring down and 3 does not go into 2. Therefore, 3 goes into 56 eighteen times with a remainder of two. This result can be written in the following form:

$$\frac{56}{3} = 18\frac{2}{3}$$

where 18 is the quotient, 2 is the remainder, and 3 is the divisor.

The process of dividing a polynomial is essentially the same. To show you how synthetic division works, let's divide $x^3 + 2x^2 - 5x + 1$ by $x - 1$.

How many times does $x - 1$ go into x^3? x^2 times. Why? Because $x \times x^2 = x^3$. The goal is to match x^3. We don't care about the -1 during this "fitting in" step. Now, $(x - 1) \times x^2 = x^3 - x^2$. This is what we put below the dividend.

$$
\begin{array}{r}
x^2 \\
x - 1 \overline{\smash{\big)}\ x^3 + 2x^2 - 5x + 1} \\
x^3 - x^2
\end{array}
$$

Finally, we subtract like we do in basic number division. Notice that we must subtract each element, so the $-x^2$ becomes $+x^2$, yielding $3x^2$. Unlike in long division with numbers, all the remaining terms from the dividend should be brought down for each step in synthetic division.

$$
\begin{array}{r}
x^2 \\
x - 1 \overline{\smash{\big)}\ x^3 + 2x^2 - 5x + 1} \\
\underline{x^3 - x^2 } \\
3x^2 - 5x + 1
\end{array}
$$

Next step. How many times does $x - 1$ go into $3x^2$? $3x$ times. Remember our goal at each step is to get the same exponent and the same coefficient as the term with the highest power. We put the $+3x$ up top and $3x \times (x - 1) = 3x^2 - 3x$ on the bottom.

$$
\begin{array}{r}
x^2 + 3x \\
x - 1 \overline{\smash{\big)}\ x^3 + 2x^2 - 5x + 1} \\
\underline{x^3 - x^2 } \\
3x^2 - 5x + 1 \\
3x^2 - 3x
\end{array}
$$

And just like last time, we subtract each term, not just the first. We then bring down the 1.

$$
\begin{array}{r}
x^2 + 3x \\
x - 1 \overline{\smash{\big)}\ x^3 + 2x^2 - 5x + 1} \\
\underline{x^3 - x^2 } \\
3x^2 - 5x + 1 \\
\underline{3x^2 - 3x } \\
- 2x + 1
\end{array}
$$

We're almost done. How many times does $x - 1$ go into $-2x + 1$? -2 times. So a -2 goes up top and $-2 \times (x - 1) = -2x + 2$ goes on the bottom.

$$
\begin{array}{r}
x^2 + 3x - 2 \\
x - 1 \overline{\smash{)}\; x^3 + 2x^2 - 5x + 1} \\
\underline{x^3 - x^2} \\
3x^2 - 5x + 1 \\
\underline{3x^2 - 3x} \\
-2x + 1 \\
-2x + 2
\end{array}
$$

Subtracting, we get -1 at the end.

$$
\begin{array}{r}
x^2 + 3x - 2 \\
x - 1 \overline{\smash{)}\; x^3 + 2x^2 - 5x + 1} \\
\underline{x^3 - x^2} \\
3x^2 - 5x + 1 \\
\underline{3x^2 - 3x} \\
-2x + 1 \\
\underline{-2x + 2} \\
-1
\end{array}
$$

We know we're done when we end up with a constant. And just as we can express $\dfrac{56}{3}$ as $18\dfrac{2}{3}$, a mixed fraction, we can express

$$
\frac{x^3 + 2x^2 - 5x + 1}{x - 1} \quad \text{as} \quad x^2 + 3x - 2 - \frac{1}{x - 1}
$$

Notice where each component is placed. The quotient is written out in front. The remainder, -1, is the numerator of the fraction and the divisor, $x - 1$, is the denominator. These placements are exactly the same as in long division with actual numbers. Get used to seeing synthetic division results in this format.

Here's another thing that's the same. The result of our long division with numbers

$$
\begin{array}{r}
1\ 8\ \text{R}\ 2 \\
3 \overline{\smash{)}\; 5\ 6}
\end{array}
$$

means that $56 = 3 \times 18 + 2$.

The same meaning applies to our synthetic division result.

$$
x^3 + 2x^2 - 5x + 1 = (x - 1)(x^2 + 3x - 2) - 1
$$

$$
\text{Dividend} = \text{Quotient} \times \text{Divisor} + \text{Remainder}
$$

Hopefully you've been able to grasp synthetic division more intuitively through the comparison with regular long division. All the parts relate to each other in the same way. Let's dive into some more examples where we can show you some shortcuts.

EXAMPLE 1: The expression $\dfrac{6x-5}{x+2}$ is equivalent to which of the following?

A) $6 - \dfrac{17}{x+2}$ B) $6 + \dfrac{7}{x+2}$ C) $\dfrac{6-5}{2}$ D) $6 - \dfrac{5}{2}$

Using synthetic division,

$$
\begin{array}{r}
6 \\
x+2 \overline{\smash{\big)}\, 6x \;-\; 5} \\
\underline{6x \;+\; 12} \\
-\;17
\end{array}
$$

The quotient is 6 and the remainder is -17. We can write this result as $6 - \dfrac{17}{x+2}$. Answer $\boxed{(A)}$.

Now how would we approach this question without using synthetic division?

We can **plug in numbers** that we make up. Let's say $x = 2$. Then $\dfrac{6x-5}{x+2} = \dfrac{6(2)-5}{2+2} = \dfrac{7}{4}$.

We now look for an answer choice that gives $\dfrac{7}{4}$ when $x = 2$. We can rule out (C) and (D) right away since they don't give $\dfrac{7}{4}$. Plugging $x = 2$ into answer (A) gives

$$
6 - \frac{17}{x+2} = 6 - \frac{17}{4} = \frac{24}{4} - \frac{17}{4} = \frac{7}{4}
$$

This confirms that the answer is indeed (A). This strategy of making up numbers and testing each answer choice can be much faster than synthetic division.

EXAMPLE 2: When $3x^2 + 4$ is divided by $x - 1$, the result is $A + \dfrac{7}{x-1}$. What is A in terms of x?

A) $3x - 4$ B) $3x - 3$ C) $3x + 3$ D) $3x + 4$

Using synthetic division,

$$
\begin{array}{r}
3x \;+\; 3 \\
x-1 \overline{\smash{\big)}\, 3x^2 \;+\; 4 } \\
\underline{3x^2 \;-\; 3x } \\
3x \;+\; 4 \\
\underline{3x \;-\; 3} \\
7
\end{array}
$$

If you followed along, you should've noticed it got a little clunky when we subtracted the $-3x$ and brought the 4 down. That's because the dividend, $3x^2 + 4$, has no x term. Still, the process is the same: subtract and bring the remaining terms down.

The quotient is $3x + 3$ and the remainder is 7. The result can be expressed as $\dfrac{3x^2 + 4}{x - 1} = 3x + 3 + \dfrac{7}{x - 1}$. Now it's easy to see that $A = 3x + 3$, answer $\boxed{(C)}$.

Again, we could've done this question by making up numbers. If $x = 2$, then

$$\frac{3x^2 + 4}{x - 1} = \frac{3(2)^2 + 4}{2 - 1} = 16$$

If we didn't know the answer was (C), we would test each answer choice with $x = 2$ until we got 16, but since we do know, we'll test (C) first for confirmation. Letting $A = 3x + 3$,

$$3x + 3 + \frac{7}{x - 1} = 3(2) + 3 + \frac{7}{2 - 1} = 9 + 7 = 16$$

Answer confirmed.

EXAMPLE 3: If the expression $\dfrac{5x^2 - 4x + 1}{x - 2}$ is written in the form $5x + 6 + \dfrac{B}{x - 2}$, where B is a constant, what is the value of B?

Based on where it is, B represents the remainder of the division.

$$
\begin{array}{r}
5x \quad + \quad 6 \\
x - 2 \overline{\big)\, 5x^2 \quad - \quad 4x \quad + \quad 1} \\
5x^2 \quad - \quad 10x \\
\hline
6x \quad + \quad 1 \\
6x \quad - \quad 12 \\
\hline
13
\end{array}
$$

We can write the result of this division as $5x + 6 + \dfrac{13}{x - 2}$, from which $B = \boxed{13}$.

This last example is perfect for demonstrating a shortcut called **the remainder theorem**, which allows us to get the remainder without going through synthetic division.

In Example 3, we divided $5x^2 - 4x + 1$ by $x - 2$. Whenever a polynomial is divided by a monomial, which is just something in the form of $ax + b$, the remainder can be found by plugging in to the polynomial the value of x that makes the monomial equal to 0. The process sounds more complicated than it is, so let's show how it's done.

What makes $x - 2$ equal to 0? $x = 2$.

Plug that into the polynomial $5x^2 - 4x + 1$.

$$5(2)^2 - 4(2) + 1 = 13$$

And that's the remainder we obtained in Example 3.

What is the remainder when $-2x^2 + 5x$ is divided by $x + 1$?

Well, what makes $x + 1$ equal to zero? $x = -1$. Plugging that into the polynomial,

$$-2(-1)^2 + 5(-1) = -7$$

Boom. -7 is the remainder.

What is the remainder when $4x^4 + 3x^2 - 4$ is divided by $2x - 1$?

What makes $2x - 1$ equal to zero? $x = \dfrac{1}{2}$.

Plugging that into the polynomial,

$$4\left(\frac{1}{2}\right)^4 + 3\left(\frac{1}{2}\right)^2 - 4 = \frac{1}{4} + \frac{3}{4} - 4 = -3$$

Boom. -3 is the remainder.

EXAMPLE 4: If the expression $\dfrac{2x^2 - 5x + 1}{x - 3}$ is written in the equivalent form $2x + 1 + \dfrac{R}{x - 3}$, what is the value of R?

R represents the remainder after dividing $2x^2 - 5x + 1$ by $x - 3$. Using the remainder theorem, we can plug in $x = 3$ into $2x^2 - 5x + 1$ to get the remainder.

$$2(3)^2 - 5(3) + 1 = 18 - 15 + 1 = \boxed{4}$$

No need for synthetic division.

One last thing about the remainder theorem. Let's say that we divide $x^2 - 3x + 2$ by $x - 2$. Plugging in 2, we see that the remainder is

$$(2)^2 - 3(2) + 2 = 0$$

Since the remainder is 0, $x - 2$ is a **factor** of $x^2 - 3x + 2$, just like 3 is a factor of 18. And indeed, if we factor $x^2 - 3x + 2$,

$$(x - 2)(x - 1)$$

we see that $x - 2$ is in fact a factor.

Don't you just love how everything in math is connected?

Some questions now become much easier. For example, is $x + 1$ a factor of $x^3 + 1$?

Well, plugging in -1, we find that the remainder is $(-1)^3 + 1 = 0$. Therefore, $x + 1$ is a factor of $x^3 + 1$.

Do note that the remainder theorem only works when we're dividing by monomials like $x + 1$. If we were dividing $x^3 + 1$ by something like $x^2 + 2$, we would have to use synthetic division. Fortunately, the SAT will never ask you to do that.

EXAMPLE 5:

$$f(x) = 3x^3 - kx^2 + 5x + 2$$

In the polynomial $f(x)$ defined above, k is a constant. If $f(x)$ is divisible by $x - 2$, what is the value of k?

A) 12   B) 9   C) 6   D) 3

If $f(x)$ is divisible by $x - 2$, then the remainder is 0 when $f(x)$ is divided by $x - 2$. In other words, $x - 2$ is a factor of $f(x)$. The remainder theorem tells us that when we plug 2 (the value that makes $x - 2$ equal to zero) into $f(x)$, we should get 0.

$$f(2) = 0$$
$$3(2)^3 - k(2)^2 + 5(2) + 2 = 0$$
$$24 - 4k + 10 + 2 = 0$$
$$36 - 4k = 0$$
$$-4k = -36$$
$$k = 9$$

Answer $\boxed{(B)}$.

EXAMPLE 6:

x	$p(x)$
-3	1
-1	0
0	5
2	-3
4	4

The table above gives the value of polynomial $p(x)$ for some values of x. Which of the following must be a factor of $p(x)$?

A) $x + 1$ B) $x - 1$ C) $x - 4$ D) $x - 5$

The remainder theorem makes this question easy. Because $p(-1) = 0$, $x + 1$ must be a factor of $p(x)$. Answer $\boxed{(A)}$. Be careful—the answer is NOT $x - 1$.

If you found this chapter confusing, feel free to skip over it and come back. It's hard to make sense of synthetic division if you haven't encountered it before. It won't show up more than once, if at all, so don't let it keep you from reviewing other topics.

CHAPTER EXERCISE: Answers for this chapter start on page 294.

A calculator should NOT be used on the following questions.

1

The expression $\dfrac{4x}{x-2}$ is equal to which of the following?

A) -2

B) $-\dfrac{8}{x-2}+4$

C) $\dfrac{8}{x-2}+4$

D) $4-2x$

2

If the expression $\dfrac{6x^2+5x+2}{2x+1}$ is written in the form $\dfrac{1}{2x+1}+Q$, what is Q in terms of x?

A) $3x-1$

B) $3x+1$

C) $6x^2+3x+1$

D) $6x^2+5x+1$

3

The expression $4x^2+5$ can be written as $A(2x-1)+R$, where A is an expression in terms of x and R is a constant. What is the value of R?

4

x	$g(x)$
-3	2
-2	3
0	-4
1	-3
3	6

The function g is defined by a polynomial. The table above shows some values of x and $g(x)$. What is the remainder when $g(x)$ is divided by $x+3$?

A) -2

B) 1

C) 2

D) 6

5

$$2z^3 - kxz^2 + 5xz + 2x - 2$$

In the polynomial above, k is a constant. If $z-1$ is a factor of the polynomial above, what is the value of k?

A calculator is allowed on the following questions.

6

When $3x^2 - 8x - 4$ is divided by $3x - 2$, the result can be expressed as $A - \dfrac{8}{3x - 2}$. What is A in terms of x?

A) $x - 4$

B) $x - 2$

C) $x + 2$

D) $x + 4$

7

The expression $2x^2 - 4x - 3$ can be written as $A(x + 1) + B$, where B is a constant. What is A in terms of x?

A) $2x + 6$

B) $2x + 2$

C) $2x - 2$

D) $2x - 6$

8

The expression $x^2 + 4x - 9$ can be written as $(ax + b)(x - 2) + c$, where $a, b,$ and c are constants. What is the value of $a + b + c$?

A) -2

B) 3

C) 7

D) 10

9

For a polynomial $p(x)$, $p(2) = 0$. Which of the following must be true about $p(x)$?

A) $2x$ is a factor of $p(x)$.

B) $2x - 2$ is a factor of $p(x)$.

C) $x - 2$ is a factor of $p(x)$.

D) $x + 2$ is a factor of $p(x)$.

10

If $p(x) = x^3 + x^2 - 5x + 3$, then $p(x)$ is divisible by which of the following?

    I. $x - 2$

    II. $x - 1$

    III. $x + 3$

A) I and II only

B) I and III only

C) II and III only

D) I, II, and III

11

If the polynomial $p(x)$ is divisible by $x - 2$, which of the following could be $p(x)$?

A) $p(x) = -x^2 + 5x - 14$

B) $p(x) = x^2 - 6x - 2$

C) $p(x) = 2x^2 + x - 8$

D) $p(x) = 3x^2 - 2x - 8$

12

If $x - 1$ and $x + 1$ are both factors of the polynomial $ax^4 + bx^3 - 3x^2 + 5x$ and a and b are constants, what is the value of a?

A) -3

B) 1

C) 3

D) 5

13

For a polynomial $p(x)$, $p\left(\dfrac{1}{3}\right) = 0$. Which of the following must be a factor of $p(x)$?

A) $3x - 1$

B) $3x + 1$

C) $x - 3$

D) $x + 3$

18
Complex Numbers

What value of x satisfies $x^2 = -1$? There were no values until mathematicians invented the imaginary number i, which represents $\sqrt{-1}$. They defined i^2 to equal -1, and from there, any other power of i can be derived.

$$i^2 = -1$$
$$i^3 = -i$$
$$i^4 = 1$$
$$i^5 = i$$
$$i^6 = -1$$
$$i^7 = -i$$
$$i^8 = 1$$

The results repeat in cycles of 4. You can use the fact that $i^4 = 1$ to simplify higher powers of i. For example,

$$i^{50} = (i^4)^{12} \times i^2 = 1 \times i^2 = -1$$

When i is used in an expression like $3 + 2i$, the expression is called a **complex number**. We add, subtract, multiply, and divide complex numbers much like we would algebraic expressions.

EXAMPLE 1: If $i = \sqrt{-1}$, which of the following is equivalent to $(3 + 5i) - (2 - 3i)$?

A) $9i$ B) $1 + 2i$ C) $1 + 8i$ D) $5 + 8i$

Just expand and combine like terms.

$$(3 + 5i) - (2 - 3i) = 3 + 5i - 2 + 3i = 1 + 8i$$

Answer $\boxed{(C)}$.

EXAMPLE 2: Given that $i = \sqrt{-1}$, what is the product $(4 + i)(5 - 2i)$?

A) $18 - 3i$ B) $22 - 3i$ C) $18 + 3i$ D) $22 + 3i$

Expanding,

$$(4 + i)(5 - 2i) = 20 - 8i + 5i - 2i^2 = 20 - 3i + 2 = 22 - 3i$$

Answer $\boxed{(B)}$.

EXAMPLE 3: Which of the following is equal to $\dfrac{2 + 3i}{1 + i}$?

A) $\dfrac{1}{2} - \dfrac{1}{2}i$ B) $\dfrac{1}{2} + \dfrac{1}{2}i$ C) $\dfrac{5}{2} - \dfrac{1}{2}i$ D) $\dfrac{5}{2} + \dfrac{1}{2}i$

When you're faced with a fraction containing i in the denominator, multiply both the top and the bottom of the fraction by the **conjugate** of the denominator. What is the conjugate, you ask? Well, the conjugate of $1 + i$ is $1 - i$. The conjugate of $5 - 4i$ is $5 + 4i$. To get the conjugate, simply reverse the sign in between.

In this example, we multiply the top and the bottom by the conjugate $1 - i$.

$$\frac{(2 + 3i)}{(1 + i)} \cdot \frac{(1 - i)}{(1 - i)} = \frac{2 - 2i + 3i - 3i^2}{1 - i + i - i^2} = \frac{2 + i - 3i^2}{1 - i^2} = \frac{5 + i}{2} = \frac{5}{2} + \frac{1}{2}i$$

The whole point of this process is to eliminate i from the denominator. The absence of i in the denominator is a good indicator that things were done correctly. The answer is $\boxed{(D)}$.

CHAPTER EXERCISE: Answers for this chapter start on page 296.

A calculator should NOT be used on the following questions.

1

For $i = \sqrt{-1}$, which of the following is equivalent to $(5 - 3i) - (-2 + 5i)$?

A) $3 - 8i$

B) $3 + 2i$

C) $7 - 8i$

D) $7 + 2i$

2

Given that $i = \sqrt{-1}$, which of the following is equal to $i(i + 1)$?

A) $i - 2$

B) $i - 1$

C) $i + 1$

D) 0

3

$$i^4 + 3i^2 + 2$$

Which of the following is equal to the expression above? (Note: $i = \sqrt{-1}$)

A) i

B) -1

C) 0

D) 1

4

$$(6 + 2i)(2 + 5i)$$

If the expression above is equivalent to $a + bi$, where a and b are constants, what is the value of a?

A) 2

B) 12

C) 22

D) 34

5

Which of the following is equal to $3(i + 2) - 2(5 - 4i)$? (Note: $i = \sqrt{-1}$)

A) $16 - 5i$

B) $-4 + 7i$

C) $-4 + 11i$

D) $16 + 11i$

6

For $i = \sqrt{-1}$, which of the following is equivalent to $3i(i + 2) - i(i - 1)$?

A) $-4 + 7i$

B) $-2 + 7i$

C) $-4 + 5i$

D) $-2 + 5i$

7

For $i = \sqrt{-1}$, which of the following is equal to i^{93}?

A) -1

B) 1

C) $-i$

D) i

154

8

Which of the following complex numbers is equivalent to $(3 - i)^2$? (Note: $i = \sqrt{-1}$)

A) $8 - 6i$

B) $8 + 6i$

C) $10 - 6i$

D) $10 + 6i$

9

$$(5 - 2i)(4 - 3i)$$

Which of the following is equal to the expression above? (Note: $i = \sqrt{-1}$)

A) $14 - 7i$

B) $14 - 23i$

C) $26 + 7i$

D) $26 - 23i$

10

Which of the following is equal to $\dfrac{1}{i} + \dfrac{1}{i^2} + \dfrac{1}{i^4}$?

(Note: $i = \sqrt{-1}$)

A) $-i$

B) i

C) 0

D) 1

11

Which of the following is equal to $\dfrac{1 - 3i}{3 + i}$? (Note: $i = \sqrt{-1}$)

A) $-i$

B) i

C) $-\dfrac{5}{4}i$

D) $\dfrac{3}{4} - \dfrac{5}{4}i$

12

Which of the following complex numbers is equivalent to $\dfrac{2 - i}{2 + i}$? (Note: $i = \sqrt{-1}$)

A) $\dfrac{3}{5} - \dfrac{4}{5}i$

B) $1 - \dfrac{4}{5}i$

C) $\dfrac{5}{3} - \dfrac{4}{3}i$

D) $1 - \dfrac{4}{3}i$

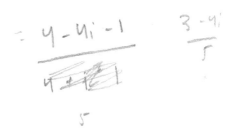

19
Absolute Value

The absolute value of x, denoted by $|x|$, is the distance x is from 0. In other words, absolute value makes everything positive. If it's positive, it stays positive. If it's negative, it becomes positive.

EXAMPLE 1: How many integer values of x satisfy $|x| < 4$?

Think of the possible numbers that work and don't forget the negative possibilities. Every integer between -3 and 3 works, a total of $\boxed{7}$ integer values.

We could've also solved this problem algebraically. Any absolute value equation like the one above can be written as
$$-4 < x < 4$$
and since x is an integer,
$$-3 \le x \le 3$$

EXAMPLE 2: How many integer values of x satisfy $|x + 1| < 5$?

Here we go through the same process. The largest possible integer for x is 3 and the smallest is -5. So $-5 \le x \le 3$, a total of $\boxed{9}$ possibilities.

Solving algebraically,
$$-5 < x + 1 < 5$$
Subtracting 1,
$$-6 < x < 4$$
$$-5 \le x \le 3$$

EXAMPLE 3: For which of the following values of x is $|2x - 5| < 0$?

A) 0   B) 2.5   C) 5   D) There is no such value of x.

Trick question. The absolute value of something can never be negative. There is no solution, answer $\boxed{(D)}$.

EXAMPLE 4: A manufacturer of cookies tests the weight of its cookie packages to ensure consistency in the product. An acceptable package of cookies must weigh between 16 ounces and 18 ounces as it comes out of production. If w is the weight of an acceptable cookie package, then which of the following inequalities correctly expresses all possible values of w?

A) $|w - 17| > 1$ B) $|w - 16| < 2$ C) $|w + 17| > 1$ D) $|w - 17| < 1$

In these types of absolute value word problems, start with the midpoint of the desired interval, 17 in this case, and subtract it from w: $|w - 17|$. Think of this as the "distance," or "error," away from the midpoint of the interval. We don't want this "error" to be greater than 1 since w would then be outside the desired interval. So our answer is $\boxed{(D)}$, $|w - 17| < 1$.

We can confirm this answer by solving the inequality. Remember that the end result should be $16 < w < 18$. Let's see if our answer gives us that result when we isolate w.

$$|w - 17| < 1$$

$$-1 < w - 17 < 1$$

Adding 17,

$$16 < w < 18$$

We have confirmed that $\boxed{(D)}$ is the correct answer.

This is the graph of $y = x$:

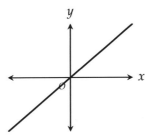

Now this is the graph of $y = |x|$:

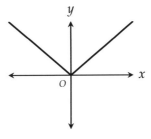

See how the graph changed? Taking the absolute value of any function makes all the negative y-values become positive y-values (points in the quadrants III and IV are reflected across the x-axis). All the positive y-values stay where they are. This V-shape is the classic absolute value graph that you should be able to recognize.

A table of values is another way to see this absolute value transformation. If $f(x) = 2x$, then compare $f(x)$ with $|f(x)|$.

x	-3	-2	-1	0	1	2	3
$f(x)$	-6	-4	-2	0	2	4	6
$|f(x)|$	6	4	2	0	2	4	6

The negative values of $f(x)$ become positive and the positive values of $f(x)$ stay positive.

EXAMPLE 5: Which of the following could be the graph of $y = |2x - 1|$?

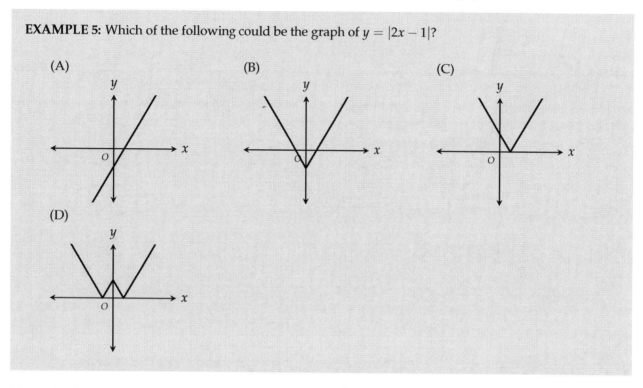

The entire function is enclosed in an absolute value and since the absolute value of something can never be negative, y must always be greater than or equal to 0. In other words, the graph must lie on or above the x-axis. That eliminates (A) and (B). In fact, (A) is the graph of $2x - 1$ without the absolute value. To get the answer, we take all the points with negative y-values in the graph of (A) and reflect them across the x-axis so that they're positive. The graph we end up with is $\boxed{(C)}$.

One great tactic that's worth mentioning here is narrowing down the answer choices by obtaining points that are easy to calculate. For example, if we let $x = 0$, then $y = |2(0) - 1| = 1$. The point $(0, 1)$ must then be on the graph, eliminating (A) and (B). Letting $y = 0$, we now find that $(0.5, 0)$ must also be on the graph. This eliminates (D) because (D) has two x-intercepts whereas the graph should only have one.

CHAPTER EXERCISE: Answers for this chapter start on page 297.

A calculator should NOT be used on the following questions.

1

If $f(x) = -2x^2 - 3x + 1$, what is the value of $|f(1)|$?

A) 3

B) 4

C) 5

D) 6

2

Which of the following expressions is equal to -5 for some value of x?

A) $|x - 6| + 2$

B) $|x - 2| - 6$

C) $|x + 2| + 6$

D) $|x + 6| - 2$

3

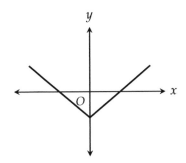

Which of the following could be the equation of the function graphed in the xy-plane above?

A) $y = -|x| - 2$

B) $y = |x| - 2$

C) $y = |x| + 2$

D) $y = |x - 2|$

4

If $|x - 3| > 10$, which of the following could be the value of $|x|$?

A) 2

B) 4

C) 6

D) 8

A calculator is allowed on the following questions.

5

How many different integer values of x satisfy $|x + 6| < 3$?

6

If $|n - 2| = 10$, what is the sum of the two possible values of n?

A) 4

B) 6

C) 12

D) 20

7

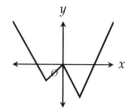

The graph of the function f is shown in the xy-plane above. Which of the following could be the graph of the function $y = |f(x)|$?

A)

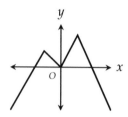

B)

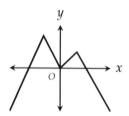

C)

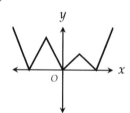

D)

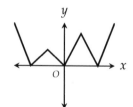

8

If $|x - 10| = b$, where $x < 10$, then which of the following is equivalent to $b - x$?

A) -10

B) 10

C) $2b - 10$

D) $10 - 2b$

9

A hot dog factory must ensure that its hot dogs are between $6\frac{1}{4}$ inches and $6\frac{3}{4}$ inches in length. If h is the length of a hot dog from this factory, then which of the following inequalities correctly expresses the accepted values of h?

A) $\left| h - 6\frac{1}{4} \right| < \frac{1}{4}$

B) $\left| h - 6\frac{1}{4} \right| < \frac{1}{2}$

C) $\left| h - 6\frac{1}{2} \right| < \frac{1}{4}$

D) $\left| h - 6\frac{1}{2} \right| > \frac{1}{4}$

10

Rolls of tape must be made to a certain length. They must contain enough tape to cover between 400 feet and 410 feet. If l is the length of a roll of tape that meets this requirement, which of the following inequalities expresses the possible values of l?

A) $|l - 400| < 10$

B) $|l - 405| > 5$

C) $|l + 405| < 5$

D) $|l - 405| < 5$

11

If $|4x - 4| = 8$ and $|5y + 10| = 15$, what is the smallest possible value of xy?

A) -20

B) -15

C) -5

D) -1

12

If $|a| < 1$, then which of the following must be true?

  I. $\dfrac{1}{a} > 1$

  II. $a^2 < 1$

  III. $a > -1$

A) III only

B) I and II only

C) II and III only

D) I, II, and III

20 Angles

Exterior Angle Theorem

An exterior angle is formed when any side of a triangle is extended. In the triangle below, $x°$ designates an exterior angle.

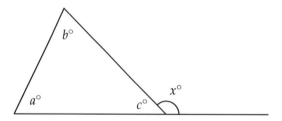

An exterior angle is always equal to the sum of the two angles in the triangle furthest from it. In this case,

$$x = a + b$$

EXAMPLE 1:

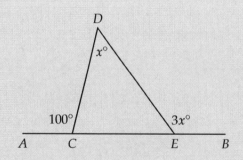

What is the value of x in the figure above?

$\angle DCE$ must be $80°$. Now there are a lot of ways to do this, but using the exterior angle theorem is the fastest:

$$80 + x = 3x$$
$$80 = 2x$$
$$\boxed{x = 40}$$

Parallel Lines

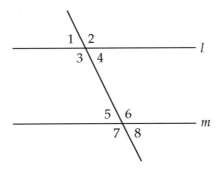

When two lines are parallel, the following are true:

- Vertical angles are equal (e.g. $\angle 1 = \angle 4$)
- Alternate interior angles are equal (e.g. $\angle 4 = \angle 5$ and $\angle 3 = \angle 6$)
- Corresponding angles are equal (e.g. $\angle 1 = \angle 5$)
- Same side interior angles are supplementary (e.g. $\angle 3 + \angle 5 = 180°$)

No need to memorize these terms. You just need to know that when two parallel lines are cut by another line, there are two sets of equal angles:

$$\angle 1 = \angle 4 = \angle 5 = \angle 8$$
$$\angle 2 = \angle 3 = \angle 6 = \angle 7$$

EXAMPLE 2:

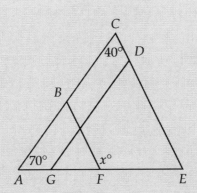

In the figure above, $\overline{AC} \parallel \overline{GD}$ and $\overline{BF} \parallel \overline{CE}$. If $\angle CAE = 70°$ and $\angle ACE = 40°$, what is the value of x?

Here is the fastest way: $\angle ACE = \angle ABF = 40°$ because they are corresponding angles ($\overline{AC}$ cuts parallel lines $\overline{BF}$ and $\overline{CE}$). Since angle x is an exterior angle to $\triangle ABF$, $x = 70 + 40 = \boxed{110°}$.

Polygons

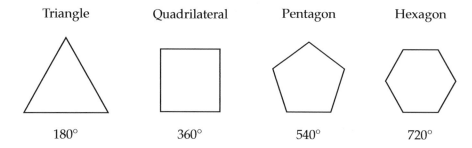

| Triangle | Quadrilateral | Pentagon | Hexagon |
| 180° | 360° | 540° | 720° |

As you can see from the polygons above, each additional side increases the sum of the interior angles by 180°. For any polygon, the sum of the interior angles is

$$180(n-2) \text{ where } n \text{ is the number of sides}$$

So for an octagon, which has 8 sides, the sum of the interior angles is $180(8-2) = 180 \times 6 = 1080°$.

A **regular polygon** is one in which all sides and angles are equal. The polygons shown above are regular. If our octagon were regular, each interior angle would have a measure of $1080° \div 8 = 135°$.

The $180(n-2)$ formula comes from the fact that any polygon can be split up into several triangles by drawing lines from any one vertex to the others.

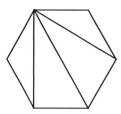

The number of triangles that results from this process is always two less than the number of sides. Count for yourself! Because each triangle contains 180°, the sum of the angles within a polygon must be $180°(n-2)$, where n is the number of sides.

EXAMPLE 3:

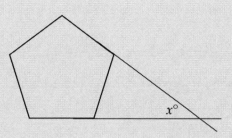

Two sides of a regular pentagon are extended as shown in the figure above. What is the value of x?

The total number of degrees in a pentagon is $180(5-2) = 540°$. So each interior angle must be $540° \div 5 = 108°$. The angles within the triangle formed by the intersecting lines must be $180 - 108 = 72°$.

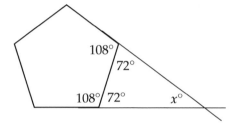

So $x = 180 - 72 - 72 = \boxed{36°}$.

CHAPTER EXERCISE: Answers for this chapter start on page 299.

A calculator should NOT be used on the following questions.

1

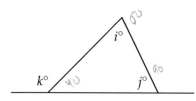

Note: Figure not drawn to scale.

In the figure above, $i = 50$ and $k = 140$. What is the value of j?

A) 60

B) 70

C) 80

D) 90

2

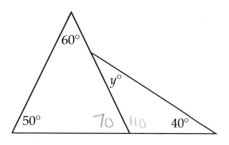

Note: Figure not drawn to scale.

In the figure above, what is the value of y?

A) 30

B) 40

C) 50

D) 70

3

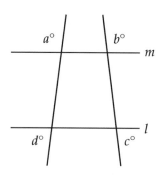

In the figure above, lines l and m are parallel. What is the value of $a + b + c + d$?

A) 270

B) 360

C) 720

D) It cannot be determined from the information given.

4

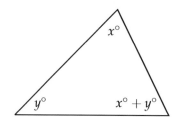

Note: Figure not drawn to scale.

In the figure above, if $x = 40$, what is the value of y?

A) 40

B) 50

C) 80

D) 90

5

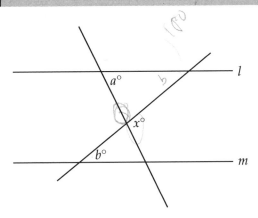

In the figure above, lines l and m are parallel. What is x in terms of a and b?

A) $a + b$

B) $a - b$

C) $b - a$

D) $180 - a - b$

6

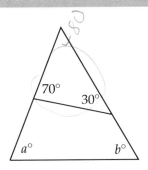

Note: Figure not drawn to scale.

In the figure above, what is the value of $a + b$?

A) 80

B) 100

C) 110

D) 120

A calculator is allowed on the following questions.

7

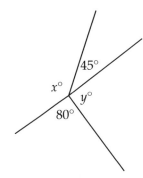

Note: Figure not drawn to scale.

In the figure above, what is the value of $x + y$?

A) 125

B) 180

C) 235

D) 280

8

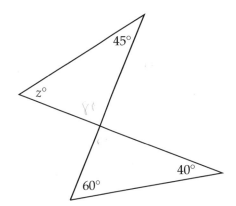

Note: Figure not drawn to scale.

In the figure above, what is the value of z?

A) 35

B) 45

C) 55

D) 80

9

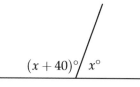

In the figure above, what is the value of x?

A) 60

B) 70

C) 75

D) 80

10

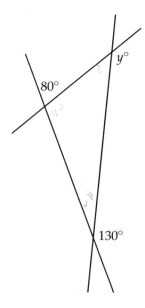

Note: Figure not drawn to scale.

In the figure above, what is the value of y?

A) 100

B) 130

C) 140

D) 150

11

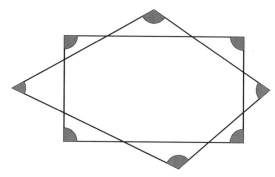

In the figure above, a rectangle and a quadrilateral overlap. What is the sum of the degree measures of the shaded angles?

A) 360

B) 540

C) 720

D) 900

12

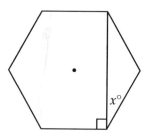

A regular hexagon is shown in the figure above. What is the value of x?

A) 15

B) 20

C) 25

D) 30

13

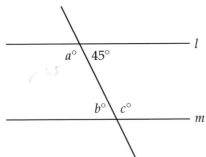

Note: Figure not drawn to scale.

In the figure above, lines l and m are parallel. Which of the following must be true?

   I. $a = 3b$ ✓
  II. $a + b = b + c$
 III. $b = 45$ ✓

A) III only
B) I and II only
C) II and III only
D) I, II, and III

14

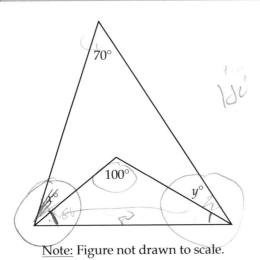

Note: Figure not drawn to scale.

In the figure above, what is the value of $x + y$?

A) 10
B) 20
C) 30
D) 50

15

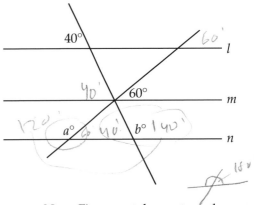

Note: Figure not drawn to scale.

In the figure above, lines l, m, and n are parallel. What is the value of $a + b$?

21 Triangles

Imagine you are trying to make a triangle with sticks of different sizes.

Can you make a triangle with any 3 sticks? No. In this case, the two shorter pieces don't connect.

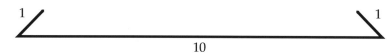

If you had sticks of size 5, 5, and 10, they would connect but only by just enough to make a straight line.

So to make a triangle, the lengths of any two sticks must add up to be greater than the third. To say it more mathematically,

For any triangle, the sum of any two sides must be greater than the third.

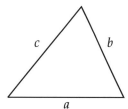

$$a + b > c$$
$$b + c > a$$
$$a + c > b$$

If the sum of two sides turns out to be equal to the third, it's enough to make a line, but NOT a triangle.

EXAMPLE 1: In $\triangle ABC$, AB has a length of 3 and BC has a length of 4. How many integer values are possible for the length of AC?

The golden rule of any geometry problem is to draw a picture:

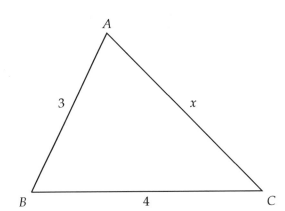

Let the length of AC be x. Based on the rule, we can come up with three equations:

$$3 + 4 > x$$
$$3 + x > 4$$
$$4 + x > 3$$

which simplify to

$$7 > x$$
$$x > 1$$
$$x > -1$$

Now if $x > 1$, then it's always going to be greater than -1. In other words, only the first and second matter. Therefore, $1 < x < 7$, and there are $\boxed{5}$ possible integer values of x.

Isosceles & Equilateral Triangles

An isosceles triangle is one that has two sides of equal length. The angles opposite those sides are equal.

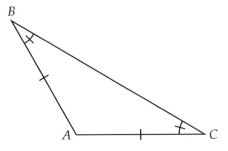

Because $AB = AC$, $\angle C = \angle B$.

In an equilateral triangle, all sides have the same length. Because equal sides imply equal angles, the angles are all $60°$.

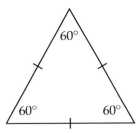

EXAMPLE 2: In an isosceles triangle, one of the angles has a measure of 50°. What is the degree measure of the greatest possible angle in the triangle?

An isosceles triangle has not only two equal sides but also two equal angles. There are two possibilities for an isosceles triangle with an angle of 50°. Another angle could be 50°, making a $50 - 50 - 80$ triangle, or the other two angles could be equal, making a $50 - 65 - 65$ triangle. Given these two possibilities, $\boxed{80°}$ is the greatest possible angle in the triangle.

EXAMPLE 3:

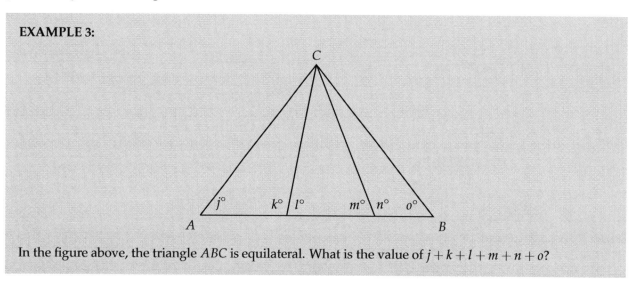

In the figure above, the triangle ABC is equilateral. What is the value of $j + k + l + m + n + o$?

Solution 1: There are 3 smaller triangles within the equilateral one. Each of these triangles has a total degree measure of 180°, for a combined total of $180° \times 3 = 540°$. We need to subtract out $\angle ACB$ to get what we want. Because triangle ABC is equilateral, $\angle ACB$ is 60°. So $540° - 60° = \boxed{480°}$.

Solution 2: Because $\triangle ABC$ is equilateral, both j and o are 60°. Because k and l form a straight line, they add up to 180°. Because m and n also form a straight line, they also add up to 180°. Adding up all our values, we get $60° + 180° + 180° + 60° = \boxed{480°}$.

Right Triangles

Right triangles are made up of two legs and the hypotenuse (the side opposite the right angle).

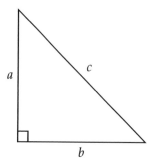

Every right triangle obeys the pythagorean theorem: $a^2 + b^2 = c^2$, where a and b are the lengths of the legs and c is the length of the hypotenuse.

EXAMPLE 4:

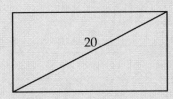

The rectangle above has a diagonal of length 20. If the base of the rectangle is twice as long as the height, what is the height?

The diagonal of any rectangle forms two right triangles. Let the height be x and the base be $2x$. Using the pythagorean theorem,

$$x^2 + (2x)^2 = 20^2$$
$$x^2 + 4x^2 = 400$$
$$5x^2 = 400$$
$$x^2 = 80$$
$$x = \sqrt{80} = \boxed{4\sqrt{5}}$$

If you take the SAT enough times, what you'll find is that certain right triangles come up repeatedly. For example, the $3 - 4 - 5$ triangle:

A set of three whole numbers that satisfy the pythagorean theorem is called a pythagorean triple. Though not necessary, it'll save you quite a bit of time and improve your accuracy if you learn to recognize the common triples that show up:

$$3, 4, 5$$
$$6, 8, 10$$
$$5, 12, 13$$
$$7, 24, 25$$
$$8, 15, 17$$

Note that the $6 - 8 - 10$ triangle is just a multiple of the $3 - 4 - 5$ triangle.

Special Right Triangles

You will have to memorize two special right triangle relationships. The first is the $45° - 45° - 90°$:

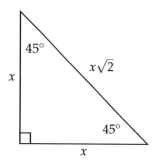

The best way to think about this triangle is that it's isosceles—the two legs are equal. We let their lengths be x. The hypotenuse, which is always the biggest side in a right triangle, turns out to be $\sqrt{2}$ times x.

We can prove this relationship using the pythagorean theorem, where h is the hypotenuse.

$$x^2 + x^2 = h^2$$

$$2x^2 = h^2$$

$$\sqrt{2x^2} = \sqrt{h^2}$$

$$x\sqrt{2} = h$$

I show you these proofs not because they will be tested on the SAT, but because they illustrate problem-solving concepts that you may have to use on certain SAT questions.

The second is the $30° - 60° - 90°$:

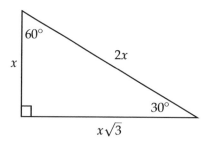

Because $30°$ is the smallest angle, the side opposite from it is the shortest. Let that side be x. The hypotenuse, the largest side, turns out to be twice x, and the side opposite $60°$ turns out to be $\sqrt{3}$ times x.

One common mistake students make is to think that because $60°$ is twice $30°$, the side opposite $60°$ must be twice as big as the side opposite $30°$. That relationship is NOT true. You cannot extrapolate the ratio of the sides from the ratio of the angles. Yes, the side opposite $60°$ is bigger than the side opposite $30°$, but it isn't twice as long.

We can prove the $30 - 60 - 90$ relationship by using an equilateral triangle. Let each side be $2x$ (we could use x but you'll see why $2x$ makes things easier in a bit):

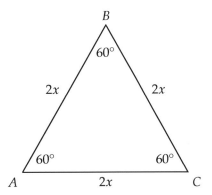

Drawing a line down the middle from B to $\overline{AC}$ creates two $30 - 60 - 90$ triangles. Because an equilateral triangle is symmetrical, AD is half of $2x$, or just x. That's why $2x$ was used—it avoids any fractions.

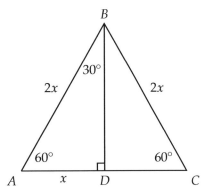

To find BD, we use the pythagorean theorem:

$$AD^2 + BD^2 = AB^2$$

$$x^2 + BD^2 = (2x)^2$$

$$BD^2 = (2x)^2 - x^2$$

$$BD^2 = 4x^2 - x^2$$

$$BD^2 = 3x^2$$

$$\sqrt{BD^2} = \sqrt{3x^2}$$

$$BD = x\sqrt{3}$$

Triangle ABD is proof of the $30 - 60 - 90$ relationship.

EXAMPLE 5:

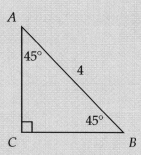

What is the area of $\triangle ACB$ shown above?

A) $\sqrt{2}$ B) $2\sqrt{2}$ C) 4   D) 8

Using the $45 - 45 - 90$ triangle relationship, $AC = BC = \dfrac{4}{\sqrt{2}}$ (the hypotenuse is $\sqrt{2}$ times greater than each leg). The area is then $\dfrac{1}{2}\left(\dfrac{4}{\sqrt{2}}\right)\left(\dfrac{4}{\sqrt{2}}\right) = \dfrac{1}{2}\left(\dfrac{16}{2}\right) = 4$.

Answer $\boxed{(C)}$.

EXAMPLE 6:

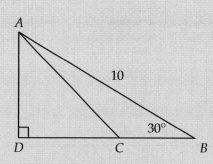

In the figure above, $AD = DC$, $\angle B = 30°$, and $AB = 10$. What is the ratio of AC to CB?

A) $\dfrac{\sqrt{2}}{\sqrt{3}-1}$ B) $\dfrac{\sqrt{3}}{\sqrt{2}-1}$ C) $\dfrac{\sqrt{2}}{\sqrt{5}-\sqrt{3}}$ D) $\dfrac{2}{3}$

Because $AD = DC$, $\triangle ADC$ is not only isosceles but also a $45 - 45 - 90$ triangle. $\triangle ADB$ is a $30 - 60 - 90$ triangle with a hypotenuse of 10. Using the $30 - 60 - 90$ relationship, AD is half the hypotenuse, 5, and $DB = 5\sqrt{3}$. Using the $45 - 45 - 90$ relationship, $AC = 5\sqrt{2}$, $DC = 5$, and $CB = DB - DC = 5\sqrt{3} - 5$.

$$\frac{AC}{CB} = \frac{5\sqrt{2}}{5\sqrt{3}-5} = \frac{\sqrt{2}}{\sqrt{3}-1}$$

Answer $\boxed{(A)}$.

Similar Triangles

When two triangles have the same angle measures, their sides are proportional:

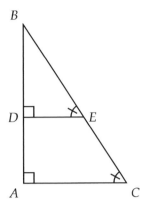

Because $\overline{DE}$ is parallel to $\overline{AC}$ in the figure above, $\angle BED$ is equal to $\angle BCA$. That makes $\triangle DBE$ similar to $\triangle ABC$. In other words, $\triangle DBE$ is just a smaller version of $\triangle ABC$. If we draw the two triangles separately and give the sides some arbitrary lengths, we can see this more clearly.

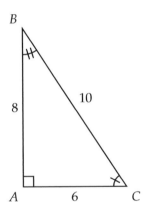
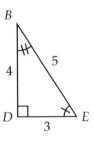

The sides of the big triangle are twice as long as the sides of the smaller one. Even if the lengths change, the ratios will remain the same:

$$\frac{AB}{BD} = \frac{AC}{DE} = \frac{BC}{BE}$$

EXAMPLE 7:

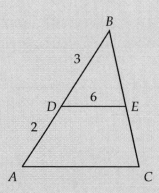

Note: Figure not drawn to scale.

PART 1: In $\triangle ABC$ above, $\overline{DE}$ is parallel to $\overline{AC}$, $AD = 2$, $DB = 3$, and $DE = 6$. What is the length of $\overline{AC}$?

PART 2: What is the ratio of the area of $\triangle BDE$ to the area of $\triangle BAC$?

A) $\dfrac{1}{4}$ B) $\dfrac{3}{5}$ C) $\dfrac{3}{4}$ D) $\dfrac{9}{25}$

Part 1 Solution: Because $\overline{DE}$ and $\overline{AC}$ are parallel, $\angle BDE$ is equal to $\angle BAC$ and $\angle BED$ is equal to $\angle BCA$. Therefore, $\triangle BDE$ and $\triangle BAC$ are similar. Setting up our ratios,

$$\frac{BD}{BA} = \frac{DE}{AC}$$

$$\frac{3}{5} = \frac{6}{AC}$$

Cross multiplying,

$$3AC = 30$$

$$AC = \boxed{10}$$

Part 2 Solution: When two triangles are similar, the ratio of their areas is equal to the square of the ratio of their sides. The ratio of the sides is $3 : 5$. Squaring that ratio, we get the ratio of the areas, $9 : 25$. Answer $\boxed{(D)}$.

Radians

A radian is simply another unit used to measure angles. Just as we have feet and meters, pounds and kilograms, we have degrees and radians.

$$\pi \text{ radians} = 180°$$

If you've never used radians before, don't be put off by the π. After all, it's just a number. We could've written

$$3.14 \text{ radians} \approx 180°$$

instead, but everything is typically expressed in terms of π when we're working with radians. Furthermore, 3.14 is only an approximation. So, given the conversion factor above, how would we convert 45° to radians?

$$45° \times \frac{\pi \text{ radians}}{180°} = \frac{\pi}{4} \text{ radians}$$

Notice that the degree units (represented by the little circles) cancel out just as they should in any conversion problem. Now how would we convert $\frac{3\pi}{2}$ to degrees? Flip the conversion factor.

$$\frac{3\pi}{2} \text{ radians} \times \frac{180°}{\pi \text{ radians}} = 270°$$

You might be wondering why we even need radians. Why not just stick with degrees? Is this another difference between the U.S. and the rest of the world, like it is with feet and meters? Nope. As we'll see in the chapter on circles, some calculations are much easier when angles are expressed in radians.

EXAMPLE 8:

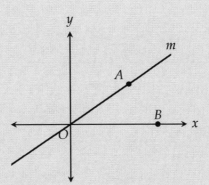

In the xy-plane above, line m passes through the origin and has a slope of $\sqrt{3}$. If point A lies on line m and point B lies on the x-axis as shown, what is the measure, in radians, of angle AOB?

A) $\frac{\pi}{6}$ B) $\frac{\pi}{5}$ C) $\frac{\pi}{4}$ D) $\frac{\pi}{3}$

179

We can draw a line down from A to the x-axis to make a right triangle. Because the slope is $\sqrt{3}$, the ratio of the height of this triangle to its base is always $\sqrt{3}$ to 1 (rise over run).

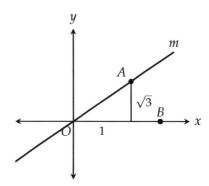

This right triangle should look familiar to you. It's the $30 - 60 - 90$ triangle. Angle AOB is opposite the $\sqrt{3}$, so its measure is $60°$. Converting that to radians,

$$60° \times \frac{\pi}{180°} = \frac{\pi}{3}$$

Answer $\boxed{(D)}$.

CHAPTER EXERCISE: Answers for this chapter start on page 301.

A calculator should NOT be used on the following questions.

1

The lengths of the sides of a right triangle are x, $x - 2$, and $x + 5$. Which of the following equations could be used to find x?

A) $x + x - 2 = x + 5$
B) $x^2 + (x + 5)^2 = (x - 2)^2$
C) $x^2 + (x - 2)^2 = (x + 5)^2$
D) $(x - 2)^2 + (x + 5)^2 = x^2$

2

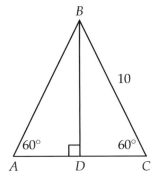

Note: Figure not drawn to scale.

In $\triangle BDC$ above, what is the length of $\overline{DC}$?

A) 3
B) 5
C) $5\sqrt{3}$
D) 8

3

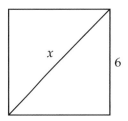

A square of side length 6 is shown in the figure above. What is the value of x?

A) $3\sqrt{2}$
B) 6
C) $6\sqrt{2}$
D) $6\sqrt{3}$

4

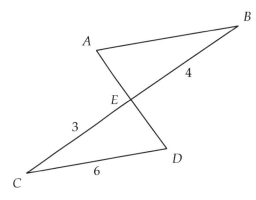

In the figure above, $\overline{AB} \parallel \overline{CD}$. What is the length of AB?

5

The lengths of two sides of a triangle are 3 and 13. What is one possible length of the third side?

6

Two angles of a triangle have the same measure. If two sides have lengths 15 and 20, what is the greatest possible value of the perimeter of the triangle?

7

Which of the following sets of the three numbers could be the side lengths of a triangle?

   I. 6, 14, 7
  II. 5, 5, 12
 III. 4, 8, 11

A) I only

B) III only

C) II and III only

D) I, II, and III

8

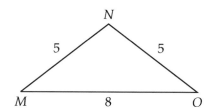

What is the area of isosceles triangle *MNO* above?

9

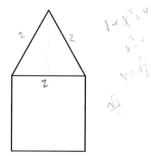

In the figure above, an equilateral triangle sits on top of a square. If the square has an area of 4, what is the area of the equilateral triangle?

A) $\sqrt{3}$

B) $\dfrac{\sqrt{3}}{2}$

C) $\dfrac{3}{4}$

D) 1

10

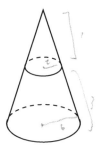

Note: Figure not drawn to scale.

In the figure above, the base of a cone has a radius of 6. The cone is sliced horizontally so that the top piece is a smaller cone with a height of 1 and a base radius of 2. What is the height of the bottom piece?

A) 1

B) 2

C) 3

D) 4

11

The lengths of three sides of a triangle are $x, y,$ and z, where $x \leq y \leq z$. If $x, y,$ and z are integers and the perimeter of the triangle is 10, what is the greatest possible value of z?

A) 4

B) 5

C) 6

D) 7

12

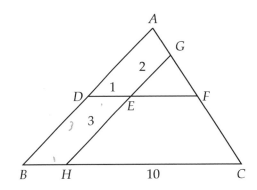

Note: Figure not drawn to scale.

In the figure above, $\overline{AB}$ is parallel to $\overline{GH}$ and $\overline{DF}$ is parallel to $\overline{BC}$. If $DE = 1, EH = 3, EG = 2,$ and $HC = 10$, what is the length of AD?

A calculator is allowed on the following questions.

13

How many radians are in $225°$?

A) $\dfrac{3\pi}{4}$

B) $\dfrac{7\pi}{6}$

C) $\dfrac{5\pi}{4}$

D) $\dfrac{3\pi}{2}$

14

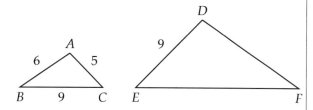

Triangle *ABC* above is similar to triangle *DEF*. What is the perimeter of triangle *DEF*?

A) 20

B) 26.8

C) 30

D) 36.2

15

The lengths of two sides of a triangle are 8 and 20. The third side has a length of p. How many positive integers are possible values of p?

A) 14

B) 15

C) 16

D) 17

16

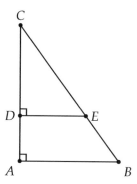

In $\triangle ABC$ above, $\angle CDE = 90°$ and $\angle A = 90°$. $AB = 9$ and $AC = 12$. If $DE = 6$, what is the length of *CE*?

A) 6

B) 8

C) 9

D) 10

17

In isosceles triangle *ABC*, $\overline{BC}$ is the shortest side. If the degree measure of $\angle A$ is a multiple of 10, what is the smallest possible measure of $\angle B$?

A) 75°

B) 70°

C) 65°

D) 60°

18

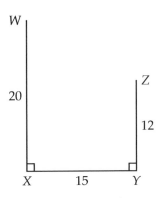

Two poles represented by $\overline{XW}$ and $\overline{YZ}$ above are 15 feet apart. One is 20 feet tall and the other is 12 feet tall. A rope joins the top of one pole to the top of the other. What is the length of the rope?

A) 12

B) 17

C) 18

D) 19

19

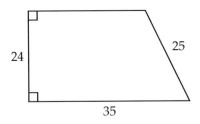

What is the perimeter of the trapezoid above?

A) 100

B) 108

C) 112

D) 116

20

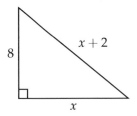

What is the value of x in the triangle above?

21

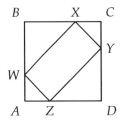

In the figure above, $ABCD$ is a square of side length 3. If $AW = AZ = CX = CY = 1$, what is the perimeter of rectangle $WXYZ$?

A) $3\sqrt{2}$

B) $4\sqrt{2}$

C) $6\sqrt{2}$

D) 8

22

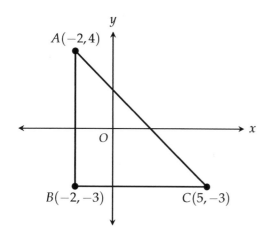

Points A, B, and C form a triangle in the xy-plane shown above. What is the measure, in radians, of angle BAC?

A) $\dfrac{\pi}{6}$

B) $\dfrac{\pi}{4}$

C) $\dfrac{\pi}{3}$

D) $\dfrac{\pi}{2}$

23

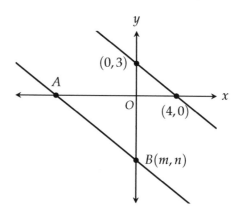

Two parallel lines are shown in the xy-plane above. If $AB = 15$ and point B has coordinates (m, n), what is the value of n?

A) -6

B) -8

C) -9

D) -12

24

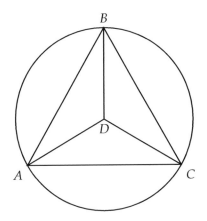

In the figure above, equilateral triangle ABC is inscribed in circle D. What is the measure, in radians, of angle ADB?

A) $\dfrac{2\pi}{3}$

B) $\dfrac{3\pi}{4}$

C) $\dfrac{4\pi}{5}$

D) $\dfrac{5\pi}{6}$

25

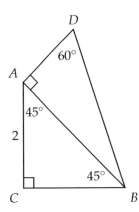

What is the length of DB in the figure above?

A) $\dfrac{2\sqrt{3}}{3}$

B) $\dfrac{2\sqrt{6}}{3}$

C) $\dfrac{4\sqrt{6}}{3}$

D) $\sqrt{3}$

26

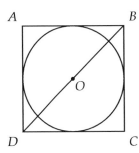

In the figure above, circle O is inscribed in the square $ABCD$. If $BD = 2$, what is the area of the circle?

A) $\dfrac{\pi}{4}$

B) $\dfrac{\pi}{2}$

C) π

D) $\dfrac{3\pi}{2}$

27

A triangle has one side of length 5 and another side of length 11. Which of the following could be the perimeter of the triangle?

   I. 20
  II. 26
 III. 30

A) II only

B) I and II only

C) II and III only

D) I, II, and III

28

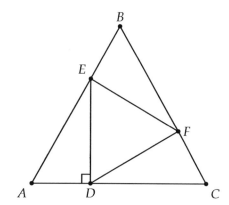

Equilateral triangle DEF is inscribed in equilateral triangle ABC such that $\overline{ED} \perp \overline{AC}$. What is the ratio of the area of $\triangle DEF$ to the area of ABC?

A) $1:4$

B) $1:3$

C) $1:2$

D) $5:8$

29

The sides of a triangle with positive area have lengths 5, 7, and a. The sides of a second triangle with positive area have lengths 5, 7, and b. Which of the following is NOT a possible value of $|a - b|$?

A) 3

B) 5

C) 7

D) 10

30

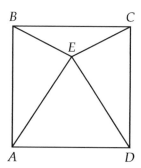

In the figure above, equilateral triangle AED is contained within square $ABCD$. What is the degree measure of $\angle BEC$?

A) $60°$

B) $100°$

C) $120°$

D) $150°$

31

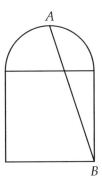

In the figure above, a semicircle sits on top of a square of side 6. Point A is at the top of the semicircle. What is the length of $\overline{AB}$?

A) $3\sqrt{5}$

B) 7

C) 9

D) $3\sqrt{10}$

32

In $\triangle ABC$, $AB = BC = 6$ and $\angle ABC = 120°$. What is the area of $\triangle ABC$?

A) $2\sqrt{3}$

B) $4\sqrt{3}$

C) $6\sqrt{3}$

D) $9\sqrt{3}$

33

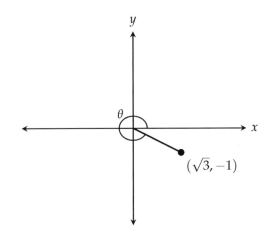

In the xy-plane above, angle θ is formed by the x-axis and the line segment shown. What is the measure, in radians, of angle θ?

A) $\dfrac{5\pi}{3}$

B) $\dfrac{7\pi}{4}$

C) $\dfrac{9\pi}{5}$

D) $\dfrac{11\pi}{6}$

34

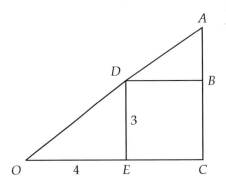

In the figure above, square $DBCE$ has a side length of 3. If $OE = 4$, what is the length of AD?

189

35

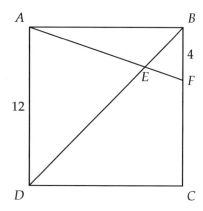

Square $ABCD$ above has a side length of 12. If $BF = 4$, what is the length of BE?

A) 3

B) $2\sqrt{2}$

C) $3\sqrt{2}$

D) $4\sqrt{2}$

36

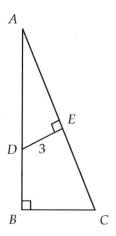

In the figure above, $AB = 12$, $AC = 13$, and $DE = 3$. What is the length of AE?

22
Circles

Circle Facts You Should Know:

Area of a circle: πr^2

Circumference of a circle: $2\pi r$

Arc Length: $\dfrac{\theta}{360} \times 2\pi r$ OR θr if θ is in radians

Area of a Sector: $\dfrac{\theta}{360} \times \pi r^2$ OR $\dfrac{1}{2}r^2\theta$ if θ is in radians

Central angles have the same measure as the arcs that they "carve out."

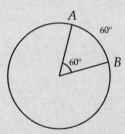

Many students confuse arc length with arc measure. The arc length is the actual distance one would travel along the circle from A to B. Arc measure is the number of degrees one turns through from A to B. You can think of it as a rotation along the circle from A to B. A full rotation is $360°$.

Inscribed angles are half the measure of the arcs that they "carve out."

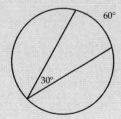

191

Angles inscribed in a semicircle are always 90°. This is just an extension of the previous fact. An angle inscribed in a semicircle carves out half a circle, or 180°, which means the angle itself is half that, or 90°.

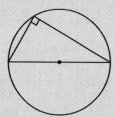

A radius drawn to a line tangent to the circle is perpendicular to that line:

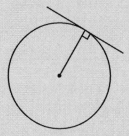

General equation of a circle in the xy-plane:

$$(x - h)^2 + (y - k)^2 = r^2$$

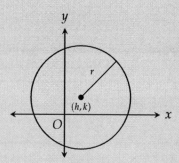

where (h, k) is the center of the circle and r is its radius.

EXAMPLE 1:

In the figure above, the outer circle's radius is twice as long as the inner circle's. What is the ratio of the area of the shaded region to the area of the unshaded region?

A) $\frac{1}{2}$ B) 1   C) 2   D) 3

Let the radius of the inner circle be r. Then the radius of the outer circle is $2r$.

Area of inner circle: πr^2
Area of outer circle: $\pi (2r)^2$
Area of shaded region: $\pi (2r)^2 - \pi r^2 = 4\pi r^2 - \pi r^2 = 3\pi r^2$

$$\frac{\text{Shaded}}{\text{Unshaded}} = \frac{3\pi r^2}{\pi r^2} = 3$$

The answer is $\boxed{(D)}$.

EXAMPLE 2:

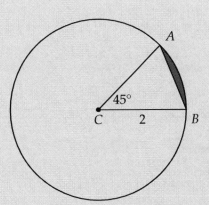

What is the area of the shaded region in the figure above?

A) $\frac{\pi}{4} - \sqrt{2}$ B) $\frac{\pi}{2} - 2\sqrt{2}$ C) $\frac{\pi}{2} - 2$ D) $\frac{\pi}{2} - \sqrt{2}$

To get the shaded area, we must subtract the area of the triangle from the area of the sector.

Area of sector: $\frac{45°}{360°} \pi r^2 = \frac{1}{8} \pi (2^2) = \frac{\pi}{2}$

Area of triangle: Draw the height from point A to base CB. This makes a $45 - 45 - 90$ triangle. Because AC is also a radius, its length is 2. Using the $45 - 45 - 90$ triangle relationship, the height is then $\frac{2}{\sqrt{2}} = \sqrt{2}$.

$$\text{Area} = \frac{1}{2}bh = \frac{1}{2}(2)(\sqrt{2}) = \sqrt{2}$$

$$\text{Area of shaded region} = \frac{\pi}{2} - \sqrt{2}$$

The answer is $\boxed{(D)}$.

EXAMPLE 3:

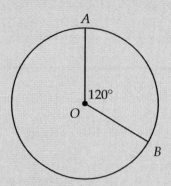

A circle with a diameter of 10 is shown in the figure above. If $\angle AOB = 120°$, what is the length of minor arc $\overset{\frown}{AB}$?

A) $\dfrac{25\pi}{3}$ B) $\dfrac{20\pi}{3}$ C) $\dfrac{10\pi}{3}$ D) $\dfrac{5\pi}{3}$

$$\frac{120°}{360°}(2\pi r) = \frac{1}{3}(2\pi \times 5) = \boxed{\frac{10\pi}{3}}$$

The answer is $\boxed{(C)}$.

EXAMPLE 4:

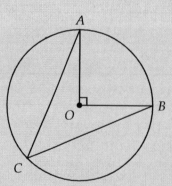

In the figure above, $\angle ACB$ is inscribed in circle O. What is the measure of angle ACB?

A) 15°   B) 30°   C) 45°   D) 60°

The measure of minor arc $\overset{\frown}{AB}$ is the same as the measure of central angle $\angle AOB$, 90°. Inscribed angle ACB is half of that, 45°. Answer $\boxed{(C)}$.

194

EXAMPLE 5:

$$x^2 - 4x + y^2 + 2y = 31$$

The equation of a circle in the xy-plane is given above. What are the coordinates of the center of the circle?

A) $(-2, -1)$ B) $(-2, 1)$ C) $(-1, 2)$ D) $(2, -1)$

To get the equation of the circle in the standard form $(x - h)^2 + (y - k)^2 = r^2$, we have to complete the square twice, once for the x's and once for the y's. If you don't know how to complete the square, you should review the quadratics chapter, which contains many examples of how to do it. Starting with x,

$$(x - 2)^2 - 4 + y^2 + 2y = 31$$

Then y,

$$(x - 2)^2 - 4 + (y + 1)^2 - 1 = 31$$
$$(x - 2)^2 + (y + 1)^2 = 36$$

From the standard form, we can see that the center is at $(2, -1)$ and the radius is 6. Answer $\boxed{(D)}$.

CHAPTER EXERCISE: Answers for this chapter start on page 307.

A calculator is allowed on the following questions.

1

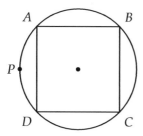

In the figure above, the square $ABCD$ is inscribed in a circle. If the radius of the circle is r, what is the length of arc APD in terms of r?

A) $\dfrac{\pi r}{4}$

B) $\dfrac{\pi r}{2}$

C) πr

D) $\dfrac{\pi r^2}{4}$

2

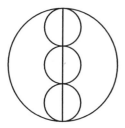

In the figure above, three congruent circles are tangent to each other and have centers that lie on the diameter of a larger circle. If the area of each of these small circles is 9π, what is the area of the large circle?

A) 36π

B) 49π

C) 64π

D) 81π

3

The circle above has area 36π and is divided into 8 congruent regions. What is the perimeter of one of these regions?

A) $6 + 1.5\pi$

B) $6 + 2\pi$

C) $12 + 1.5\pi$

D) $12 + 2\pi$

4

Which of the following is an equation of a circle in the xy-plane with center $(-2, 0)$ and an area of 49π?

A) $(x - 2)^2 + y^2 = 7$

B) $(x + 2)^2 + y^2 = 7$

C) $(x - 2)^2 + y^2 = 49$

D) $(x + 2)^2 + y^2 = 49$

196

5

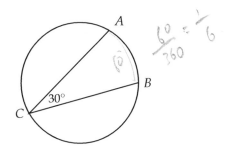

Note: Figure not drawn to scale.

In the figure above, $\angle ACB$ is inscribed in a circle. The length of minor arc $\overarc{AB}$ is what fraction of the circumference of the circle?

A) $\dfrac{1}{3}$

B) $\dfrac{1}{4}$

C) $\dfrac{1}{6}$

D) $\dfrac{1}{12}$

6

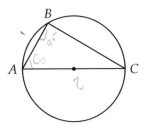

In the figure above, AC is a diameter of the circle and the length of AB is 1. If the radius of the circle is 1, what is the measure, in degrees, of $\angle BAC$?

7

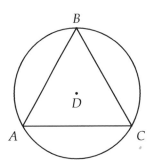

In the figure above, equilateral triangle ABC is inscribed in circle D. If the area of circle D is 36π, what is the length of minor arc $\overarc{AB}$?

A) 2π

B) 3π

C) 4π

D) 6π

8

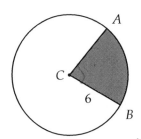

In the figure above, circle C has a radius of 6. If the area of the shaded sector is 10π, what is the measure, in radians, of angle ACB?

A) $\dfrac{2\pi}{5}$

B) $\dfrac{4\pi}{9}$

C) $\dfrac{5\pi}{9}$

D) $\dfrac{5\pi}{8}$

9

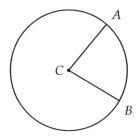

In the figure above, a circle has center C and radius 5. If the measure of central angle ACB is between $\dfrac{\pi}{4}$ and $\dfrac{\pi}{2}$ radians, what is one possible integer value of the length of minor arc $\overset{\frown}{AB}$?

10

In the figure above, four circles, each with radius 4, are tangent to each other. What is the area of the shaded region?

A) $16 - 4\pi$

B) $64 - 4\pi$

C) $64 - 8\pi$

D) $64 - 16\pi$

11

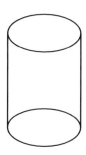

The base of a right circular cylinder shown above has a radius of 4. The height is 5. What is the surface area of the cylinder?

A) 40π

B) 60π

C) 72π

D) 81π

12

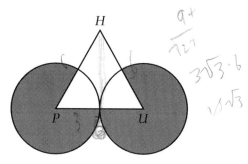

In the figure above, circle P and circle U each have a radius of 3 and are tangent to each other. If $\triangle PHU$ is equilateral, what is the area of the shaded region?

A) 10π

B) 12π

C) 14π

D) 15π

13

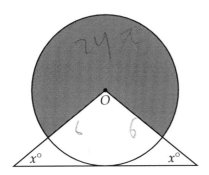

Note: Figure not drawn to scale.

If the area of the shaded region in the figure above is 24π and the radius of circle O is 6, what is the value of x?

A) 15

B) 30

C) 45

D) 60

14

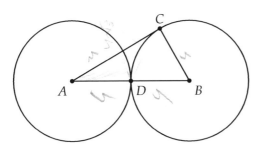

In the figure above, circle A is tangent to circle B at point D. If the circles each have a radius of 4 and $\overline{AC}$ is tangent to circle B at point C, what is the area of triangle ABC?

A) 8

B) $8\sqrt{2}$

C) $8\sqrt{3}$

D) 16

15

$$(x + 2)^2 + (y + 4)^2 = 4$$

The equation of a circle in the xy-plane is given above. Which of the following must be true?

   I. The center of the circle is at $(2, 4)$.

   II. The circle is tangent to the x-axis.

   III. The circle is tangent to the y-axis.

A) II only

B) III only

C) I and II only

D) I, II, and III

23 Trigonometry

We illustrate the three trigonometric functions you need to know with a $5 - 12 - 13$ right triangle.

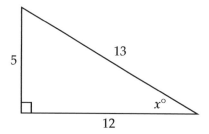

$$\sin x = \frac{\text{opposite}}{\text{hypotenuse}} = \frac{5}{13} \qquad \cos x = \frac{\text{adjacent}}{\text{hypotenuse}} = \frac{12}{13} \qquad \tan x = \frac{\text{opposite}}{\text{adjacent}} = \frac{5}{12}$$

It's important to see these trigonometric functions as if they were just ordinary numbers. After all, they're just ratios. For example, $\sin 30°$ is always equal to $\frac{1}{2}$. Why? Because all right triangles with a $30°$ angle are similar. The ratios of the sides stay the same.

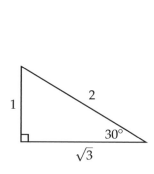 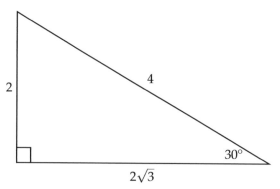

Many students over-complicate trigonometry because they treat $\sin x, \cos x$, and $\tan x$ differently than regular numbers. Perhaps because of the notation, students sometimes make mistakes like the following:

$$\frac{\sin 2x}{x} = \sin 2$$

200

The above is not possible because $\sin 2x$ is one "entity." You cannot separate sin and $2x$ and treat them independently just like you can't separate $f(x)$ into f and x.

> The definitions of sine, cosine, and tangent are best memorized through the acronym **SOH-CAH-TOA**, S for sine (opposite over hypotenuse), C for cosine (adjacent over hypotenuse), and T for tangent (opposite over adjacent).

Aside from the definitions, you should also memorize the following very important identity:

$$\sin x = \cos(90° - x)$$

The reverse is also true.

$$\cos x = \sin(90° - x)$$

Expressed in radians,

$$\sin x = \cos\left(\frac{\pi}{2} - x\right) \qquad \text{and} \qquad \cos x = \sin\left(\frac{\pi}{2} - x\right)$$

Now, the sign of each of the trig functions depends on the quadrant in which the angle terminates.

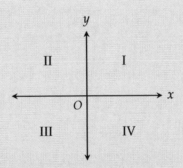

- Sine, cosine, and tangent are all positive in the first quadrant.
- Only sine is positive in the second quadrant.
- Only tangent is positive in the third quadrant.
- Only cosine is positive in the fourth quadrant.

These are best memorized through the acronym **ASTC** (All Students Take Calculus). All the functions are positive in the first quadrant, only sine is positive in the second, and so on.

To find the value of a trig function for an angle without a calculator,

1. Determine what the sign of the result should be (positive or negative).

2. Find the reference angle (the acute angle you get by drawing a straight line to the x-axis). If the angle is $225°$, for example, the reference angle is $225° - 180° = 45°$:

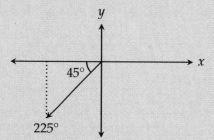

Don't memorize any formulas for finding the reference angle. Just draw a line to the x-axis and figure it out yourself!

3. Use your $45 - 45 - 90$ or $30 - 60 - 90$ special right triangles to get the trig value for the reference angle. The SAT won't ask you to calculate trig values for angles that aren't in these special right triangles unless you're able to use your calculator.

4. Make sure your result has the correct sign from step one.

Let's do a couple simple examples.

1. What is the value of $\sin 330°$?

Since $330°$ is in the fourth quadrant and sine is negative in the fourth quadrant, the result should be negative. Now let's find the reference angle with the help of a diagram:

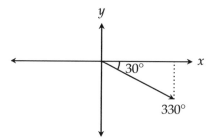

The reference angle is $360° - 330° = 30°$. Using the $30 - 60 - 90$ triangle,

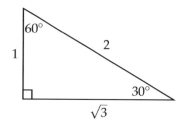

$$\sin 30° = \frac{\text{opp}}{\text{hyp}} = \frac{1}{2}$$

Since the result should be negative, $\sin 330° = \boxed{-\dfrac{1}{2}}$.

2. What is the value of $\cos 135°$?

Since 135° is in the second quadrant and cosine is negative in the second quadrant, the result should be negative. Next, we find the reference angle:

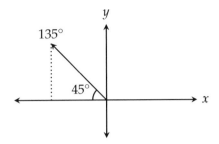

The reference angle is $180° - 135° = 45°$. Using the $45 - 45 - 90$ triangle,

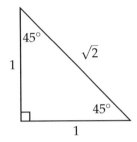

$$\cos 45° = \frac{\text{adj}}{\text{hyp}} = \frac{1}{\sqrt{2}} = \frac{\sqrt{2}}{2}$$

Since the result should be negative, $\cos 135° = \boxed{-\dfrac{\sqrt{2}}{2}}$.

3. What is the value of $\tan 210°$?

Since 210° is in the third quadrant and tangent is positive in the third quadrant, the result should be positive. Next, we find the reference angle:

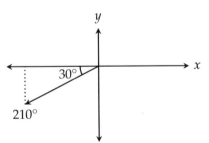

The reference angle is $210° - 180° = 30°$. Using the $30 - 60 - 90$ triangle shown earlier,

$$\tan 30° = \frac{1}{\sqrt{3}} = \frac{\sqrt{3}}{3}$$

Since the result should be positive, $\tan 210° = \boxed{\dfrac{\sqrt{3}}{3}}$.

Finally, you should memorize the following values for 0° and 90°:

$$\sin 0° = 0 \qquad \sin 90° = 1$$
$$\cos 0° = 1 \qquad \cos 90° = 0$$
$$\tan 0° = 0 \qquad \tan 90° = \text{undefined}$$

Expressing 90° in radians,

$$\sin\left(\frac{\pi}{2}\right) = 1$$
$$\cos\left(\frac{\pi}{2}\right) = 0$$
$$\tan\left(\frac{\pi}{2}\right) = \text{undefined}$$

CHAPTER EXERCISE: Answers for this chapter start on page 309.

A calculator should NOT be used on the following questions.

1

If $\cos 40° = a$, what is $\sin 50°$ in terms of a?

A) a

B) $\dfrac{1}{a}$

C) $90 - a$

D) $a\sqrt{2}$

2

In a right triangle, one angle measures $x°$ such that $\tan x° = 0.75$. What is the value of $\cos x°$?

3

$$\sin\theta + \cos(90 - \theta) + \cos\theta + \sin(90 - \theta)$$

For any angle θ, which of the following is equivalent to the expression above?

A) 0

B) $2\sin\theta$

C) $2\cos\theta$

D) $2(\sin\theta + \cos\theta)$

4

In right triangle ABC, the measure of $\angle C$ is $90°$ and $AB = 30$. If $\cos A = \dfrac{5}{6}$, what is the length of AC?

5

If $\tan x = m$, what is $\sin x$ in terms of m?

A) $\dfrac{1}{\sqrt{m^2 + 1}}$

B) $\dfrac{1}{\sqrt{1 - m^2}}$

C) $\dfrac{m}{\sqrt{m^2 + 1}}$

D) $\dfrac{m}{\sqrt{1 - m^2}}$

6

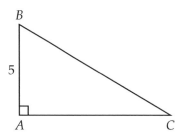

Given that $AB = 5$ and $\tan B = \dfrac{4}{3}$ in the right triangle above, what is the value of $\sin B + \cos B$?

A calculator is allowed on the following questions.

7

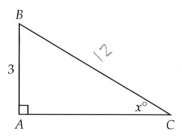

If $\sin x = 0.25$, what is the length of BC in the triangle above?

8

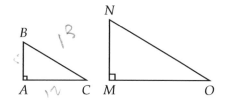

In the figure above, right triangle ABC is similar to right triangle MNO, with vertices A, B, and C corresponding to vertices M, N, and O, respectively. If $\tan B = 2.4$, what is the value of $\cos N$?

9

$$\cos 32 = \sin(5m - 12)$$

In the equation above, the angle measures are in degrees. If $0° < m < 90°$, what is the value of m?

10

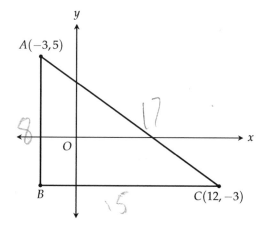

Right triangle ABC is shown in the xy-plane above. What is the value of $\cos C$?

A) $\dfrac{8}{17}$

B) $\dfrac{8}{15}$

C) $\dfrac{13}{15}$

D) $\dfrac{15}{17}$

11

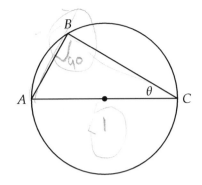

In the figure above, AC is a diameter of the circle. If $AC = 1$, which of the following gives the area of triangle ABC in terms of θ?

A) $\dfrac{\theta}{2}$

B) $\dfrac{\tan \theta}{2}$

C) $2 \sin \theta$

D) $\dfrac{\sin \theta \cos \theta}{2}$

12

Given that $\sin \theta - \cos \theta = 0$, where θ is the radian measure of an angle, which of the following could be true?

   I. $0 < \theta < \dfrac{\pi}{2}$

   II. $\dfrac{\pi}{2} < \theta < \pi$

   III. $\pi < \theta < \dfrac{3\pi}{2}$

A) I only

B) II only

C) I and III only

D) I, II, and III

24
Reading Data

The SAT loves to test your ability to read graphs and charts. Fortunately, these are typically the easiest questions because they never involve too much math. Most of them just test you on simple arithmetic with the extra step of having to interpret a graph. Practice away!

CHAPTER EXERCISE: Answers for this chapter start on page 311.

A calculator is allowed on the following questions.

1

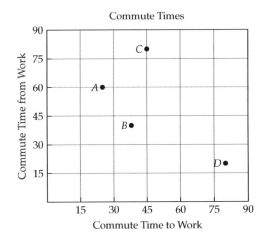

For four work days, Alex plotted the commute time *to* work and the commute time *from* work in the grid above. For which of the four days was the total commute time to and from work the greatest?

A) *A*

B) *B*

C) *C*

D) *D*

2

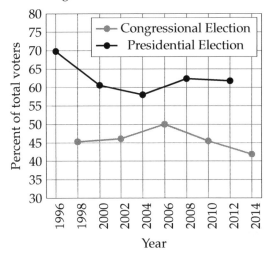

The graph above shows the voter turnout for each year a congressional election or a presidential election was held. In which two year period was the difference in voter turnout between the congressional election and the presidential election the smallest?

A) 1996 to 1998

B) 2000 to 2002

C) 2004 to 2006

D) 2008 to 2010

3

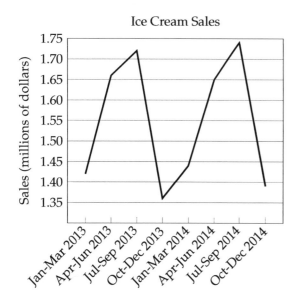

According to the line graph above, ice cream sales were highest both in 2013 and in 2014 during which three month period?

A) January to March

B) April to June

C) July to September

D) October to December

4

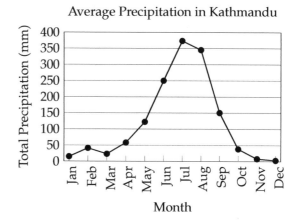

The line graph above shows the monthly precipitation in Kathmandu last year. According to the graph, the total precipitation in September was what percentage of the total precipitation in June?

A) 40%

B) 50%

C) 60%

D) 75%

5

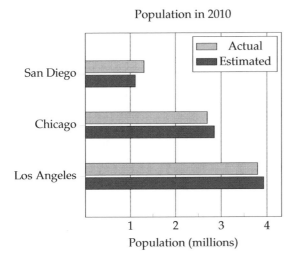

Population in 2010

Population (millions)

Researchers created the graph above to compare their population estimates with the actual populations of different cities in 2010. For which of the cities did the researchers underestimate the population?

  I. San Diego
 II. Chicago
III. Los Angeles

A) I only

B) I and II only

C) II and III only

D) I, II, and III

6

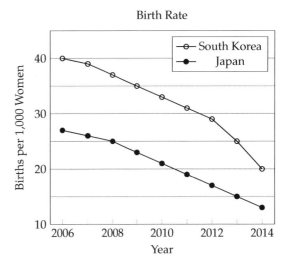

Birth Rate

Based on the graph, which of the following best describes the general trend in birth rates in South Korea and Japan from 2006 to 2014?

A) Each year, birth rates decreased in both South Korea and Japan.

B) Each year, birth rates increased in both South Korea and Japan.

C) Each year, birth rates increased in South Korea but decreased in Japan.

D) Each year, birth rates decreased in South Korea but increased in Japan.

7

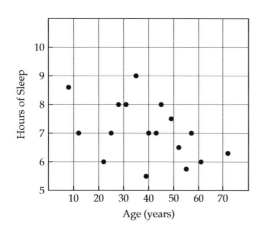

In a certain study, researchers created the scatterplot above to summarize the ages of the participants and the number of hours of sleep they required each night. Which of the following is the closest to the age, in years, of the participant who required the least amount of sleep each night?

A) 35

B) 40

C) 55

D) 60

8

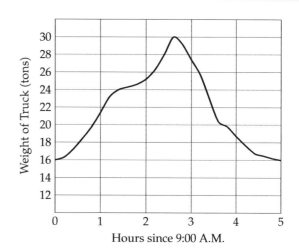

Starting at 9:00 A.M. each day, Musa picks up packages at various locations until his trailer truck reaches its maximum capacity. He then delivers all the packages that he picked up that day. The graph above shows the weight of his truck at different points during the day. What is the maximum weight Musa's truck can hold, in tons?

A) 14

B) 16

C) 24

D) 30

9

Annual Salt Production in the U.S.

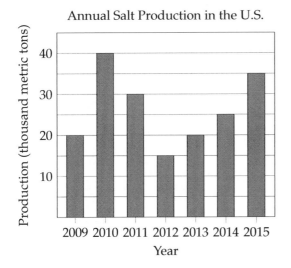

Based on the graph above, for which of the following two consecutive years was the percent increase in U.S. annual salt production the same as the percent decrease from 2010 to 2011?

A) 2009 to 2010

B) 2012 to 2013

C) 2013 to 2014

D) 2014 to 2015

10

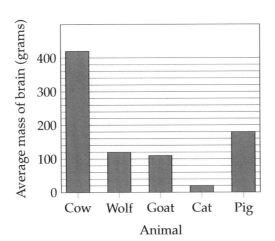

According to the graph above, the average mass of a wolf's brain is what fraction of the average mass of a pig's brain?

11

Video Game Console Sales in 2015

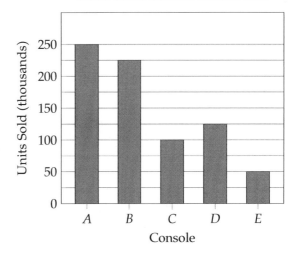

The graph above shows the number of units sold in 2015 for five different video game consoles. The prices of consoles A, B, C, D, and E are $100, $150, $200, $250, and $300, respectively. Which of the five consoles generated the most total revenue?

A) A

B) B

C) D

D) E

12

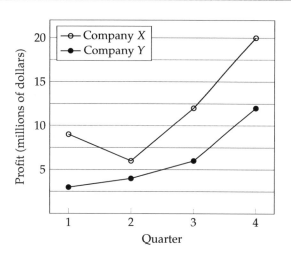

The graph above shows the profit of Company X and Company Y in each quarter of last year. In which quarter was Company X's profit twice Company Y's?

A) 1

B) 2

C) 3

D) 4

13

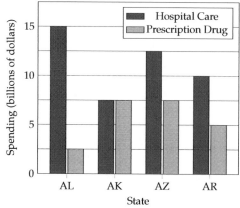

The graph above shows the health care spending of four different states, Alabama (AL), AK (Alaska), AZ (Arizona), and AR (Arkansas) in 2013. Based on the graph, which state had the highest combined hospital care and prescription drug spending in 2013?

A) Alabama

B) Alaska

C) Arizona

D) Arkansas

14

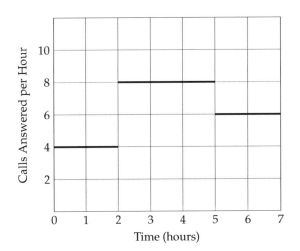

Jeremy works at a call center. The graph above shows the average number of calls he answered per hour during his 7-hour work shift. What is the total number of calls he answered during his shift?

15

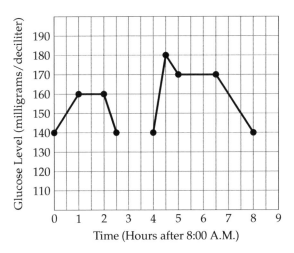

On the day of a medical evaluation, Greg ate breakfast at 8:00 A.M. and lunch at 12:00 P.M. During each meal, doctors recorded his glucose levels in the graph above until they were able to calculate the *glucose recovery time*, the time it took for the body's glucose level to return to its initial value at the start of the meal. According to the graph, by how many hours was Greg's glucose recovery time after lunch greater than his glucose recovery time after breakfast?

A) 1.5

B) 2

C) 3

D) 5.5

16

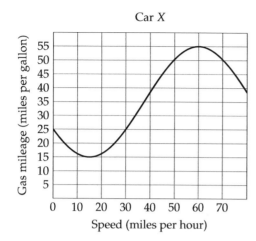

Car *X*

The graph above shows the gas mileage for Car *X* at different speeds. Based on the graph, how many gallons of gas are needed to drive Car *X* for 5 hours at a constant speed of 30 miles per hour?

25 Probability

Generally speaking, probability can be defined as

$$\frac{\text{number of target outcomes}}{\text{number of total possible outcomes}}$$

Nearly all probability questions on the SAT will involve tables of data. So for the purposes of the SAT, probability can more narrowly be defined as

$$\frac{\text{number in target group}}{\text{number in group under consideration}}$$

EXAMPLE 1:

	Beef	Chicken
First Class	18	27
Coach	62	138

The table above summarizes the meat preferences of passengers on a particular flight. If a first class passenger is chosen at random from this flight, what is the probability that the passenger chosen prefers beef?

A) $\frac{9}{40}$ B) $\frac{2}{5}$ C) $\frac{3}{5}$ D) $\frac{2}{3}$

The number of first class passengers is $18 + 27 = 45$. This is the group under consideration. The number of first class passengers who prefer beef is 18. This is the target group.

$$\frac{\text{number in target group}}{\text{number in group under consideration}} = \frac{18}{45} = \frac{2}{5}$$

Answer $\boxed{(B)}$.

EXAMPLE 2: The manager of a large assembly line uses the table below to keep track of the number of vehicles that are produced during different shifts in the day.

	Cars	Trucks	Total
First shift	173	126	299
Second shift	182	143	325
Third shift	165	109	274
Total	520	378	898

If a vehicle is selected at random at the end of the day, which of the following is closest to the probability that the vehicle will be either a car produced during the first shift or a truck produced during the third shift?

A) 0.193   B) 0.314   C) 0.352   D) 0.421

In this question, the group under consideration includes all the vehicles, a total of 898 at the end of the day. The target group includes cars produced during the first shift and trucks produced during the third shift, a total of $173 + 109 = 282$ vehicles.

$$\frac{\text{number in target group}}{\text{number in group under consideration}} = \frac{282}{898} \approx 0.314$$

Answer $\boxed{(B)}$.

CHAPTER EXERCISE: Answers for this chapter start on page 313.

A calculator is allowed on the following questions.

1

	Violation Type			
	Speeding	Stop sign	Parking	Total
Truck	68	39	17	124
Car	83	51	26	160
Total	151	90	43	284

A district police department records driving violations by type and vehicle in the table above. According to the record, which of the following is closest to the proportion of stop sign violations committed by truck drivers?

A) 0.137

B) 0.315

C) 0.433

D) 0.567

$$\frac{39}{90}$$

▼

Questions 2-3 refer to the following information.

The table below shows the number of workers in California with at least one year of experience in five different construction-related occupations.

| | Years of Experience | | | | | |
	1	2	3	4	5+	Total
Painter	22,491	26,973	29,086	33,861	37,061	149,472
Roofer	23,908	27,634	30,932	34,146	39,718	156,338
Welder	27,062	29,812	32,784	36,902	42,680	169,240
Plumber	28,637	33,119	36,670	40,083	45,376	183,885
Carpenter	24,396	28,806	34,867	37,418	43,922	169,409
Total	126,494	146,344	164,339	182,410	208,757	828,344

2

Based on the table, if a plumber in California is chosen at random, which of the following is closest to the probability that the plumber has at least four years of experience?

A) 0.10

B) 0.22

C) 0.25

D) 0.46

3

If a worker with at least four years of experience is chosen at random from those included in the table, which of the following is closest to the probability that the person is a plumber?

A) 0.10

B) 0.22

C) 0.25

D) 0.46

▲

4

Color	Red	Blue	Black	White	Silver
Percent	20%	33%	10%	14%	

A car manufacturer produces cars in red, blue, black, white, and silver. The incomplete table above shows the percentage of cars it produces in each color. If a car from the manufacturer is chosen at random, what is the probability that the car's color is red or silver?

A) 23%

B) 33%

C) 37%

D) 43%

5

	Won	Lost	Total
Underdog	10	35	45
Favorite	25	5	30
Total	35	40	75

The table above shows the results of a baseball team, categorized by whether the team was considered the favorite (expected to win) in the game or the underdog (expected to lose). What fraction of the games in which the team was considered the underdog did the team win?

A) $\dfrac{2}{5}$

B) $\dfrac{2}{7}$

C) $\dfrac{2}{9}$

D) $\dfrac{2}{15}$

6

	Week 1	Week 2	Week 3	Week 4	Total
Box springs	35	40		55	
Mattresses	47	61	68		198
Total	82	101	88	77	348

A store manager summarizes the number of box spring and mattress units sold over four weeks at a bedding store in the incomplete table above. Weeks 2 and 3 accounted for what fraction of all box spring units sold?

A) $\dfrac{2}{15}$

B) $\dfrac{4}{15}$

C) $\dfrac{2}{5}$

D) $\dfrac{4}{5}$

7

Country	Gold	Silver	Bronze	Total
USA	46	29	29	104
China	38	27	23	88
Russia	24	26	32	82
Great Britain	29	17	19	65
Germany	11	19	14	44
Total	148	118	117	383

The table above shows the distribution of medals awarded at the 2012 London Summer Olympics. If an Olympic medalist is to be chosen at random from one of the countries in the table, which country gives the highest probability of selecting a Bronze medalist?

A) USA

B) Russia

C) Great Britain

D) Germany

8

Number of Fish Species

	Cartilaginous	Bony
Philippines	400	800
New Caledonia	300	1,200

All fish can be categorized as either cartilaginous or bony. The data in the table above were produced by biologists studying the fish species in the Philippines and New Caledonia. Assuming that each fish species has an equal chance of being caught, the probability of catching a cartilaginous fish in the Philippines is how much greater than the probability of catching one in New Caledonia?

A) $\dfrac{2}{15}$

B) $\dfrac{1}{4}$

C) $\dfrac{3}{10}$

D) $\dfrac{1}{3}$

9

	Lightning-caused fires	Human-caused fires	Total
East Africa	55	65	120
South Africa	30	70	100
Total		135	220

The incomplete table above summarizes the number of wildfires that occurred in two regions of Africa in 2014 by cause. Based on the table, what fraction of all wildfires in East Africa in 2014 were human-caused?

A) $\dfrac{11}{24}$

B) $\dfrac{13}{27}$

C) $\dfrac{13}{24}$

D) $\dfrac{11}{15}$

10

	Defective	Not defective	Total
Assembly Line *A*	300	5,700	6,000
Assembly Line *B*	500	3,500	4,000
Total	800	9,200	10,000

A manufacturer uses two assembly lines to produce air conditioners. The results of each assembly line's quality control are shown in the table above. If a refrigerator from the manufacturer turns out to be defective, what is the probability that the refrigerator was produced by Assembly Line *A*?

A) 5%

B) 37.5%

C) 60%

D) 62.5%

11

	Type of Residence			
Family members	Apartment	Duplex	Single residence	Total
1	10	22	3	35
2	20	12	13	45
3	8	8	12	28
4 or more	8	4	18	30
Total	46	46	46	138

The table above summarizes the distribution of living situations for residences in a neighborhood. If a duplex in the neighborhood is to be inspected at random, what is the probability that the residence is occupied by no more than 2 family members?

A) $\dfrac{2}{23}$

B) $\dfrac{6}{23}$

C) $\dfrac{17}{69}$

D) $\dfrac{17}{23}$

12

	Number of soil samples	Percent of samples with Chemical A
Area A	450	8%
Area B	550	6%

The data in the table above were produced by ecologists who collected soil samples from two areas to determine whether they were contaminated with Chemical A. Based on the table, what proportion of the soil samples were contaminated with Chemical A?

A) 0.067

B) 0.069

C) 0.070

D) 0.072

13

	Test negative	Test positive	Total
Has virus	30	370	400
Does not have virus	550	50	600
Total	580	420	1,000

The table above shows the results of a test that is designed to give a positive indicator when patients are infected with a certain virus and a negative indicator when they are not infected. According to the results, what is the probability that the test gives the incorrect indicator?

A) 5%

B) 8%

C) 10%

D) 12%

14

	Cured	Not cured
Drug	90	25
Sugar Pill	30	75

The incomplete table above shows the results of a study in which doctors gave patients experiencing back pain either a drug or a sugar pill. Three times as many patients were cured from the drug than from the sugar pill. For every 2 patients cured by the sugar pill, 5 patients were not cured by the sugar pill. According to the results, if a patient is given a sugar pill, what is the probability that the person will be cured of back pain?

A) $\dfrac{1}{4}$

B) $\dfrac{2}{7}$

C) $\dfrac{3}{10}$

D) $\dfrac{2}{5}$

15

	Gym equipment	Computers	Total
Juniors	240	300	540
Seniors	80	160	240
Total		460	

The principal of a school is deciding whether to spend a budget surplus on new gym equipment or computers. The incomplete table above summarizes the preferences among junior and senior class students. If a senior from the school is chosen at random, the probability that the student prefers gym equipment is $\dfrac{1}{3}$. How many seniors are at the school?

26
Statistics I

Consider this list of numbers:

$$5, 6, 2, 2, 2, 7$$

The **mean** of the list is the average:

$$\frac{5 + 6 + 2 + 2 + 2 + 7}{6} = \boxed{4}$$

The **median** is the number in the middle when the list is in order. For example, the median for $1, 2, 3, 4, 5$ is 3. For our particular list, which looks like

$$2, 2, 2, 5, 6, 7$$

when ordered, there is no single middle number we can consider the median. When that happens, the median is the average of the two middle numbers:

$$\frac{2 + 5}{2} = \boxed{3.5}$$

Now what if the list were 100 numbers long? How would you determine the median? Take half to get 50. The 50th and 51st numbers would be the ones in the middle you would average.

For an ordered list of 101 numbers, take half to get 50.5. Round up. The 51st number is the median.

Seems a little counterintuitive, right? If you find this hard to memorize, just keep the smallest case in your back pocket. For a list of 3 numbers, the second one is obviously the median. How would we get this mathematically? Take half of 3 to get 1.5. Round up to 2, which designates the second number. For a list of 4 numbers, the median is the average of the second and third numbers. Take half of 4 to get 2. This designates the second and third numbers.

In both cases, we "rounded up." When there was an odd number of numbers, we rounded 1.5 up to 2. When there was an even number of numbers, we rounded 2 up to 3, which indicated that two numbers would contribute to the median. This technique may seem a bit odd, but many students have found it helpful in quickly finding the median of a large batch of numbers.

The **mode** is the number that shows up the most often. In our particular list, it's $\boxed{2}$.

The **range** is the difference between the biggest number in the list and the smallest number:

$$7 - 2 = \boxed{5}$$

The **standard deviation** is a measure of how spread out a list of numbers is. In other words, how much they "deviate" from the mean. The standard deviation is lower when more numbers are closer to the mean. The standard deviation is higher when more numbers are spread out away from the mean. For example, our list

$$2, 2, 2, 5, 6, 7$$

would have a higher standard deviation than the following list

$$5, 5, 5, 5, 6, 7$$

because the second list is more tightly clustered around the mean. It turns out that the standard deviation of our list is 2.28 and the standard deviation of the second list is 0.83. Don't worry about how we got these values—you'll never be asked to calculate the standard deviation on the SAT. Just know how to compare one list's standard deviation with another's as we just did.

EXAMPLE 1:

Daily Hours Spent Playing Sports

The histogram above summarizes the daily number of hours spent playing sports for 80 students at a school.

PART 1: What is the mean daily number of hours spent playing sports for the 80 students?

PART 2: What is the median daily number of hours spent playing sports for the 80 students?

Part 1 Solution: Sum up the total number of hours for every student. Then divide that by the number of students.

$$\frac{\text{Total hours}}{\text{Number of students}} = \frac{(0 \times 5) + (1 \times 35) + (2 \times 15) + (3 \times 25)}{80} = \frac{140}{80} = \boxed{1.75}$$

Part 2 Solution: In a group of 80 students, the 40th and 41st students are the two in the middle (the histogram already orders the students by their hours so we don't have to). The first 5 students spend 0 hours playing sports each day. The next 35 students spend 1 hour. This group includes the 40th student, so the 40th student spends 1 hour. The next 15 students spend 2 hours. Now this group includes the 41st student, so the 41st student spends 2 hours. Taking the average,

$$\frac{\text{Daily hours spent by 40th student} + \text{Daily hours spent by 41st student}}{2} = \frac{1+2}{2} = \boxed{1.5}$$

EXAMPLE 2:

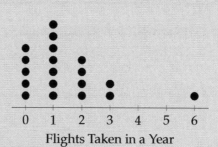

Flights Taken in a Year

The dot plot above summarizes the number of flights taken in a year by 19 college students. If the student who took 6 flights in a year is removed from the data, which of the following correctly describes the changes to the statistical measures of the data?

   I. The mean decreases.
  II. The median decreases.
 III. The range decreases.

   A) III only

   B) I and II only

   C) I and III only

   D) I, II, and III

The student who took 6 flights in a year is called an **outlier**, an extreme data point that is far outside where most of the data lies. Because this outlier is greater than the rest of the data, it brings the average (mean) up. It also increases the range since there is a larger gap between the minimum (0) and the maximum (6).

When this outlier is removed, the mean decreases and the range decreases. The median, however, is unaffected. To confirm this, let's calculate it. Before the outlier is removed, there are 19 students, and the median is represented by the 10th student, who took one flight. After the outlier is removed, there are 18 students, and the median is represented by the 9th and 10th students, both of whom took one flight. So the median of 1 does not change. And in fact, outliers typically affect the mean but not the median. Answer $\boxed{(C)}$.

EXAMPLE 3: The average weight of a group of pandas is 200 pounds. Another panda, weighing 230 pounds, joins the group, raising the average weight of the entire group to 205 pounds. How many pandas were in the original group?

Once in a while, you will get a word problem that involves averages. These questions have less to do with statistics and more to do with algebra, but because we cover averages in this chapter, we decided to cover these types of word problems here as well.

When dealing with average questions on the SAT, think in terms of sums or totals. You can always find the sum by multiplying the average with the number of subjects.

Let the number of pandas in the original group be x. The total weight of the original group is then $200x$. When another panda joins the group, the number of pandas is $x + 1$ and the total weight is $205(x + 1)$.

Since that panda weighs 230 pounds,

$$200x + 230 = 205(x + 1)$$
$$200x + 230 = 205x + 205$$
$$-5x = -25$$
$$x = 5$$

There were $\boxed{5}$ pandas in the original group.

EXAMPLE 4:

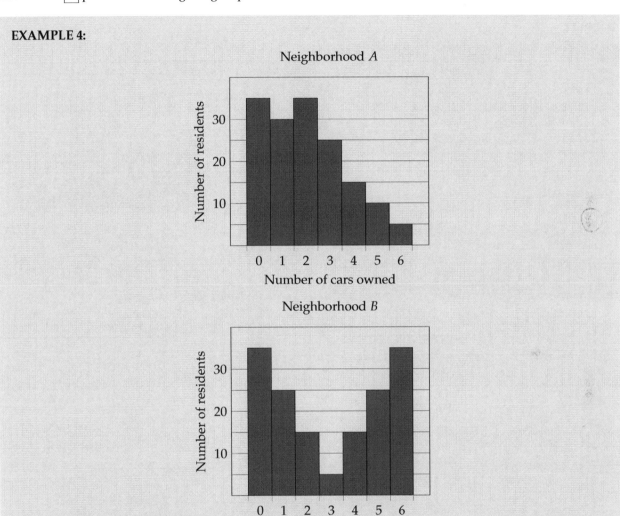

The bar charts above summarize the number of cars that residents from two neighborhoods, A and B, own. Which of the following correctly compares the standard deviation of the number of cars owned by residents in each of the neighborhoods?

A) The standard deviation of the number of cars owned by residents in Neighborhood A is larger.

B) The standard deviation of the number of cars owned by residents in Neighborhood B is larger.

C) The standard deviation of the number of cars owned by residents in Neighborhood A and Neighborhood B is the same.

D) The relationship cannot be determined from the information given.

Most of the data for Neighborhood B are at the ends and are much more spread out from the mean, which, because the bar graph is symmetrical, we can estimate to be 3 cars. The data for Neighborhood A, on the other hand, are more clustered towards the low end, where the mean is. Therefore, the standard deviation for Neighborhood B is larger. Answer $\boxed{(B)}$.

CHAPTER EXERCISE: Answers for this chapter start on page 315.

A calculator is allowed on the following questions.

1

The average height of 14 students in one class is 63 inches. The average height of 21 students in another class is 68. If the two classes are combined, what is the average height, in inches, of the students in the combined class?

A) 64.5

B) 65

C) 66

D) 66.5

2

Kristie has taken five tests in science class. The average of all five of Kristie's test scores is 94. The average of her last three test scores is 92. What is the average of her first two test scores?

A) 95

B) 96

C) 97

D) 98

3

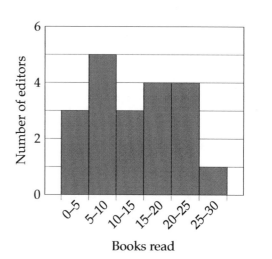

Books read

The histogram above shows the number of books read last year by 20 editors at a publishing company. Which of the following could be the median number of books read by the 20 editors?

A) 7

B) 12

C) 17

D) 22

4

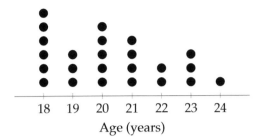

Miss World Titleholders

18   19   20   21   22   23   24
Age (years)

The dotplot above shows the distribution of ages for 24 winners of the Miss World beauty pageant at the time they were crowned. Based on the data, which of the following is closest to the average (arithmetic mean) age of the winning Miss World pageant contestant?

A) 19

B) 20

C) 21

D) 22

5

Locks are sections of canals in which the water level can be mechanically changed to raise and lower boats. The table below shows the number of locks for 10 canals in France.

Name	# Locks
Aisne	27
Alsace	25
Rhone	5
Centre	30
Garonne	23
Lalinde	27
Midi	32
Oise	27
Vosges	93
Sambre	29

Removing which of the following two canals from the data would result in the greatest decrease in the standard deviation of the number of locks in each canal?

A) Aisne and Lalinde

B) Alsace and Garonne

C) Centre and Midi

D) Rhone and Vosges

6

The tables below give the distribution of travel times between two towns for Bus A and Bus B over the same 40 days.

Bus A

Travel time (minutes)	Frequency
44	5
45	10
47	15
48	10

Bus B

Travel time (minutes)	Frequency
25	5
30	10
35	15
40	10

Which of the following statements is true about the data shown for these 40 days?

A) The standard deviation of travel times for Bus A is smaller.

B) The standard deviation of travel times for Bus B is smaller.

C) The standard deviation of travel times is the same for Bus A and Bus B.

D) The standard deviation of travel times for Bus A and Bus B cannot be compared with the data provided.

7

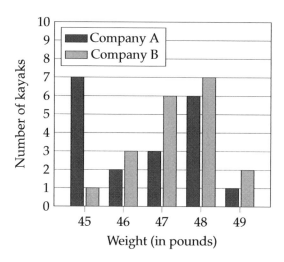

The bar chart above shows the distribution of weights (to the nearest pound) for 19 kayaks made by Company A and 19 kayaks made by Company B. Which of the following correctly compares the median weight of the kayaks made by each company?

A) The median weight of the kayaks made by Company A is smaller.

B) The median weight of the kayaks made by Company B is smaller.

C) The median weight of the kayaks is the same for both companies.

D) The relationship cannot be determined from the information given.

8

Temperature (°F)	Frequency
60	3
61	4
63	4
67	10
70	7

The table above gives the distribution of low temperatures for a city over 28 days. What is the median low temperature, in degrees Fahrenheit (°F), of the city for these 28 days?

67

9

A shoe store surveyed a random sample of 50 customers to better estimate which shoe sizes should be kept in stock. The store found that the median shoe size of the customers in the sample is 10 inches. Which of the following statements must be true?

A) The sum of all the shoe sizes in the sample is 500 inches.

B) The average of the smallest shoe size and the largest shoe size in the sample is 10 inches.

C) The difference between the smallest shoe size and the largest shoe size in the sample is 10 inches.

D) At least half of the customers in the sample have shoe sizes greater than or equal to 10 inches.

10

A food company hires an independent research agency to determine its product's shelf life, the length of time it may be stored before it expires. Using a random sample of 40 units of the product, the research agency finds that the product's shelf life has a range of 3 days. Which of the following must be true about the units in the sample?

A) All the units expired within 3 days.

B) The unit with the longest shelf life took 3 days longer to expire than the unit with the shortest shelf life.

C) The mean shelf life of the units is 3 more than the median.

D) The median shelf life of the units is 3 more than the mean.

11

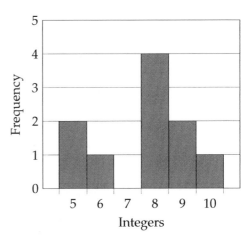

Integers

The graph above shows the frequency distribution of a list of randomly generated integers between 5 and 10. Which of the following correctly gives the mean and the range of the list of integers?

A) Mean = 7.6, Range = 4

B) Mean = 7.6, Range = 5

C) Mean = 8.2, Range = 4

D) Mean = 8.2, Range = 5

12

Quiz	1	2	3	4	5	6	7
Score	87	75	90	83	98	87	91

The table above shows the scores for Jay's first seven math quizzes. Which of the following are true about his scores?

I. The mode is greater than the median.
II. The median is greater than the mean.
III. The range is greater than 20.

A) II only

B) III only

C) II and III

D) I, II, and III

13

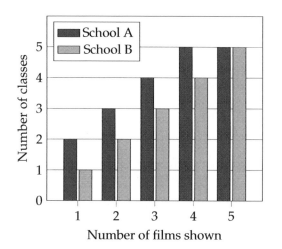

Number of films shown

The bar chart above shows the number of films shown in class over the past year for 19 classes in School A and 15 classes in School B. Which of the following correctly compares the mean and median number of films shown in each class for the two schools?

A) The mean and median number of films shown in each class are both greater in School A.

B) The mean and median number of films shown in each class are both greater in School B.

C) The mean number of films shown in each class is greater in School A, but the median is the same in both schools.

D) The mean number of films shown in each class is greater in School B, but the median is the same in both schools.

14

Calories in Meals				
500	500	520	550	550
550	550	600	600	900

The table above lists the number of calories in each of Mary's last 10 meals. If a 900-calorie meal that she had today is added to the values listed, which of the following statistical measures of the data will not change?

  I.   Median
  II. Mode
  III. Range

A) I and II only

B) I and III only

C) II and III only

D) I, II, and III

15

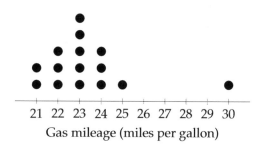

Gas mileage (miles per gallon)

The dotplot above gives the gas mileage (in miles per gallon) of 15 different cars. If the dot representing the car with the greatest gas mileage is removed from the dotplot, what will happen to the mean, median, and standard deviation of the new data set?

A) Only the mean will decrease.

B) Only the mean and standard deviation will decrease.

C) Only the mean and median will decrease.

D) The mean, median, and standard deviation will decrease.

16

Snowfall (in inches)					
45	48	49	50	52	54
55	57	57	57	58	59
60	60	61	61	65	90

The table above lists the amounts of snowfall, to the nearest inch, experienced by 18 different cities in the past year. The outlier measurement of 90 inches is an error. Of the mean, median, and range of the values listed, which will change the most if the 90-inch measurement is replaced by the correct measurement of 20 inches?

A) Mean

B) Median

C) Range

D) None of them will change.

27
Statistics II

The goal of statistics is to be able to make predictions and estimations based on limited time and information. For example, a statistician might want to estimate the mean weight of all female raccoons in the United States. The problem is that it's impossible to survey the entire female raccoon population. In fact, by the time that could be accomplished, not only would the data be out of date but there would be new females in the population. Instead, a statistician takes a random sample of female raccoons to make an estimation of what the actual mean might be. In other words, the **sample** mean is used to estimate the **population** mean. Using a sample to predict something about the entire population is a common theme in statistics and in SAT questions.

EXAMPLE 1: A pet food store chose 1,000 customers at random and asked each customer how many pets he or she has. The results are shown in the table below.

Number of pets	Number of customers
1	600
2	200
3	100
4 or more	100

There are a total of 18,000 customers in the store's database. Based on the survey data, what is the expected total number of customers who own 2 pets?

Using the sample data, we can estimate the total number who own 2 pets to be

$$18,000 \times \frac{200}{1,000} = \boxed{3,600}$$

EXAMPLE 2:

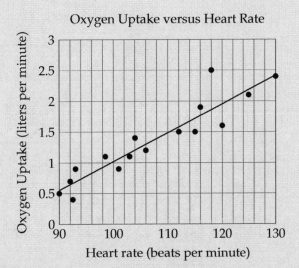

The scatterplot above shows the relationship between heart rate and oxygen uptake at 16 different points during Kyle's exercise routine. The line of best fit is also shown.

PART 1: Based on the line of best fit, what is Kyle's predicted oxygen uptake at a heart rate of 110 beats per minute?

PART 2: What is the oxygen uptake, in liters per minute, of the measurement represented by the data point that is farthest from the line of best fit?

Part 1 Solution: Using the line of best fit, we can see that at a heart rate of 110 beats per minute (along the x-axis), the oxygen uptake is $\boxed{1.5}$ liters per minute.

Using the line of best fit to make a prediction can be dangerous, especially when

- we are making a prediction outside the scope of our data set (predicting the oxygen uptake at a heart rate of 250 beats per minute, for example—you'd probably be dead).
- there are outliers that may heavily influence the line of best fit (see Part 2).
- the data is better modeled by a quadratic or exponential curve rather than a linear one. In this case, a linear model looks to be the right one, but something like compound interest may look linear at first even though it's exponential growth.

Part 2 Solution: From the scatterplot, we can see that the data point farthest away from the line of best fit is at 118 along the x-axis. The point represents an oxygen uptake of $\boxed{2.5}$ liters per minute.

Note that this data point is likely an outlier, which can heavily influence the line of best fit and throw off our predictions. Outliers should be removed from the data if they represent special cases or exceptions.

Not only will you be asked to make predictions using the line of best fit, but you'll also be asked to interpret its slope and y-intercept. We'll use the data from this example in the next one to show you how these concepts are tested.

EXAMPLE 3:

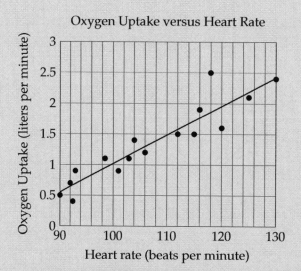

The scatterplot above shows the relationship between heart rate and oxygen uptake at 16 different points during Kyle's exercise routine. The line of best fit is also shown.

PART 1: Which of the following is the best interpretation of the slope of the line of best fit in the context of this problem?

A) The predicted increase in Kyle's oxygen uptake, in liters per minute, for every one beat per minute increase in his heart rate

B) The predicted increase in Kyle's heart rate, in beats per minute, for every one liter per minute increase in his oxygen uptake

C) Kyle's predicted oxygen uptake in liters per minute at a heart rate of 0 beats per minute

D) Kyle's predicted heart rate in beats per minute at an oxygen uptake of 0 liters per minute

PART 2: Which of the following is the best interpretation of the *y*-intercept of the line of best fit in the context of this problem?

A) The predicted increase in Kyle's oxygen uptake, in liters per minute, for every one beat per minute increase in his heart rate

B) The predicted increase in Kyle's heart rate, in beats per minute, for every one liter per minute increase in his oxygen uptake

C) Kyle's predicted oxygen uptake in liters per minute at a heart rate of 0 beats per minute

D) Kyle's predicted heart rate in beats per minute at an oxygen uptake of 0 liters per minute

Part 1 Solution: As we learned in the linear model questions in the interpretation chapter, the slope is the increase in *y* (oxygen uptake) for each increase in *x* (heart rate). The only difference now is that it's a *predicted* increase. The answer is $\boxed{(A)}$.

Part 2 Solution: The *y*-intercept is the value of *y* (oxygen uptake) when *x* (the heart beat) is 0. The answer is $\boxed{(C)}$. Note that this value would have no significance in real life since you would be dead at a heart rate of 0. This again illustrates the danger of predicting values outside the scope of the sample data.

EXAMPLE 4: Malden is a town in the state of Massachusetts. A real estate agent randomly surveyed 50 apartments for sale in Malden and found that the average price of each apartment was $150,000. Another real estate agent intends to replicate the survey and will attempt to get a smaller margin of error. Which of the following samples will most likely result in a smaller margin of error for the mean price of an apartment in Malden, Massachusetts?

A) 30 randomly selected apartments in Malden

B) 30 randomly selected apartments in all of Massachusetts

C) 80 randomly selected apartments in Malden

D) 80 randomly selected apartments in all of Massachusetts

The answer is $\boxed{(C)}$. The margin of error refers to the room for error we give to an estimate. For example, we could say the mean price of an apartment in Malden is $150,000 with a margin of error of $10,000. This implies that the true mean price of all apartments in Malden is likely between $140,000 and $160,000. This interval is called a **confidence interval** (see Example 6).

To get a smaller margin of error in Example 4, we should first only select from apartments in Malden. Selecting apartments from all of Massachusetts not only introduces more variability to the data but also strays from the original intent of the survey, which is to find the average price of Malden apartments. Secondly, we should use a larger sample size. This is common sense. The more apartments we survey, the more accurate our data and our estimations are and the lower our margin of error is.

In fact, the margin of error for any estimate from an experiment depends on two factors:

- Sample size

- Variability in the data (often measured by standard deviation)

The larger the sample size and the less variable the data is, the lower the margin of error. We typically can't control the standard deviation of the data (how spread out it is), but we can control the sample size. So why don't researchers always use huge sample sizes? Because it's too costly and time-consuming to gather data from everyone and everywhere.

EXAMPLE 5: Researchers conducted an experiment to determine whether exercise improves student exam scores. They randomly selected 200 students who exercise at least once a week and 200 students who do not exercise at least once a week. After tracking the students' academic performances for a year, the researchers found that the students who exercise at least once a week performed significantly better on the same exams than the students who do not. Based on the design and results of the study, which of the following is an appropriate conclusion?

A) Exercising at least once a week is likely to improve exam scores.

B) Exercising three times a week improves exam scores more than exercising just once a week.

C) Any student who starts exercising at least once a week will improve his or her exam scores.

D) There is a positive association between exercise and student exam scores.

This question deals with a classic case of **association** (also called correlation) vs. **causation**. Just because students who exercise got better exam scores doesn't mean that exercise *causes* an improvement in exam scores. It's just *associated* with an improvement in exam scores. Perhaps students who exercise just have more discipline or they have more demanding parents who make them study harder. Due to the way the experiment was designed, we can't tell what the underlying factor is.

Therefore, answer (A) is wrong because it implies causation. Answer (B) is wrong because it not only implies causation but also implies that the frequency of exercise matters, something that wasn't tracked in the experiment. Answer (C) is wrong because it suggests a completely certain outcome. Even if exercise DID improve exam scores, not every single student who starts exercising will improve their scores. There might be students for whom exercising makes their scores worse. Any conclusion drawn from sample data is a generalization and should not be regarded as a truth for every individual.

The answer is $\boxed{(D)}$. There is a positive association between exercise and student exam scores.

One of the things the researchers did correctly was to take random samples from each group. The key word is **random**. If the samples weren't random, we wouldn't even have been able to conclude that there is a positive association between exercise and exam scores. Why? Let's say the researchers picked 30 students from the tennis team for the exercise group and 30 students who just play video games all day for the non-exercise group. Definitely not random. Now, did the exercise group do better on their exams because they exercise or because they play tennis? Or was it the video games that made the non-exercise group perform worse? Because the selection wasn't random, we can't tell how each factor influences the result. When the selection is random, all the factors except the one we're testing are "averaged out."

Now what if the researchers wanted to see whether exercise does indeed *cause* an improvement in exam scores. What should they have done differently? The answer is **random assignment**. Instead of randomly selecting 200 students from one group that already exercises regularly and 200 students from another group that does not, they should have just randomly selected 400 students. The next step would be to randomly assign each student to exercise or not. Everyone in the exercise group is forced to exercise at least once a week and everyone in the non-exercise group is not allowed to exercise. If the exercise group performs better on the exams, then we can conclude that exercise causes an improvement in exam scores. Of course, conducting this type of experiment can be extremely difficult, which is why proving causation can be such a monumental task.

The following list summarizes the conclusions you can draw from different experimental designs involving two variables (e.g. exercise and exam scores).

1. Subjects not selected at random & Subjects not randomly assigned

    - Results cannot be generalized to the population.

    - Cause and effect cannot be proven.

    - Example: Researchers want to see whether medication X is effective in treating the flu. People with the flu from Town A receive medication X. People with the flu from Town B receive a placebo (sugar pill). More people in the medication X group experience a reduction in flu symptoms. The generalization that medication X is associated with a reduction in flu symptoms cannot be made since it was only tested in Town A and Town B (sample was not randomly selected from the general population). There may be something special about Town A and Town B. No cause and effect relationship can be established because the medication was not randomly assigned. Perhaps Town A experienced a less severe flu epidemic.

2. Subjects not selected at random & Subjects randomly assigned

    - Results cannot be generalized to the population.

    - Cause and effect can be proven.

    - Example: Researchers want to see whether medication X is effective in treating the flu. People with the flu from Town A and Town B are randomly assigned to either medication X or a placebo (sugar pill). More people in the medication X group experience a reduction in flu symptoms. The generalization that medication X is effective for everyone cannot be made since it was only tested in Town A and Town B (sample was not randomly selected from the general population). Perhaps only one particular strain of the flu exists in Town A and Town B. A cause and effect relationship can be established because the medication was randomly assigned. For the people in Town A and

Town B, we can conclude that medication X *causes* a reduction in flu symptoms. Note that this is still just a generalization—as with any other medication, medication X does not guarantee you will definitely get better, even if you live in Town A or Town B.

3. Subjects selected at random & Subjects not randomly assigned

   - Results can be generalized to the population.

   - Cause and effect cannot be proven.

   - Example: Researchers want to see whether medication X is effective in treating the flu. People with the flu from the general population are randomly selected. They are given the choice of a new medication (medication X) or a traditional medication (really a sugar pill). More people in the medication X group experience a reduction in flu symptoms. We can generalize that people who choose to receive medication X fare better than those who don't. However, no cause and effect relationship can be established because the medication was not randomly assigned. We don't know whether the reduction in symptoms is due to the medication or a difference between those who volunteered and those who didn't.

4. Subjects selected at random & Subjects randomly assigned

   - Results can be generalized to the population.

   - Cause and effect can be proven.

   - Example: Researchers want to see whether medication X is effective in treating the flu. People with the flu from the general population are randomly selected. Using a coin toss (heads or tails), researchers randomly assign each person to either medication X or a placebo (sugar pill). More people in the medication X group experience a reduction in flu symptoms. We can conclude that medication X *causes* a reduction in flu symptoms. This conclusion can be generalized to the entire population of people with the flu.

EXAMPLE 6: Environmentalists are testing pH levels in a forest that is being harmed by acid rain. They analyzed water samples from 40 rainfalls in the past year and found that the mean pH of the water samples has a 95% confidence interval of 3.2 to 3.8. Which of the following conclusions is the most appropriate based on the confidence interval?

   A) 95% of all the forest rainfalls in the past year have a pH between 3.2 and 3.8.

   B) 95% of all the forest rainfalls in the past decade have a pH between 3.2 and 3.8.

   C) It is plausible that the true mean pH of all the forest rainfalls in the past year is between 3.2 and 3.8.

   D) It is plausible that the true mean pH of all the forest rainfalls in the past decade is between 3.2 and 3.8.

If you don't know what a confidence interval is, don't worry. You'll never need to calculate one and the SAT makes these questions very easy. All a confidence interval does is tell you where the true mean (or some other statistical measure) for the population is likely to be (e.g. between 3.2 and 3.8). Even though the SAT only brings up 95% confidence intervals, there are 97% and 99% (any percentage) confidence intervals. The higher the confidence, the more likely the true mean falls within the interval. So in the example above, we can be quite confident that the true mean pH of all the forest rainfalls in the past year is between 3.2 and 3.8. Answer (C) . The answer is not (D) because we cannot draw conclusions about the past decade when all the samples were gathered from the past year.

A confidence interval does NOT say anything about the rainfalls themselves. You cannot say that any one rainfall has a 95% chance of having a pH between 3.2 and 3.8, and you cannot say that 95% of all the forest rainfalls in the past year had a pH between 3.2 and 3.8. Always remember that a confidence interval applies only to the mean, which is a statistical measurement, NOT an individual data point or a group of data points.

Secondly, a 95% confidence interval does not imply that there is a 95% chance it contains the true mean. Even though confidence intervals are computed for the mean, you cannot say that the interval of 3.2 to 3.8 has a 95% chance of containing the true mean pH.

So what does it mean in statistics to be 95% confident in something? If the experiment were repeated again and again, each with 40 water samples, 95% of those experiments would give us a confidence interval that contains the true mean. In other words, the confidence interval given in the example is the result of just one experiment. Another run of the same experiment (another 40 samples) would produce a different confidence interval. Keep on getting these confidence intervals and 95% of them will contain the true mean. So the 95% pertains to all the confidence intervals generated by repeated experiments, NOT the chance that any one confidence interval contains the true mean. Again, don't worry about how confidence intervals are calculated, but be aware that this is how "confidence" is defined in statistics.

CHAPTER EXERCISE: Answers for this chapter start on page 317.

A calculator is allowed on the following questions.

1

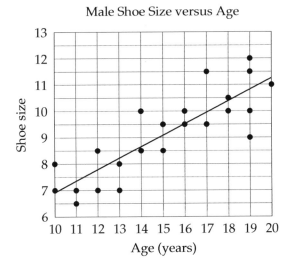

Male Shoe Size versus Age

The scatterplot above shows the relationship between age, in years, and shoe size for 24 males between 10 and 20 years old. The line of best fit is also shown. Based on the data, how many 19 year old males had a shoe size greater than the one predicted by the line of best fit?

A) 1
B) 2
C) 3
D) 4

2

In a survey of 400 seniors, x percent said that they plan on majoring in physics. One university has used this data to estimate the number of physics majors it expects for its entering class of 3,300 students. If the university expects 66 physics majors, what is the value of x?

3

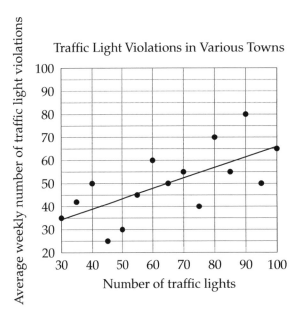

Traffic Light Violations in Various Towns

The scatterplot above shows the number of traffic lights in 15 towns and the average weekly number of traffic light violations that occur in each town. The line of best fit is also shown. Based on the line of best fit, which of the following is the predicted average weekly number of traffic light violations in a town with 75 traffic lights?

A) 40
B) 50
C) 55
D) 60

4

A university wants to determine the dietary preferences of the students in its freshman class. Which of the following survey methods is most likely to provide the most valid results?

A) Selecting a random sample of 600 students from the university

B) Selecting a random sample of 300 students from the university's freshman class

C) Selecting a random sample of 600 students from the university's freshman class

D) Selecting a random sample of 600 students from one of the university's freshman dining halls

5

Two candidates are running for governor of a state. A recent poll reports that out of a random sample of 250 voters, 110 support Candidate A and 140 support Candidate B. An estimated 500,000 state residents are expected to vote on election day. According to the poll, Candidate B is expected to receive how many more votes than Candidate A?

A) 60,000

B) 130,000

C) 220,000

D) 280,000

6

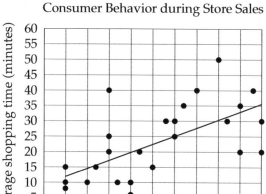

Consumer Behavior during Store Sales

Shopping time refers to the time a customer spends in one store. The scatterplot above shows the average shopping time, in minutes, of customers at 26 different stores offering various discounts. The line of best fit is also shown. Which of the following is the best interpretation of the meaning of the y-intercept of the line of best fit?

A) The predicted average shopping time, in minutes, of customers at a store offering no discount

B) The predicted average shopping time, in minutes, of customers at a store offering a 50% discount

C) The predicted increase in the average shopping time, in minutes, for each one percent increase in the store discount

D) The predicted average number of customers at a store offering no discount

7

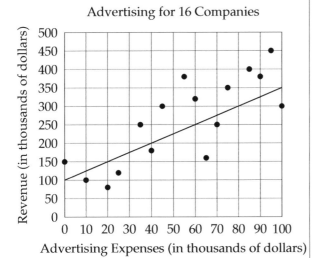

The scatterplot above shows the relationship between revenue and advertising expenses for 16 companies. The line of best fit is also shown. Which of the following is the best interpretation of the meaning of the slope of the line of best fit?

A) The expected increase in revenue for every one dollar increase in advertising expenses

B) The expected increase in revenue for every one thousand dollar increase in advertising expenses

C) The expected increase in advertising expenses for every one thousand dollar increase in revenue

D) The expected revenue of a company that has no advertising expenses

8

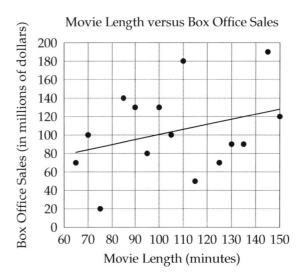

The scatterplot above plots the lengths of 15 movies against their box office sales. The line of best fit is also shown. Which of the following is the best interpretation of the meaning of the slope of the line of best fit?

A) The expected decrease in box office sales per minute increase in movie length

B) The expected increase in box office sales per minute increase in movie length

C) The expected decrease in box office sales per 10-minute increase in movie length

D) The expected increase in box office sales per 10-minute increase in movie length

9

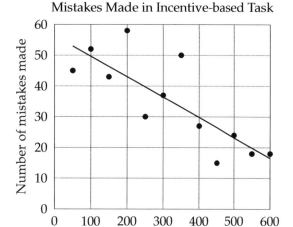

Mistakes Made in Incentive-based Task

In a psychological study, researchers asked participants to each complete a difficult task for a cash prize, the amount of which varied from participant to participant. The results of the study, as well as the line of best fit, are shown in the scatterplot above. Which of the following is the best interpretation of the meaning of the *y*-intercept of the line of best fit?

A) The expected decrease in the number of mistakes made per dollar increase in the cash prize

B) The expected increase in the number of mistakes made per dollar increase in the cash prize

C) The expected dollar amount of the cash prize required for a person to complete the task with 0 mistakes

D) The expected number of mistakes a person makes in completing the task when no cash prize is offered

10

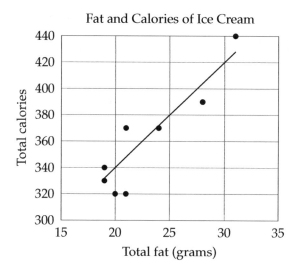

Fat and Calories of Ice Cream

The scatterplot above shows the fat content and calorie counts of 8 different cups of ice cream. Based on the line of best fit to the data shown, what is the expected increase in the number of calories for each additional gram of fat in a cup of ice cream?

A) 5

B) 8

C) 20

D) 40

11

A record of driving violations by type and vehicle is shown below.

	Violation Type			
	Speeding	Stop Sign	Parking	Total
Truck	68	39	17	124
Car	83	51	26	160
Total	151	90	43	284

If the data is used to estimate driving violation information about 2,000 total violations in a certain state, which of the following is the best estimate of the number of speeding violations committed by cars in the state?

A) 479

B) 585

C) 1063

D) 1099

12

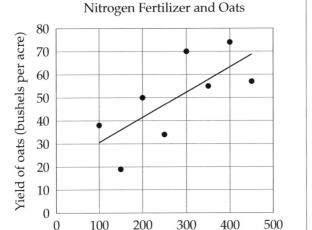

Nitrogen Fertilizer and Oats

The scatterplot above shows the amount of nitrogen fertilizer applied to 8 oat fields and their yields. The line of best fit is also shown. Which of the following is closest to the amount of nitrogen applied, in pounds per acre, to the oat field whose yield is best predicted by the line of best fit?

A) 200

B) 350

C) 400

D) 450

13

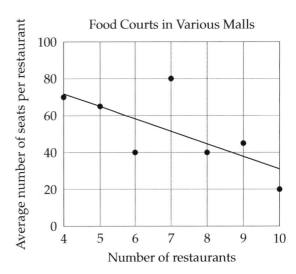

Food Courts in Various Malls

The scatterplot above shows the distribution of seats for the restaurants in 7 different mall food courts. The line of best fit is also shown. According to the data, what is the total number of seats at the food court represented by the data point that is farthest from the line of best fit?

A) 200

B) 240

C) 320

D) 560

14

Researchers must conduct an experiment to see whether a new vaccine is effective in relieving certain allergies. They have selected a random sample of 100 allergy patients. Some of the patients are assigned to the new vaccine while the rest are assigned to the traditional treatment. Which of the following methods of assigning each patient's treatment is most likely to lead to a reliable conclusion about the effectiveness of the new vaccine?

A) Females are assigned to the new vaccine.

B) Those who have more than one allergy are assigned to the new vaccine.

C) The patients divide themselves evenly into two groups. A coin is tossed to decide which group receives the new vaccine.

D) Each patient is assigned a random number. Those with an even number are assigned to the new vaccine.

15

A basketball manufacturer selects a random sample of its basketballs each week to ensure a consistent air pressure within them is maintained. In Week 1, the sample had a mean air pressure of 8.2 psi (pounds per square inch) and a margin of error of 0.1 psi. In Week 2, the sample had a mean air pressure of 7.7 psi and a margin of error of 0.3 psi. Based on these results, which of the following is a reasonable conclusion?

A) Most of the basketballs produced in Week 1 had an air pressure under 8.2 psi, whereas most of the basketballs produced in Week 2 had an air pressure under 7.7 psi.

B) The mean air pressure of all the basketballs produced in Week 1 was 0.5 psi more than the mean air pressure of all the basketballs produced in Week 2.

C) The number of basketballs in the Week 1 sample was more than the number of basketballs in the Week 2 sample.

D) It is very likely that the mean air pressure of all the basketballs produced in Week 1 was less than the mean air pressure of all the basketballs produced in Week 2.

16

A student is assigned to conduct a survey to determine the mean number of servings of vegetables eaten by a certain group of people each day. The student has not yet decided which group of people will be the focus of this survey. Selecting a random sample from which of the following groups would most likely give the smallest margin of error?

A) Residents of the same city

B) Customers of a certain restaurant

C) Viewers of the same television show

D) Students who are following the same daily diet plan

17

The length of a blue-spotted salamander's tail can be used to estimate its age. A biologist selects 80 blue-spotted salamanders at random and finds that the average length of their tails has a 95% confidence interval of 5 to 6 inches. Which of the following conclusions is the most appropriate based on the confidence interval?

A) 95% of all blue-spotted salamanders have a tail that is between 5 and 6 inches in length.

B) 95% of all salamanders have a tail that is between 5 and 6 inches in length.

C) The true average length of the tails of all blue-spotted salamanders is likely between 5 and 6 inches.

D) The true average length of the tails of all salamanders is likely between 5 and 6 inches.

18

An economist conducted research to determine whether there is a relationship between the price of food and population density. He collected data from a random sample of 100 U.S. cities and found significant evidence that the price of food is lower in places with a high population density. Which of the following conclusions is best supported by these results?

A) In U.S. cities, there is a positive association between the price of food and population density.

B) In U.S. cities, there is a negative association between the price of food and population density.

C) In U.S. cities, a decrease in the price of food is caused by an increase in the population density.

D) In U.S. cities, an increase in the population density is caused by a decrease in the price of food.

28 Volume

The volume of all regular solids can be found using the following formula:

$$\text{Volume} = \text{Area of base} \times \text{height}$$

That's why the volume of a cube is $V = s^3$ (the area of the base is s^2 and the height is s)

The volume of a rectangular box/prism is $V = lwh$ (the area of the base is lw and the height is h)

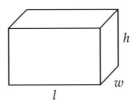

And the volume of a cylinder is $V = \pi r^2 h$ (the area of the base is πr^2 and the height is h)

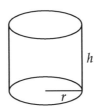

Even though the SAT gives you these formulas at the beginning of each math section, they should be memorized, in addition to the volume of a cone

$$V = \frac{1}{3}\pi r^2 h$$

and the volume of a sphere

$$V = \frac{4}{3}\pi r^3$$

But what if we have a hollowed-out cylinder? What's the volume of that?

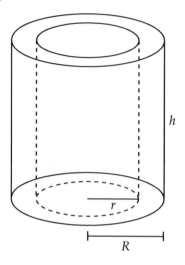

Well, if we look at the base, it's just a ring.

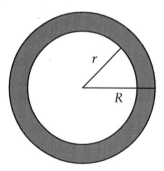

The area of the ring is the outer circle minus the inner circle.

$$\pi R^2 - \pi r^2 = \pi(R^2 - r^2)$$

To get the volume, we multiply this area by the height.

$$V = \pi(R^2 - r^2)h$$

CHAPTER EXERCISE: Answers for this chapter start on page 319.

A calculator is allowed on the following questions.

1

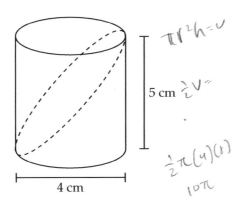

5 cm

4 cm

In the figure above, a cylindrical block of wood is sliced into two pieces as shown by the dashed curve. What is the volume of the top piece in cubic centimeters?

A) 10π

B) 15π

C) 20π

D) 40π

2

James wants to cover a rectangular box with wrapping paper. The box has a square base with an area of 25 square inches. The volume of the box is 100 cubic inches. How many square inches of wrapping paper will James need to exactly cover all faces of the box, including the top and the bottom?

A) 120

B) 130

C) 150

D) 160

3

What is the volume of a cube with surface area $24a^2$?

A) $4a^2$

B) $8a^2$

C) $8a^3$

D) $16a^3$

4

A cylindrical water tank with a base radius of 4 feet and a height of 6 feet can be filled in 3 hours. At that rate, how many hours will it take to fill a cylindrical water tank with a base radius of 6 feet and a height of 8 feet?

A) 4.5

B) 6

C) 7.5

D) 9

5

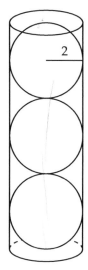

A container in the shape of a right circular cylinder shown above is just large enough to fit exactly 3 tennis balls each with a radius of 2 inches. If the container were emptied out and filled to the top with water, what would be the volume of water, in cubic inches, held by the container?

A) 16π

B) 24π

C) 32π

D) 48π

4π

24π

6

An aquarium has an 80 inch by 25 inch rectangular base and a height of 30 inches. The aquarium is filled with water to a depth of 20 inches. If a solid block with a volume of 5,000 in^3 is completely submerged in the aquarium, by how many inches does the water level rise?

7

A cube with a side length of 5 inches is painted black on all six faces. The entire cube is then cut into smaller cubes with sides of 1 inch. How many small cubes do <u>not</u> have any black paint on them?

A) 27

B) 31

C) 36

D) 48

8

Yuna finds a box with an open top. Each side is 8 inches long. If she fills this box with identical 2 in by 2 in by 2 in cubes, how many of these cubes will be touching the box?

A) 40

B) 48

C) 52

D) 56

9

A 3 × 4 × 5 solid block is made up of 1 × 1 × 1 unit cubes. The outside surface of the block is painted black. How many unit cubes have exactly one face painted black?

A) 16

B) 18

C) 20

D) 22

10

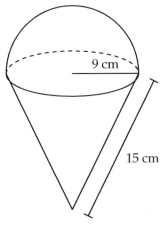

A food manufacturer produces packages of frozen ice cream cones. Each ice cream cone consists of a right circular cone that is filled with ice cream until a hemisphere is formed above the cone as shown in the figure above. The right circular cone has a base radius of 9 cm and a slant height of 15 cm. What is the volume of ice cream, in cubic centimeters, the manufacturer uses for each ice cream cone?

A) 729π

B) 810π

C) 891π

D) 960π

11

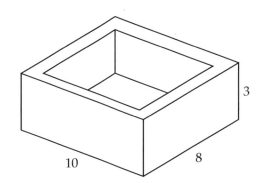

A crate that is 10 inches long, 8 inches wide, and 3 inches high is shown above. The floor and the four walls are all one inch thick. How many one-inch cubical blocks can fit inside the crate?

A) 84

B) 96

C) 120

D) 144

12

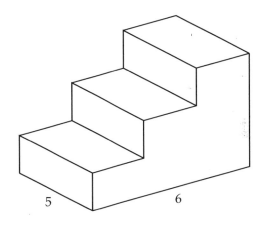

Note: Figure not drawn to scale.

The concrete staircase shown above is built from a rectangular base that is 5 meters long and 6 meters wide. The three steps have equal dimensions and each one has a rise of 0.2 meters. If the density of concrete is 130 kilograms per cubic meter, what is the mass of the concrete staircase in kilograms? (Density is mass divided by volume)

A) 1,420

B) 1,560

C) 1,820

D) 2,040

29
Answers to the Exercises

Chapter 1: Exponents & Radicals

EXERCISE 1:

1. 1

2. −1

3. 1

4. −1

5. 1

6. −1

7. −1

8. −27

9. −27

10. 27

11. −36

12. 64

13. −72

14. 108

15. −648

16. 1

17. $\frac{1}{6}$

18. $\frac{1}{4}$

19. 1

20. 9

21. $\frac{1}{9}$

22. 125

23. $\frac{1}{125}$

24. 49

25. $\frac{1}{49}$

26. 1,000

27. $\frac{1}{1,000}$

EXERCISE 2:

1. $6x^5$

2. $\dfrac{8}{k^2}$

3. $15x^2$

4. -21

5. $\dfrac{1}{8x^6}$

6. $-\dfrac{9b^5}{a^3}$

7. $\dfrac{n^4}{2}$

8. a^4b^6

9. $\dfrac{y^2}{x^2}$

10. x^3

11. $\dfrac{x^6}{y^3}$

12. $\dfrac{3u^2}{4}$

13. $-8u^3v^3$

14. x^5

15. $3x^8$

16. x

17. x^9

18. $\dfrac{2}{x^3}$

19. $36m^8$

20. $\dfrac{1}{a^6}$

21. b^{12}

22. $\dfrac{m^4}{n}$

23. x^2

24. $\dfrac{1}{mn^2}$

25. k

26. $\dfrac{m^6}{n^9}$

27. $x^5y^7z^9$

EXERCISE 3:

1. $2\sqrt{3}$

2. $4\sqrt{6}$

3. $3\sqrt{5}$

4. $3\sqrt{2}$

5. $6\sqrt{3}$

6. $15\sqrt{3}$

7. $4\sqrt{2}$

8. $10\sqrt{2}$

9. $2\sqrt{2}$

10. $8\sqrt{2}$

11. $x = 50$

12. $x = 5$

13. $x = 2$

14. $x = 8$

15. $x = 21$

16. $x = \dfrac{1}{2}$

17. $x = 6$

18. $x = 6$

CHAPTER EXERCISE:

1. $\boxed{B}$

$$a^{-\frac{1}{2}} = 3$$

$$\frac{1}{a^{\frac{1}{2}}} = 3$$

$$1 = 3\sqrt{a}$$

$$\frac{1}{3} = \sqrt{a}$$

$$\frac{1}{9} = a$$

2. $\boxed{C}$ It's obvious that there will be a bunch of 1's, but how many? Well, how many even numbers are there between 2 and 50? If we take the list

$$2, 4, 6, \ldots, 48, 50$$

and divide each element by 2,

$$1, 2, 3, \ldots, 24, 25$$

we can clearly see that there are 25 numbers. Therefore, n is the sum of twenty-five 1's. The answer is 25.

3. $\boxed{D}$

$$2^{2(2n+3)} = 2^{3(n+5)}$$
$$2(2n+3) = 3(n+5)$$
$$4n + 6 = 3n + 15$$
$$n = 9$$

4. $\boxed{A}$

$$\frac{2^x}{2^y} = 2^3$$
$$2^{x-y} = 2^3$$
$$x - y = 3$$
$$x = y + 3$$

5. $\boxed{C}$

$$3^{x-3} = \frac{3^x}{3^3} = \frac{10}{3^3} = \frac{10}{27}$$

6. $\boxed{D}$ Multiply both equations together. The left hand side gives $x^5 y^5$. The right hand side gives 80.

7. $\boxed{B}$ To avoid any trickiness, it's best to plug in numbers. Let $a = 2$ and $b = 2$. Going through each choice,

A) $(-4)^2 = 16$

B) $(-4)^4 = 256$

C) $(2 \cdot 2)^2 = 16$

D) $2 \cdot 2^4 = 2 \cdot 16 = 32$

(B) is the largest.

8. $\boxed{B}$ The $2a$ means raised to the $2a$ power and the b on the bottom means the bth root.

9. $\boxed{D}$ Cube both sides of the first equation,

$$(x^2)^3 = (y^3)^3$$
$$x^6 = y^9$$

Now y^9 can be replaced by x^6,

$$x^{3z} = y^9$$
$$x^{3z} = x^6$$
$$3z = 6$$
$$z = 2$$

10. $\boxed{C}$

$$2^{x+3} - 2^x = k(2^x)$$
$$(2^x)(2^3) - 2^x = k(2^x)$$
$$2^x(2^3 - 1) = k(2^x)$$
$$2^x(7) = k(2^x)$$
$$7 = k$$

11. $\boxed{B}$

$$\sqrt{x\sqrt{x}} = \sqrt{x \cdot x^{\frac{1}{2}}} = \sqrt{x^{\frac{3}{2}}} = (x^{\frac{3}{2}})^{\frac{1}{2}} = x^{\frac{3}{4}}$$

Therefore, $a = \dfrac{3}{4}$

12. $\boxed{A}$ Squaring both sides ("unsimplifying" will get you the same result),

$$(2\sqrt{x+2})^2 = (3\sqrt{2})^2$$
$$4(x+2) = 18$$
$$4x + 8 = 18$$
$$4x = 10$$
$$x = 2.5$$

13. $\boxed{C}$

$$x^{ac} \cdot x^{bc} = x^{30}$$
$$x^{ac+bc} = x^{30}$$
$$ac + bc = 30$$
$$(a+b)c = 30$$
$$5c = 30$$
$$c = 6$$

14. $\boxed{8,000}$ Multiply the first equation by n to get

$$n^4 = nx$$

Substitute this into the left side of the second equation,

$$nx = 20x$$

$$n = 20$$

Using the first equation,
$x = n^3 = (20)^3 = 8,000$

15. $\boxed{111}$

$$x^7 y^6 = 3$$

Multiply both sides by xy,

$$x^8 y^7 = 3xy$$

We do this to make the following substitution,

$$3xy = 333$$

$$xy = 111$$

Chapter 2: Percent

CHAPTER EXERCISE:

1. $\boxed{D}$ $32,000(1.15) = 36,800$

2. $\boxed{B}$ $\dfrac{0.5}{16} = 0.03125 \approx 3.1\%$

3. $\boxed{C}$ Let $z = 100$. Then $x = 1.50(100) = 150$ and $y = 1.20(100) = 120$. x is

$$\frac{150 - 120}{120} = \frac{30}{120} = 25\%$$

larger than y.

4. $\boxed{A}$ Each year, Veronica keeps whatever she has in her account plus the interest on that amount. Because m is a percentage, we can convert it to a decimal by dividing it by 100, giving us $0.01m$. Therefore, $x = 1 + 0.01m$.

5. $\boxed{D}$ $\dfrac{\text{new value} - \text{old value}}{\text{old value}} \times 100\% =$
$\dfrac{2,690 - 2,140}{2,140} \times 100\% \approx 25.7\%$

6. $\boxed{D}$ Let the original price of the book be $100. Then James bought the book at $100(1 - 0.20)(1 - 0.30) = 100(0.80)(0.70) = \$56$, which is $\dfrac{56}{100} = 56\%$ of the original price.

7. $\boxed{A}$ Let x be the number of pistachios at the start. At the end of each day, what's left is $1 - 0.40 = 0.60$ of the day's starting amount. Over two days,

$$x(0.60)(0.60) = 27$$
$$0.36x = 27$$
$$x = 75$$

8. $\boxed{D}$ Let x be the sales tax (as a decimal for now). We'll convert it to a percent at the end.

$$105.82(.90)(1 + x) = 100$$
$$1 + x = \frac{100}{(105.82)(.90)}$$
$$x = \frac{100}{(105.82)(.90)} - 1 = 0.05 = 5\%$$

9. $\boxed{56}$

$$A = (1.25)(B)$$
$$70 = (1.25)(B)$$
$$56 = B$$

10. $\boxed{C}$ Kyle ate $20(1.20) = 24$ pounds of chicken wings and $15(1.40) = 21$ pounds of hot dogs. That's a total of $24 + 21 = 45$ pounds of food. John had $20 + 15 = 35$ pounds of food. The percent increase from John to Kyle is

$$\frac{45 - 35}{35} \approx .29 = 29\%$$

11. $\boxed{C}$ Let her starting card count be x. A loss of 18 percent reduces her total to $(0.82)x$. From there, an increase of 36 percent gets the total to $(1.36)(0.82)x$. Now,

$$(1.36)(0.82)x = n$$
$$x = \frac{n}{(1.36)(0.82)}$$

12. $\boxed{B}$ $12,000(0.94)^{10} \approx 6,460$.

13. $\boxed{B}$ Simple interest means that Kyle will receive the same amount each year based on his initial investment of \$2,000. He'll receive $2,000(0.06)$ in interest each year for a total of $2,000(0.06)t$ after t years. He'll also get back his initial investment. Therefore, the total amount he receives after t years is

$$2,000 + 2,000(0.06)t = 2,000(1 + 0.06t)$$

14. $\boxed{100}$ Since scarves and ties make up 80% of the accessories, the 40 belts must account for 20%. Letting the total number of accessories be x,

$$20\% \text{ of } x = 40$$

$$\frac{1}{5}x = 40$$

$$x = 200$$

There are 200 accessories in the store. Hopefully you're able to get this without having to make an equation, but there's no harm in a little algebra! Now we can determine that there are $\frac{1}{5} \times 200 = 40$ scarves and $\frac{3}{5} \times 200 = 120$ ties. Half of the 120 ties (60 ties) are replaced with scarves, so the store will end up with $40 + 60 = 100$ scarves.

15. $\boxed{C}$ The total amount in the savings account after 5 years will be $3,000(1.06)^5$, but the interest earned will be $3,000(1.06)^5 - 3,000$. The total amount in the checking account after 5 years will be $1,000(1.01)^5$, but the interest earned will be $1,000(1.01)^5 - 1,000$. With a larger initial deposit and a higher interest rate, it's obvious the savings account will have earned more interest. The difference in earned interest will be $(3,000(1.06)^5 - 3,000) - (1,000(1.01)^5 - 1,000)$.

16. $\boxed{D}$ Compounded once every 2 years, interest is earned $\frac{t}{2}$ times in t years. The annual interest rate of 4% must be doubled to get the rate earned over a 2 year span. Therefore, the correct expression is $k(1.08)^{\frac{t}{2}}$.

17. $\boxed{C}$ The percent change is the new minus the old over the old times 100. Notice that the P's cancel out.

$$\frac{P\left(1 + \dfrac{r}{100}\right)^5 - P}{P} \times 100 = \left[\left(1 + \frac{r}{100}\right)^5 - 1\right] \times 100$$

Chapter 3: Exponential vs. Linear Growth

CHAPTER EXERCISE:

1. $\boxed{B}$ With exponential growth, we need to calculate the percent increase, which turns out to be $\dfrac{25 - 20}{20} = 0.25$. Therefore, the rate is 1.25, and the growth can be modeled by $P = 20(1.25)^t$.

2. $\boxed{A}$ The constant increase is $125 - 100 = 25$. Therefore, the slope is 25 and the y-intercept (the initial population) is 100.

3. $\boxed{D}$ The population of trees is experiencing exponential decay at a rate of $1 - 0.04 = 0.96$. The decrease happens once every 4 years, so the rate should be applied $\dfrac{t}{4}$ times.

4. $\boxed{C}$ Scatterplot C is the closest to forming a straight line.

5. $\boxed{C}$ Keep track of the total amount she has received: $3, 9, 27, 81$. Because the total amount she has received triples each day, the relationship is exponential growth.

6. $\boxed{B}$ Each month, Albert loses a book. Because this is a constant decrease, the relationship is linear decay (decreasing linear).

7. $\boxed{D}$ The cell count doubles every hour so the rate, r, is 2. The initial count is 80 so $c = 80$.

8. $\boxed{C}$ Five percent of the original square footage is a constant. It doesn't change, which would make it linear growth.

Chapter 4: Proportion

CHAPTER EXERCISE:

1. $\boxed{D}$

$$P_{old} = \frac{V^2}{R}$$

$$P_{new} = \frac{(0.5V)^2}{R} = \frac{0.25V^2}{R} = 0.25P_{old}$$

The electric power drops to a fourth of what it was.

2. $\boxed{B}$ The area of a square is $A = s^2$, where s is the length of each side.

$$A_{new} = (1.10s)^2 = (1.10)^2s^2 = 1.21s^2 = 1.21A_{old}$$

The new area is 21% greater.

3. $\boxed{D}$

$$V_{old} = \frac{1}{3}\pi r^2 h$$

$$V_{new} = \frac{1}{3}\pi(0.80r)^2(1.10h) = (0.80)^2(1.10)\left(\frac{1}{3}\pi r^2 h\right) = 0.704V_{old}$$

The volume of the cone decreases by $1 - 0.704 = 0.296 = 29.6\%$.

4. $\boxed{B}$

$$A_{old} = \frac{1}{2}(b_1 + b_2)h$$

$$A_{new} = \frac{1}{2}\left(\frac{1}{2}b_1 + \frac{1}{2}b_2\right)(2h) = \left(\frac{1}{2}\right)(2)\left[\frac{1}{2}(b_1 + b_2)h\right] = \frac{1}{2}(b_1 + b_2)h = A_{old}$$

Notice how $\frac{1}{2}$ was factored out from b_1 and b_2. The area stays the same.

5. $\boxed{B}$ Let r be the radius of Kevin's sphere, and let x be the factor the radius of Calvin's sphere is greater by.

$$V_{Kevin} = \frac{4}{3}\pi r^3$$

$$V_{Calvin} = \frac{4}{3}\pi(xr)^3 = x^3\left(\frac{4}{3}\pi r^3\right) = x^3 V_{Kevin}$$

$$x^3 = 4$$

$$x = \sqrt[3]{4} \approx 1.59$$

6. $\boxed{B}$ The area of the original triangle is $\frac{1}{2}(s)(s) = \frac{1}{2}s^2$

$$A_{new} = \frac{1}{2}(xs)^2 = x^2\left(\frac{1}{2}s^2\right) = x^2 A_{old}$$

$$x^2 = 0.64$$

$$x = .80$$

s must have been decreased by $1 - .80 = 0.20 = 20\%$.

7. $\boxed{D}$

$$L_{other\,star} = 4\pi d^2 b$$

$$L_{star} = 4\pi(3d)^2(2b) = (3)^2(2)(4\pi d^2 b) = 18L_{other\,star}$$

8. $\boxed{C}$ Let x be the fraction that Star A's distance is of Star B's.

$$L_{Star\,A} = \frac{1}{9}L_{Star\,B}$$

$$4\pi(xd)^2 b = \frac{1}{9}(4\pi d^2 b)$$

$$x^2(4\pi d^2 b) = \frac{1}{9}(4\pi d^2 b)$$

$$x^2 = \frac{1}{9}$$

$$x = \frac{1}{3}$$

Chapter 5: Rates

CHAPTER EXERCISE:

1. $\boxed{14}$ For one week, Tim's diet plan would require a protein intake of $7 \times 60 = 420$ grams. Since each protein bar provides 30 grams of protein, he would need to buy $420 \div 30 = 14$ protein bars.

2. $\boxed{A}$ Over 6 years, the screen size increased by a total of $18.5 - 15.5 = 3$ inches. That's $3 \div 6 = 0.5$ inches each year.

3. $\boxed{B}$ The pressure increases by $70 - 50 = 20$ atm while the submarine descends $-900 - (-700) = -200$ meters. That's $20 \div 200 = 0.1$ atm per meter, or 1 atm per 10 meters.

4. $\boxed{3}$ The pool has a capacity of $5 \times 300 = 1,500$ gallons. At an increased rate of 500 gallons per hour, it would only take $1,500 \div 500 = 3$ hours to fill the pool.

5. $\boxed{B}$

$$20 \; \text{apples} \times \frac{d \; \text{dollars}}{a \; \text{apples}} = \frac{20d}{a} \; \text{dollars}$$

6. $\boxed{C}$ The racecar burned $22 - 18 = 4$ gallons of fuel in $7 - 4 = 3$ laps. To get to 6 gallons left, the racecar will have to consume $18 - 6 = 12$ more gallons. That's

$$12 \; \text{gallons} \times \frac{3 \; \text{laps}}{4 \; \text{gallons}} = 9 \; \text{more laps}$$

which is Lap $7 + 9 = 16$.

7. $\boxed{100}$ It took 2.5 hours for $65 - 40 = 25$ boxes to be unloaded. There are 3.5 hours from 3:30PM to 7:00PM. In 3.5 hours, $3.5 \; \text{hours} \times \dfrac{25 \; \text{boxes}}{2.5 \; \text{hours}} = 35$ more boxes will be unloaded. That's a total of $65 + 35 = 100$ boxes.

8. $\boxed{A}$ Amy spends $\dfrac{d}{4}$ dollars each week on fruit. Therefore, it will take her $100 \div \dfrac{d}{4} = \dfrac{400}{d}$ weeks to spend $100 on fruit.

9. $\boxed{A}$ The first 150 miles took $150 \div 30 = 5$ hours. The next 200 miles took $200 \div 50 = 4$ hours. His average speed, total distance over total time, was $(150 + 200)/(5 + 4) \approx 38.89$ miles per hour.

10. $\boxed{120}$ Average speed is just total distance over total time. The total distance, in inches, was $2400 \times 12 = 28,800$. The total time, in seconds, was $4 \times 60 = 240$. $28,800 \div 240 = 120$ inches per second.

11. $\boxed{432}$

$$12 \; \text{minutes} \times \frac{90 \; \text{words}}{2.5 \; \text{minutes}} = 432 \; \text{words}$$

12. $\boxed{8}$ The painter can cover an area of $\pi(3)^2 = 9\pi$ in 2 minutes. A circular region with a radius of 6 feet has an area of $\pi(6)^2 = 36\pi$.

$$36\pi \times \frac{2 \; \text{minutes}}{9\pi} = 8 \; \text{minutes}$$

13. $\boxed{C}$ The clock falls behind by 8 minutes every hour. There are 6.5 hours between 4:00 AM and 10:30 AM, so the clock falls behind by $8 \times 6.5 = 52$ minutes. The correct time is then 52 minutes past 10:30 AM, which is 11:22 AM.

14. $\boxed{60}$

$$180 \text{ in commission} \times \frac{100 \text{ in products}}{15 \text{ in commission}} \times \frac{1 \text{ jar}}{20 \text{ in products}} = 60 \text{ jars}$$

15. $\boxed{B}$

$$2 \text{ hours} \times \frac{60 \text{ minutes}}{1 \text{ hour}} \times \frac{32 \text{ kilometers}}{14.5 \text{ minutes}} \approx 265 \text{ kilometers}$$

16. $\boxed{A}$ Two liters is equivalent to $2 \times 33.8 = 67.6$ ounces, which will fill $67.6 \div 12 \approx 5.63$ plastic cups. So at most, 5 plastic cups can be completely filled.

17. $\boxed{B}$ What makes this question a little tricky is that we don't know the distance Brett travels each month or the number of gallons he uses each month. Let's say he needs 2 gallons of gas each month (you can make up any number you want). That means he travels $30 \times 2 = 60$ miles each month and each gallon costs $160 \div 2 = 80$ dollars (ridiculous, I know). Now if he switches to the new car, he'll only need $60 \div 40 = 1.5$ gallons of gas each month (distance of 60 miles divided by the 40 miles per gallon). Because the price of gas stays the same, that will cost him $1.5 \times 80 = 120$ dollars each month.

18. $\boxed{B}$ An 8 inch by 10 inch piece of cardboard has an area of $8 \times 10 = 80$ square inches. A 16 inch by 20 inch piece of cardboard has an area of $16 \times 20 = 320$ square inches.

$$320 \text{ square inches} \times \frac{2 \text{ dollars}}{80 \text{ square inches}} = 8 \text{ dollars}$$

19. $\boxed{48}$ Each jar of honey costs $9 \div 4 = 2.25$ dollars. She can sell each jar for $15 \div 3 = 5$ dollars. That's a profit of $5 - 2.25 = 2.75$ dollars per jar. To make a profit of 132 dollars, she would have to sell $132 \div 2.75 = 48$ jars.

20. $\boxed{B}$ Working at the slowest pace, Jason would take $100 \div 6 \approx 16.67$ hours. Working at the fastest pace, he would take $100 \div 8 = 12.5$ hours. The only answer choice between those two numbers is 16.

21. $\boxed{28}$

$$6 \text{ cups} \times \frac{16 \text{ ounces}}{1 \text{ cup}} \times \frac{29.6 \text{ mL}}{1 \text{ ounce}} \times \frac{1 \text{ student}}{100 \text{ mL}} \approx 28.4 \text{ students}$$

Since it wouldn't make sense to have four-tenths of a student, the most that can be accommodated is 28 students.

Chapter 6: Expressions

CHAPTER EXERCISE:

1. $\boxed{A}$ We factor out $6xy$ from both terms to get $6xy(x+y)$.

2. $\boxed{B}$ The common denominator is $4a$. $\dfrac{1}{a} + \dfrac{3}{4} = \dfrac{4}{4a} + \dfrac{3a}{4a} = \dfrac{4+3a}{4a}$

3. $\boxed{B}$ Expanding,
$$(x^2 + y)(y + z) = x^2y + x^2z + y^2 + yz$$

4. $\boxed{C}$ Divide the top and bottom by 4 to get $\dfrac{1+2x}{3x}$. Another way to get the same answer is to split the fractions and reduce.

5. $\boxed{D}$ $3x^4 - 3 = 3(x^4 - 1) = 3(x^2 + 1)(x^2 - 1) = 3(x^2 + 1)(x + 1)(x - 1)$

6. $\boxed{B}$ The expression follows the $(a+b)^2 = a^2 + 2ab + b^2$ pattern, where $a = x + 1$ and $b = y + 1$. Therefore, the expression is equivalent to $((x+1) + (y+1))^2 = (x + y + 2)^2$.

7. $\boxed{D}$ $\dfrac{xy - x^2}{xy - y^2} = \dfrac{x(y - x)}{y(x - y)} = \dfrac{-x(x - y)}{y(x - y)} = -\dfrac{x}{y}$

8. $\boxed{C}$ Adding the two fractions in the denominator,

$$\frac{x - 1}{2} + \frac{x + 5}{3} = \frac{3(x - 1) + 2(x + 5)}{6} = \frac{5x + 7}{6}$$

Now, 1 over this result means we can flip it: $\dfrac{6}{5x + 7}$.

9. $\boxed{B}$

$$\frac{2 + \dfrac{1}{x}}{2 - \dfrac{1}{x}} = \frac{\dfrac{2x}{x} + \dfrac{1}{x}}{\dfrac{2x}{x} - \dfrac{1}{x}} = \frac{\dfrac{2x + 1}{x}}{\dfrac{2x - 1}{x}} = \frac{2x + 1}{x} \times \frac{x}{2x - 1} = \frac{2x + 1}{2x - 1}$$

10. $\boxed{C}$ First factor out an 8 from both terms. Then use the formula $a^2 - b^2 = (a - b)(a + b)$.

$$8x^2 - \frac{1}{2}y^2 = 8\left(x^2 - \frac{1}{16}y^2\right) = 8\left(x - \frac{1}{4}y\right)\left(x + \frac{1}{4}y\right)$$

Therefore, $c = \dfrac{1}{4}$.

11. $\boxed{B}$ Combining like terms, we get $3x^3 + (8x^2 + 7x^2) + (-4x - 11x) - 7 = 3x^3 + 15x^2 - 15x - 7$.

12. $\boxed{C}$ Combining like terms, $5a - 2a = 3a$ and $3\sqrt{a} - 5\sqrt{a} = -2\sqrt{a}$.

13. $\boxed{\dfrac{3}{2}}$ $\dfrac{9(2y)^2 + 2(6y)^2}{8(3y)^2} = \dfrac{36y^2 + 72y^2}{72y^2} = \dfrac{1}{2} + 1 = \dfrac{3}{2}$

Chapter 7: Constructing Models

CHAPTER EXERCISE:

1. $\boxed{A}$ In the first y hours, the carpenter lays $(x)(y) = xy$ bricks. In the $2y$ hours thereafter, he lays $\left(\dfrac{x}{2}\right)(2y) = xy$ bricks. Altogether, that's $xy + xy = 2xy$ bricks.

2. $\boxed{B}$ The setup fees amount to $100c$, \$100 for each customer. The monthly cost for all the customers amounts to $50c$, \$50 for each customer. Over m months, the monthly charges add up to $50c \times m$, or $50cm$. The total charge is therefore $100c + 50cm$.

3. $\boxed{D}$ The compound's temperature increases by $\dfrac{d}{m}$ degrees per minute. So after x minutes, the temperature increases by $\dfrac{d}{m}x$, or $\dfrac{dx}{m}$. The final temperature is then $t + \dfrac{dx}{m}$.

4. $\boxed{B}$ The reduced price of each souvenir after the first is $0.6a$. After the first souvenir, there are $n - 1$ souvenirs that James will purchase at the reduced price. Therefore, the total cost is $a + (n - 1)(0.6a)$.

5. $\boxed{D}$ The bakers make $3xy$ cupcakes each day. Over 4 days, they will make a total of $4 \times 3xy = 12xy$ cupcakes. The number of boxes needed is the total number of cupcakes divided by the number of cupcakes that can fit in each box: $\dfrac{12xy}{x} = 12y$.

6. $\boxed{B}$ For mn students, the total number of slices must be $2mn$. Since there are 8 slices in each pizza, the school must order $\dfrac{2mn}{8} = \dfrac{mn}{4}$ pizzas.

7. $\boxed{B}$ The store's monthly total cost is $3,000 + 2,500x$. For an entire year, we multiply by 12 months: $c = 12(3,000 + 2,500x)$.

8. $\boxed{B}$ The vendor sold $0.38 \times 8,000 = 3,040$ tickets in the first 5 hours. That's a rate of $\dfrac{3,040}{5} = 608$ tickets per hour. Since the initial number of available tickets was 8,000, $N(t) = 8,000 - 608t$.

9. $\boxed{C}$ Test each of the answer choices by plugging in the values from the table. Answer A works for Monday $(c(7.2) = 30(7.2) + 400 = 616)$ but not for any of the other days. Answer B works for Saturday $(c(8.5) = 60(8.5) + 210 = 720)$ but not for any of the other days. Answer D does not give the correct value of c for any of the given values of s. Only answer C gives the correct value of c for each of the given values of s. These types of questions require you to be thorough. Don't just test one case and choose the first thing that "works." You have to evaluate all the answer choices.

10. $\boxed{D}$ Since Mike's distance from home increases during his commute, we're looking for a graph that goes up and to the right. Since his distance from home increases slowly at first and then more quickly later, we're also looking for the graph to go from a low slope (less steep) to a high slope (more steep). Only the graph in answer D meets these conditions.

Chapter 8: Manipulating & Solving Equations

EXERCISE 1:

1. $r = \pm\sqrt{\dfrac{A}{\pi}}$

2. $r = \dfrac{C}{2\pi}$

3. $b = \dfrac{2A}{h}$

4. $w = \dfrac{V}{lh}$

5. $h = \dfrac{V}{\pi r^2}$

6. $r = \pm\sqrt{\dfrac{V}{\pi h}}$

7. $b = \pm\sqrt{c^2 - a^2}$

8. $s = \sqrt[3]{V}$

9. $h = \dfrac{S - 2\pi r^2}{2\pi r}$

10. $a = \dfrac{bc}{d}$

11. $d = \dfrac{bc}{a}$

12. $m = \dfrac{y - b}{x}$

13. $y_2 = m(x_2 - x_1) + y_1 = mx_2 - mx_1 + y_1$

14. $x_1 = \dfrac{mx_2 - y_2 + y_1}{m}$

15. $a = \dfrac{v^2 - u^2}{2s}$

16. $y = \pm\sqrt{\dfrac{bx}{a}}$

17. $g = \dfrac{4\pi^2 L}{t^2}$

18. $p = \dfrac{A^2}{\pi^2 r^2} - q$

19.

$$X = \dfrac{X + 1}{Y + Z}$$
$$X(Y + Z) = X + 1$$
$$XY + XZ - X = 1$$
$$X(Y + Z - 1) = 1$$
$$X = \boxed{\dfrac{1}{Y + Z - 1}}$$

20.

$$x(y + 2) = y$$
$$xy + 2x = y$$
$$2x = y - xy$$
$$2x = y(1 - x)$$
$$\boxed{\dfrac{2x}{1 - x}} = y$$

21. First, cross-multiply.

$$2ac = ab + b$$
$$2ac - ab = b$$
$$a(2c - b) = b$$
$$a = \boxed{\dfrac{b}{2c - b}}$$

22. $\boxed{\dfrac{3t}{2}}$

23. Divide both sides by 3 to get $x + 2y = \boxed{\dfrac{7z}{3}}$

24. Multiply both sides by 2 to get $2x + 10 = \boxed{4b}$

25. Since $2t = \dfrac{a - 1}{a}$, we can multiply both sides by 2 to get $4t = \boxed{\dfrac{2(a - 1)}{a}}$

26. Cross multiply.

$$3(p - h) = 2(p + h)$$
$$3p - 3h = 2p + 2h$$
$$p = 5h$$
$$\frac{p}{h} = \boxed{5}$$

27. Cross multiply.

$$2(1 + 2r) = 1 - t$$
$$2 + 4r = 1 - t$$
$$t = \boxed{-1 - 4r}$$

28. Square both sides to get $(x^y)^2 = x^{2y} = \boxed{z^2}$

29. $p = \boxed{\dfrac{4^{x+1}}{(x^3 - x^2)(x^5 - x^4)}}$

30. $m = \boxed{\dfrac{2^x\left(x^3 - \dfrac{1}{x}\right) + \dfrac{1}{x^2}}{x^2 + 1}}$

31. $n = \boxed{\dfrac{1}{x\left(\dfrac{\sqrt{x}+1}{5x^2 - 3} - x^3\right)}}$

32. $a = \boxed{\dfrac{5(c + 1)^3 - c}{b^2 + 2}}$

33.

$$k(x^2 + 4) + ky = \frac{7x^2 + 3}{2}$$
$$k(x^2 + 4 + y) = \frac{7x^2 + 3}{2}$$
$$k = \boxed{\frac{7x^2 + 3}{2(x^2 + 4 + y)}}$$

34.

$$ax + 3a + x + 3 = b$$
$$a(x + 3) + (x + 3) = b$$
$$(x + 3)(a + 1) = b$$
$$x + 3 = \frac{b}{a + 1}$$
$$x = \boxed{\frac{b}{a + 1} - 3}$$

CHAPTER EXERCISE:

1. $\boxed{D}$
$$(a+b)^3 = (-2)^3 = -8$$

2. $\boxed{0}$ The answer should be obvious just by looking at it. Testing $n = 0$ gives us:
$$(0-4)^2 = (0+4)^2$$
$$(-4)^2 = (4)^2$$
$$16 = 16$$

We could also expand and solve like so:
$$(n-4)(n-4) = (n+4)(n+4)$$
$$n^2 - 8n + 16 = n^2 + 8n + 16$$
$$-16n = 0$$
$$n = 0$$

3. $\boxed{B}$
$$\frac{b}{ac} = 1$$
$$b = ac$$

If $b = ac$, then $b - ac$ must equal 0.

4. $\boxed{D}$ If $3x - 8 = -23$, then $3x = -15$. Multiplying both sides by 2, $6x = -30$ and $6x - 7 = -37$.

5. $\boxed{A}$ Cross multiply.
$$\frac{4}{9} = \frac{8}{3}m$$
$$12 = 72m$$
$$\frac{1}{6} = m$$

6. $\boxed{A}$
$$3x + 1 = -8$$
$$3x = -9$$
$$x = -3$$
$$(x+2)^3 = (-3+2)^3 = (-1)^3 = -1$$

7. $\boxed{A}$ Cross multiply to get $12 = kx + 2x$. Then,
$$k = \frac{12 - 2x}{x}$$

8. $\boxed{9}$ Note that
$$(-6)^2 = 36$$
which happens when $x = -3$. Then $x^2 = (-3)^2 = 9$.

9. $\boxed{A}$
$$f = p\left(\frac{(1+i)^n - 1}{i}\right)$$
$$fi = p((1+i)^n - 1)$$
$$\frac{fi}{(1+i)^n - 1} = p$$

10. $\boxed{A}$ Multiply both sides by 2 to get $\frac{m}{n} = 4$, which means $\frac{n}{m} = \frac{1}{4}$. Then,
$$\frac{n}{2m} = \frac{1}{2} \cdot \frac{n}{m} = \frac{1}{2} \cdot \frac{1}{4} = \frac{1}{8}$$

11. $\boxed{C}$ If $x^2 - 12 = 4$, then $x^2 = 16$ and $x = \pm 4$. Since $x < 0$, $x = -4$.

12. $\boxed{17}$ If $x^2 + 7 = 21$, then $x^2 = 14$ and $x^2 + 3 = 14 + 3 = 17$.

13. $\boxed{8}$ $x^2 + 5x - 24 = 0$ can be factored as $(x+8)(x-3) = 0$. The two possible solutions are then -8 and 3. Since $k < 0$, $k = -8$ and $|k| = 8$.

14. $\boxed{3}$ Because this is a no calculator question, guess and check is a valid strategy. You can also do the following:
$$x^2(x^4 - 9) = 8x^4$$
$$x^6 - 9x^2 - 8x^4 = 0$$
$$x^2(x^4 - 8x^2 - 9) = 0$$
$$x^2(x^2 - 9)(x^2 + 1) = 0$$
$$x^2(x+3)(x-3)(x^2 + 1) = 0$$

Because $x > 0$, x must be 3 for the equation above to be true.

15. $\boxed{77}$

$$\frac{2\sqrt{x+4}}{3} = 6$$

$$2\sqrt{x+4} = 18$$

$$\sqrt{x+4} = 9$$

$$x+4 = 81$$

$$x = 77$$

16. $\boxed{36}$

$$20 - \sqrt{x} = \frac{2}{3}\sqrt{x} + 10$$

$$10 = \frac{5}{3}\sqrt{x}$$

$$6 = \sqrt{x}$$

$$36 = x$$

17. $\boxed{C}$ Cross multiply.

$$\frac{x}{6} = \frac{x+12}{42}$$

$$42x = 6x + 72$$

$$36x = 72$$

$$x = 2$$

Now, $\dfrac{6}{x} = \dfrac{6}{2} = 3$.

18. $\boxed{C}$

$$d = a\left(\frac{c+1}{24}\right)$$

$$\frac{a}{2} = a\left(\frac{c+1}{24}\right)$$

$$\frac{1}{2} = \frac{c+1}{24}$$

$$12 = c+1$$

$$11 = c$$

19. $\boxed{B}$

$$3(x - 2y) - 3z = 0$$

$$3x - 6y - 3z = 0$$

$$3x = 6y + 3z$$

$$x = 2y + z$$

20. $\boxed{1}$

$$xy^2 + x - y^2 - 1 = 0$$

$$x(y^2 + 1) - (y^2 + 1) = 0$$

$$(y^2 + 1)(x - 1) = 0$$

Since $y^2 + 1$ is always positive, x must equal 1.

21. $\boxed{C}$

$$a = \frac{m_2 g - \mu m_1 g}{m_1 + m_2}$$

$$a(m_1 + m_2) = m_2 g - \mu m_1 g$$

$$a(m_1 + m_2) - m_2 g = -\mu m_1 g$$

$$\frac{m_2 g - a(m_1 + m_2)}{m_1 g} = \mu$$

22. $\boxed{A}$ Because the 2's cancel out, the acceleration stays the same.

$$a_{new} = \frac{2m_2 g - \mu(2m_1)g}{2m_1 + 2m_2} = \frac{2(m_2 g - \mu m_1 g)}{2(m_1 + m_2)}$$

$$= a_{old}$$

23. $\boxed{A}$ Divide both sides by P and take the tth root of both sides.

$$V = P(1 - r)^t$$

$$\frac{V}{P} = (1 - r)^t$$

$$\sqrt[t]{\frac{V}{P}} = 1 - r$$

$$r = 1 - \sqrt[t]{\frac{V}{P}}$$

24. $\boxed{A}$ From the previous question, we know that $r = 1 - \sqrt[t]{\dfrac{V}{P}}$. Because V is half P, $\dfrac{V}{P} = \dfrac{1}{2}$.

Thus, $r = 1 - \sqrt[5]{\dfrac{1}{2}} \approx 0.13$

Chapter 9: More Equation Solving Strategies

CHAPTER EXERCISE:

1. $\boxed{B}$ Expand the right side.

$$(2x+3)(ax-5) = 12x^2 + bx - 15$$
$$2ax^2 + 3ax - 10x - 15 = 12x^2 + bx - 15$$
$$2ax^2 + (3a-10)x - 15 = 12x^2 + bx - 15$$

Comparing both sides, $2a = 12$ and $b = 3a - 10$, which yields $a = 6$ and $b = 3a - 10 = 3(6) - 10 = 8$.

2. $\boxed{49}$ Expand the left side:

$$x^2 + 6xy + 9y^2 = x^2 + 9y^2 + 42$$
$$\cancel{x^2} + 6xy + \cancel{9y^2} = \cancel{x^2} + \cancel{9y^2} + 42$$
$$6xy = 42$$
$$xy = 7$$
$$x^2y^2 = 49$$

3. $\boxed{5}$ Multiply both sides by b.

$$ab + a = a + 5b$$
$$ab = 5b$$
$$a = 5$$

4. $\boxed{2}$ Multiply both sides by $x(x-4)$.

$$(x-4) - x = x(x-4)$$
$$-4 = x^2 - 4x$$
$$0 = x^2 - 4x + 4$$
$$0 = (x-2)^2$$

We can see that $x = 2$.

5. $\boxed{A}$ Expanding the right side,

$$4x^2 + mx + 9 = 4x^2 + 4nx + n^2$$

Comparing both sides, we see that

$$9 = n^2 \text{ and } m = 4n$$

Therefore, $n = -3$ and $m = 4(-3) = -12$

$$m + n = -12 + (-3) = -15$$

6. $\boxed{D}$ Multiply both sides by xyp.

$$\frac{1}{x} + \frac{1}{y} = \frac{1}{p}$$

$$yp + xp = xy$$

$$yp = xy - xp$$

$$yp = x(y - p)$$

$$\frac{yp}{y - p} = x$$

7. $\boxed{D}$

$$(2x + a)(3x + b) = 6x^2 + cx + 7$$

$$6x^2 + 3ax + 2bx + ab = 6x^2 + cx + 7$$

$$6x^2 + (3a + 2b)x + ab = 6x^2 + cx + 7$$

Comparing both sides, $3a + 2b = c$ and $ab = 7$. The two possibilities are $a = 1, b = 7$ and $a = 7, b = 1$. Therefore, $c = 3a + 2b = 3(1) + 2(7) = 17$ and $c = 3a + 2b = 3(7) + 2(1) = 23$.

8. $\boxed{C}$ Multiply both sides by $2x + 1$.

$$12x^2 + mx + 23 = 6x(2x + 1) - 18(2x + 1) + 41$$

$$12x^2 + mx + 23 = 12x^2 + 6x - 36x - 18 + 41$$

$$12x^2 + mx + 23 = 12x^2 - 30x + 23$$

Comparing both sides, $m = -30$.

9. $\boxed{D}$ Expand the left side of the equation.

$$(x^3 + kx^2 - 3)(x - 2) = x^4 + kx^3 - 3x - 2x^3 - 2kx^2 + 6$$

$$= x^4 + (k - 2)x^3 - 2kx^2 - 3x + 6$$

Comparing this to $x^4 + 7x^3 - 18x^2 - 3x + 6$, we can see that $k - 2 = 7$ and $-2k = -18$. In both cases, $k = 9$.

10. $\boxed{3}$ Multiply both sides by $(n - 1)(n + 1)$.

$$3(n + 1) + 2n(n - 1) = 3(n + 1)(n - 1)$$

$$3n + 3 + 2n^2 - 2n = 3(n^2 - 1)$$

$$2n^2 + n + 3 = 3n^2 - 3$$

$$0 = n^2 - n - 6$$

$$0 = (n - 3)(n + 2)$$

$n = 3$ or -2. Because $n > 0$, $n = 3$.

11. $\boxed{4 \text{ or } 6}$ Multiply both sides by $(x+2)(x-2)$.

$$12(x-2) - 2(x+2) = (x+2)(x-2)$$
$$12x - 24 - 2x - 4 = x^2 - 4$$
$$10x - 28 = x^2 - 4$$
$$0 = x^2 - 10x + 24$$
$$0 = (x-6)(x-4)$$

So the two possible solutions are 4 and 6.

12. $\boxed{\dfrac{11}{2}}$ Notice that $x^2 - 1 = (x+1)(x-1)$ on the right hand side. It's then easy to see that we should multiply both sides by $(x+1)(x-1)$

$$4(x+1) + 2(x-1) = 35$$
$$4x + 4 + 2x - 2 = 35$$
$$6x + 2 = 35$$
$$6x = 33$$
$$x = \frac{11}{2}$$

Chapter 10: Systems of Equations

CHAPTER EXERCISE:

1. $\boxed{B}$ Substituting the second equation into the first,

$$3(1 - 3y) - 5y = -11$$
$$3 - 9y - 5y = -11$$
$$3 - 14y = -11$$
$$-14y = -14$$
$$y = 1$$

Finally, $x = 1 - 3(1) = -2$.

2. $\boxed{D}$ From the first equation, $y = 20 - 2x$. Plugging this into the second equation,

$$6x - 5(20 - 2x) = 12$$
$$6x - 100 + 10x = 12$$
$$16x = 112$$
$$x = 7$$

We already know the answer is (D) at this point, but just in case, $y = 20 - 2(7) = 6$.

3. $\boxed{B}$ Add the two equations to get $7x - 7y = 35$. Dividing both sides by 7, $x - y = 5$. We can multiply both sides by -1 to get $y - x = -5$.

4. $\boxed{C}$ The fastest way to do this problem is to subtract the second equation from the first, which yields $x + y = 9$.

5. $\boxed{C}$ In the first equation, we can move $3x$ to the right hand side to get $y = -5x + 8$. Substituting this into the second equation,

$$-3x + 2(-5x + 8) = -10$$
$$-3x - 10x + 16 = -10$$
$$-13x = -26$$
$$x = 2$$

Then, $y = -5(2) + 8 = -2$. Finally, $xy = (2)(-2) = -4$.

6. $\boxed{C}$ If the two lines intersect at the point $(2,8)$, then $(2,8)$ is a solution to the system. Plugging the point into the equation of the second line, we can solve for b,

$$y = -bx$$
$$8 = -b(2)$$
$$-4 = b$$

Plugging the point into the equation of the first line,

$$y = ax + b$$
$$8 = a(2) - 4$$
$$12 = 2a$$
$$6 = a$$

7. $\boxed{A}$ The two graphs do not intersect at all, so there are no solutions.

8. $\boxed{B}$ From the first equation, we can isolate y to get $y = -5x - 2$. Substituting this into the second equation,

$$2(2x - 1) = 3 - 3(-5x - 2)$$
$$4x - 2 = 3 + 15x + 6$$
$$4x - 2 = 15x + 9$$
$$-11 = 11x$$
$$-1 = x$$

Finally, $y = -5(-1) - 2 = 3$.

9. $\boxed{B}$ Divide the first equation by 2 to get $x - 2y = 4$. We can't get the coefficients to match (-2 vs. 2 for the y's). Therefore, the system has one solution. In fact, we can even solve this system by adding the two equations to get $2x = 8$, $x = 4$, which makes $y = 0$.

10. $\boxed{C}$ To get the same coefficients, multiply the first equation by -2 to get $-4x + 10y = -2a$. Now we can see that $-2a = -8$, $a = 4$.

11. $\boxed{A}$ Multiply the first equation by -3 to get $-3ax - 6y = -15$. The constant a cannot be -1. Otherwise, the second equation's coefficients would then be equal to the first equation's coefficients, resulting in a system with no solution.

12. $\boxed{B}$ First, multiply the first equation by 3 to get rid of the fraction: $12x - y = -24$. Next, substitute the second equation into the first,

$$12x - (4x + 16) = -24$$
$$12x - 4x - 16 = -24$$
$$8x = -8$$
$$x = -1$$

Finally, $y = 4(-1) + 16 = 12$.

13. $\boxed{10}$ We can isolate x in the second equation to get $x = y - 18$. Substituting this into the first equation,

$$y = 0.5(y - 18) + 14$$
$$y = 0.5y - 9 + 14$$
$$0.5y = 5$$
$$y = 10$$

14. $\boxed{C}$ To match the coefficients, multiply the first equation by 18 to get $6x - 3y = 72$. We can then see that $a = 3$ if the system is to have no solution.

15. $\boxed{D}$ Divide the first equation by 3 to get $x - 2y = 5$. Divide the second equation by -2 to get $x - 2y = 5$. They're the same, so there are an infinite number of solutions.

16. $\boxed{C}$ For a system to have infinitely many solutions, the equations must essentially be the same. Looking at the constants, we can make them match by multiplying the second equation by 2. The equations then look like this:

$$mx - 6y = 10$$
$$4x - 2ny = 10$$

Now it's easy to see that $m = 4$ and $2n = 6$, $n = 3$. Finally, $\dfrac{m}{n} = \dfrac{4}{3}$.

17. $\boxed{9}$ Plugging the first equation into the second,

$$\sqrt{4x} - (\sqrt{x} + 3) = 3$$
$$2\sqrt{x} - \sqrt{x} - 3 = 3$$
$$\sqrt{x} = 6$$
$$x = 36$$

Therefore, $y = \sqrt{36} + 3 = 9$.

18. $\boxed{B}$ Let $s, m,$ and l be the weights of small, medium, and large jars, respectively. Based on the information, we can create the following two equations:

$$16s = 2m + l$$
$$4s + m = l$$

To get the weight of the large jar in terms of the weight of the small jar, we need to get rid of m, the weight of the medium jar. We could certainly use elimination, but here, we'll use substitution. Isolating m in the second equation, $m = l - 4s$. Substituting this into the first equation, we get

$$16s = 2(l - 4s) + l$$
$$16s = 2l - 8s + l$$
$$24s = 3l$$
$$8s = l$$

Eight small jars are needed to match the weight of one large jar.

19. $\boxed{D}$ Since there were 30 questions, James must have had 30 answers, $x + y = 30$. The points he earned from correct answers total $5x$. The points he lost from incorrect answers total $2y$. Therefore, $5x - 2y = 59$.

20. $\boxed{5}$ Let a and b be the number points you get for hitting regions A and B, respectively. From the information, we can form the following two equations:

$$a + 2b = 18$$
$$2a + b = 21$$

To solve for b, multiply the first equation by 2 and subtract to get $3b = 15$, $b = 5$.

21. $\boxed{D}$ Let r and c be the number of rectangular tables and circular tables, respectively, at the restaurant. Based on the information, we can make the following two equations:

$$4r + 8c = 144$$
$$r + c = 30$$

To solve for r, multiply the second equation by 8 and subtract to get $-4r = -96$, $r = 24$.

22. $\boxed{8}$ To find the point(s) where two graphs intersect, solve the system consisting of their equations. In this problem, that system is

$$y = x^2 - 7x + 7$$
$$y = 2x - 1$$

Substituting the first equation into the second, we get

$$x^2 - 7x + 7 = 2x - 1$$
$$x^2 - 9x + 8 = 0$$
$$(x - 1)(x - 8) = 0$$
$$x = 1 \text{ or } 8$$

So the x-coordinates of the points of intersection are 1 and 8. Since the question already gave us the point $(1, 1)$, p must be equal to 8.

23. $\boxed{9 \text{ or } 16}$ First, add 11 to both sides of the second equation to get $y = x + 11$. Then substitute this in for y in the first equation:

$$x^2 - 2x = x + 11 - 1$$
$$x^2 - 3x - 10 = 0$$
$$(x + 2)(x - 5) = 0$$
$$x = -2 \text{ or } 5$$

When $x = -2$, $y = -2 + 11 = 9$. When $x = 5$, $y = 5 + 11 = 16$. The solutions to the system are then $(-2, 9)$ and $(5, 16)$. Therefore, the possible values of y are 9 and 16.

Chapter 11: Inequalities

CHAPTER EXERCISE:

1. $\boxed{A}$

$$-x - 4 > 4x - 14$$
$$-5x > -10$$
$$x < 2$$

Of the answer choices, only -1 is a solution.

2. $\boxed{D}$ Multiply both sides by 4 to get rid of the fractions.

$$\frac{3}{4}x - 4 > \frac{1}{2}x - 10$$
$$3x - 16 > 2x - 40$$
$$x > -24$$

3. $\boxed{C}$ The shaded region falls below the horizontal line $y = 3$, so $y < 3$. The shaded region also stays above $y = x$, so $y > x$.

4. $\boxed{B}$ Let's say Jerry's estimate, m, is 100 marbles. If the actual number of marbles is within 10 of that estimate, then the actual number must be at least 90 and at most 110. Using variables, $m - 10 \le n \le m + 10$.

5. $\boxed{A}$ Setting up the inequality,

$$M \ge N$$
$$12P + 100 \ge -3P + 970$$
$$15P \ge 870$$
$$P \ge 58$$

6. $\boxed{7}$

$$3(n - 2) > -4(n - 9)$$
$$3n - 6 > -4n + 36$$
$$7n > 42$$
$$n > 6$$

Since n is an integer, the least possible value of n is 7.

7. $\boxed{B}$ The shaded region is below the horizontal line $y = 3$ but above the horizontal line $y = -3$. Therefore, $y \ge -3$ and $y \le 3$.

8. $\boxed{A}$ The time Harry spends on the bus is $\frac{8}{x}$ hours and the time he spends on the train is $\frac{16}{y}$ hours. Since the total number of hours is never greater than 1, $\frac{8}{x} + \frac{16}{y} \le 1$.

9. $\boxed{C}$ If the distributor contracts out to Company A for x hours, then it contracts out to Company B for $10 - x$ hours. Company A then produces $80x$ cartons and Company B produces $140(10 - x)$ cartons. Setting up the inequality,
$$80x + 140(10 - x) > 1,100$$

10. $\boxed{D}$ The line going from the bottom-left to the top-right must be $y = \dfrac{3}{2}x + 2$ and the line going from the top-left to the bottom-right must be $y = -2x + 5$ (based on the slopes and y-intercepts). Answer (D) correctly shades in the region above $y = \dfrac{3}{2}x + 2$ and below $y = -2x + 5$.

11. $\boxed{D}$ Plug in $x = 1$, $y = 20$ into the first inequality to get $20 > 15 + a$, $5 > a$. Do the same for the second inequality to get $20 < 5 + b$, $15 < b$. So, a is less than 5 and b is greater than 15. The difference between the two must be more than $15 - 5 = 10$. Among the answer choices, 12 is the only one that is greater than 10.

12. $\boxed{C}$ One manicure takes $1/3$ of an hour. One pedicure takes $1/2$ an hour. The total number of hours she spends doing manicures and pedicures must be less than or equal to 30, so $\dfrac{1}{3}m + \dfrac{1}{2}p \leq 30$. She earns $25m$ for the manicures and $40p$ for the pedicures. Altogether, $25m + 40p \geq 900$.

13. $\boxed{D}$ From the given inequality, $x \leq 3k + 12$. Subtracting 12 from both sides gives $x - 12 \leq 3k$, which confirms that I is always true.

From the given inequality, $3k + 12 \geq k$, which means $2k \geq -12$, $k \geq -6$, so II must also be true.

From the given inequality, $k \leq x$. Subtracting k from both sides gives $0 \leq x - k$. Therefore, III must also be true.

14. $\boxed{\dfrac{9}{4} < x < \dfrac{10}{3}}$ Let's solve these separately. First,
$$-\frac{20}{3} < -2x + 4$$
$$-20 < -6x + 12$$
$$-32 < -6x$$
$$\frac{16}{3} > x$$

Now for the second part,
$$-2x + 4 < -\frac{9}{2}$$
$$-4x + 8 < -9$$
$$-4x < -17$$
$$x > \frac{17}{4}$$

Putting the two results together, $\dfrac{17}{4} < x < \dfrac{16}{3}$. Therefore, $\dfrac{9}{4} < x - 2 < \dfrac{10}{3}$.

15. $\boxed{D}$ If the area is at least 300, then $xy \geq 300$. The perimeter of the rectangular garden is $2x + 2y$, so $2x + 2y \geq 70$, which reduces to $x + y \geq 35$.

16. $\boxed{C}$ I is not always true because of negative values. Take $a = -5$ and $b = 2$ for example. $a < b$, but $a^2 > b^2$. II is definitely true. It's the equivalent of multiplying both sides by 2. III is also true. It's the equivalent of multiplying both sides by -1, which necessitates a sign change.

Chapter 12: Word Problems

CHAPTER EXERCISE:

1. $\boxed{D}$ The square of the sum of x and y is $(x + y)^2$. The product of x and y is xy. The question asks for the difference: $(x + y)^2 - xy$

2. $\boxed{32}$

$$98 - X = 3(X - 10)$$
$$98 - X = 3X - 30$$
$$-4X = -128$$
$$X = 32$$

3. $\boxed{18}$

$$\sqrt{x} + 5 = 9$$
$$\sqrt{x} = 4$$
$$x = 16$$

$$x + 2 = 18$$

4. $\boxed{5 \text{ or } 10}$ Based on the information, we can form the equation $4x + 10y = 60$. Now it's just a matter of guess and check. Since x and y are integers, it won't be long before we find something that works. For example, $x = 5, y = 4$ is one possible solution.

5. $\boxed{18}$ The width of the monitor is $\frac{1}{3}x$. Since the perimeter of a rectangle is twice the length plus twice the width,

$$2x + 2\left(\frac{1}{3}x\right) = 48$$
$$2x + \frac{2}{3}x = 48$$
$$\frac{8}{3}x = 48$$
$$x = 48 \cdot \frac{3}{8} = 18$$

6. $\boxed{D}$ Susie bought $2x$ pounds of salmon and y pounds of trout. The total cost is then

$$(3.50)(2x) + 5y = 77$$
$$7x + 5y = 77$$

Since x and y must be integers, we can plug each answer choice into the equation above to see if we get an integer value for x. When $y = 4$, for example, $x \approx 8.14$, which is not an integer. The answer turns out to be 7. When $y = 7, x = 6$.

7. $\boxed{15}$ The 35% nickel alloy contains $2(0.35) = 0.7$ grams of nickel. The x% nickel alloy contains $\frac{x}{100} \cdot 6 = 0.06x$ grams of nickel. When combined, these alloys formed $2 + 6 = 8$ grams of a 20% nickel alloy, which must contain $8(0.20) = 1.6$ grams of nickel. Setting up an equation, we get

$$0.7 + 0.06x = 1.6$$
$$0.06x = 0.9$$
$$6x = 90$$
$$x = 15$$

8. $\boxed{A}$

$$8 + 5x = 2(x - 5)$$
$$8 + 5x = 2x - 10$$
$$3x = -18$$
$$x = -6$$

9. $\boxed{60}$ Converting 75% and 85% to fractions in the equation below,

$$\frac{3}{4}(68) = \frac{17}{20}n$$

$$51 = \frac{17}{20}n$$

$$51\left(\frac{20}{17}\right) = n$$

$$60 = n$$

10. $\boxed{7}$

$$\frac{4+N}{15+N} = \frac{1}{2}$$

Cross multiplying,

$$2(4+N) = 15+N$$

$$8+2N = 15+N$$

$$N = 7$$

11. $\boxed{48}$ They start with the same number x. Once Alice gives 16 to Julie, Alice is left with $x-16$ and Julie then has $x+16$.

$$x+16 = 2(x-16)$$

$$x+16 = 2x-32$$

$$-x = -48$$

$$x = 48$$

12. $\boxed{C}$ The fraction of students who take math is $1 - \frac{1}{4} - \frac{1}{6} - \frac{1}{8} = \frac{11}{24}$. Let x be the total number of students.

$$\frac{11}{24}x = 33$$

$$x = 72$$

13. $\boxed{D}$ Let x be the number of trades. Each trade, Ian has a net gain of 1 card while Jason has a net loss of 1 card.

$$20 + x = 44 - x$$

$$2x = 24$$

$$x = 12$$

14. $\boxed{D}$ Making an equation to figure out x,

$$3x - 3 = 21$$

$$3x = 24$$

$$x = 8$$

$$8 + \frac{1}{2}(8) = 12$$

15. $\boxed{90}$ Three times the price of a shirt is 120. Since a tie, which costs 30, is k less than that, k must be $120 - 30 = 90$. As an equation,

$$\text{tie} = 3(\text{shirt}) - k$$

$$30 = 3(40) - k$$

$$30 = 120 - k$$

$$k = 90$$

16. $\boxed{16}$ Let the width of the board be w. Then its length is $2w$. Since the area of a rectangle is its length times its width,

$$(2w)(w) = 128$$

$$2w^2 = 128$$

$$w^2 = 64$$

$$w = \sqrt{64} = 8$$

Finally, the length is $2w = 2(8) = 16$.

17. $\boxed{D}$ Let the number of \$5 coupons given out be x. Then the number of \$3 coupons given out is $3x$, and the number of \$1 coupons given out is $2(3x) = 6x$.

$$5(x) + 3(3x) + 1(6x) = 360$$

$$5x + 9x + 6x = 360$$

$$20x = 360$$

$$x = 18$$

The number of \$3 coupons given out is then $3x = 3(18) = 54$.

18. $\boxed{C}$ Let x be the number of seashells that Carl has. Bob then has $\frac{1}{2}x$ seashells and Alex has $\frac{3}{2}x$ seashells. Since Alex and Bob together have 60 seashells,

$$\frac{1}{2}x + \frac{3}{2}x = 60$$
$$2x = 60$$
$$x = 30$$

Carl has 30 seashells.

19. $\boxed{40}$ Jessica runs at a rate of 4 yards per second. Let t be the time it takes for Jessica to overtake Yoona. We can make an equation with the left side being Yoona's distance and the right side being Jessica's distance.

$$30 + t = 4t$$
$$30 = 3t$$
$$10 = t$$

It takes 10 seconds for Jessica to catch up to Yoona. In that time, Jessica runs $4(10) = 40$ yards.

20. $\boxed{121}$ Let the side length of the original patio be s. Then the renovated patio has a length of $s + 4$ and a width of $s - 5$. Setting up an equation for the area of the renovated patio, we get

$$(s + 4)(s - 5) = 90$$
$$s^2 - s - 20 = 90$$
$$s^2 - s - 110 = 0$$
$$(s - 11)(s + 10) = 0$$

Since the side length s must be a positive number, $s = 11$, which means the original area of the patio was $s^2 = (11)^2 = 121$ square feet.

Chapter 13: Lines

CHAPTER EXERCISE:

1. $\boxed{B}$ A vertical line that intersects the x-axis at 3 has an equation of $x = 3$.

2. $\boxed{C}$

$$\frac{y_2 - y_1}{x_2 - x_1} = \frac{1}{3}$$

$$\frac{n - 1}{5 - (-1)} = \frac{1}{3}$$

$$\frac{n - 1}{6} = \frac{1}{3}$$

$$n - 1 = 2$$

$$n = 3$$

3. $\boxed{A}$ The slope of line l is $\dfrac{8 - 5}{6 - (-3)} = \dfrac{3}{9} = \dfrac{1}{3}$.

Using point-slope form,

$$y - y_1 = m(x - x_1)$$

$$y - 8 = \frac{1}{3}(x - 6)$$

$$y = \frac{1}{3}x + 6$$

At this point, we test each answer choice by plugging in the x-coordinate and verifying the y-coordinate. Only answer (A) works.

4. $\boxed{C}$ The graph of line l goes up three units for every two units to the right, which means its slope is $\dfrac{3}{2}$. A parallel line must have the same slope. Only answer choice (C) gives an equation of a line with the same slope.

5. $\boxed{6.5 \text{ or } \dfrac{13}{2}}$ From the graph, we can see that f goes up 1 unit for every 2 units to the right, which means its slope is $\dfrac{1}{2}$. Since g is perpendicular to f, the slope of g must be -2 (the negative reciprocal). Since g passes through the point $\left(1, \dfrac{5}{2}\right)$, we can use point-slope form to find the equation of g:

$$y - y_1 = m(x - x_1)$$

$$y - \frac{5}{2} = -2(x - 1)$$

$$y = -2x + 2 + \frac{5}{2}$$

$$y = -2x + \frac{9}{2}$$

Finally, $g(-1) = -2(-1) + \dfrac{9}{2} = 2 + 4\dfrac{1}{2} = 6\dfrac{1}{2}$. A quicker way would've been to work backwards from the point $\left(1, \dfrac{5}{2}\right)$, knowing that the slope is -2. So on the graph of g, 1 unit to the left brings us to $\left(0, \dfrac{5}{2} + 2\right) = \left(0, 4\dfrac{1}{2}\right)$, and 1 more unit to the left brings us to $\left(-1, 4\dfrac{1}{2} + 2\right) = \left(-1, 6\dfrac{1}{2}\right)$. Therefore, $g(-1) = 6.5$.

6. $\boxed{B}$

$$\frac{y_2 - y_1}{x_2 - x_1} = \frac{2 - 0}{0 - 4} = \frac{2}{-4} = -\frac{1}{2}$$

7. $\boxed{B}$ From the graph, slope m is positive and y-intercept b is negative. Therefore, $mb < 0$.

8. $\boxed{D}$ The line $y = -2x - 2$ has a slope of -2 and a y-intercept of -2. Line l must have a slope that is the negative reciprocal of -2, which is $\dfrac{1}{2}$. Since they have the same y-intercept, the equation of line l must be $y = \dfrac{1}{2}x - 2$.

9. $\boxed{B}$ The line we're looking for must have a slope that is the negative reciprocal of $\dfrac{1}{2}$, which is -2.

$$y = -2x + b$$

Plugging in the point $(1, 5)$,

$$5 = -2(1) + b$$

$$7 = b$$

Now that we have b, the line is $y = -2x + 7$.

10. $\boxed{D}$

$$\frac{10 - 4}{x - 1} = \frac{2}{3}$$

$$\frac{6}{x - 1} = \frac{2}{3}$$

Cross multiplying,

$$2(x - 1) = 18$$
$$2x - 2 = 18$$
$$2x = 20$$
$$x = 10$$

11. $\boxed{1.6 \text{ or } \dfrac{8}{5}}$ First, plug the point $(2, 6)$ into the equation of the line so that we can solve for a:

$$a(2) - \frac{1}{3}(6) = 8$$

$$2a - 2 = 8$$

$$2a = 10$$

$$a = 5$$

So the equation of the line is $5x - \dfrac{1}{3}y = 8$.

The x-intercept always has a y-coordinate of 0, so if we plug in 0 for y, we get $5x = 8$, which gives $x = \dfrac{8}{5} = 1.6$.

12. $\boxed{A}$ One easy way to approach this problem is to make up numbers for a and b. Let $a = 1$ and $b = 2$ so that $\dfrac{a}{b} = \dfrac{1}{2}$. Since the second line is perpendicular to the first, $\dfrac{d}{e} = -2$, which satisfies the condition in answer choice (A).

Chapter 14: Interpreting Linear Models

CHAPTER EXERCISE:

1. $\boxed{A}$ The slope is -3, which means the water level decreases by 3 feet each day.

2. $\boxed{B}$ The value 18 refers to the slope of -18, which means the number of loaves remaining decreases by 18 each hour. This implies that the bakery sells 18 loaves each hour.

3. $\boxed{C}$ The y-intercept of 500 means that when $n = 0$ (when there were no videos on the site), there were 500 members.

4. $\boxed{B}$ The number 2 refers to the slope of -2, which means two fewer teaspoons of sugar should be added for every teaspoon of honey already in the beverage. Don't be fooled by answers (C) and (D), which "reverse" the x and the y (h and s, in this case). The slope is always the change in y for each unit increase in x, not the other way around.

5. $\boxed{A}$ The salesperson earns a commission, but on what? The amount of money he or she brings in. To get that, we must multiply the number of cars sold by the average price of each car. Since x and c already represent the commission rate and the number of cars sold, respectively, the number 2,000 must represent the average price of each car.

6. $\boxed{C}$ The number 2,000 refers to the slope, which means a town's estimated population increases by 2,000 for each additional school in the town.

7. $\boxed{A}$ The number 4 refers to the slope of -4, which means an increase of $1°$ C decreases the number of hours until a gallon of milk goes sour by 4. In other words, the milk goes sour 4 hours faster.

8. $\boxed{B}$ When $t = 0$, there is no time left in the auction. The auction has finished. Therefore, the 900 is the final auction price of the lamp.

9. $\boxed{A}$ Because it's the slope, the 1.30 can be thought of as the exchange rate, converting U.S. dollars into euros. But after the conversion, 1.50 is subtracted away, which means you get 1.50 euros less than you should have. Therefore, the best interpretation of the 1.50 y-intercept is a 1.50 euro fee the bank charges to do the conversion.

10. $\boxed{.4}$ To see the answer more clearly, we can put the equation into $y = mx + b$ form: $t = \frac{2}{5}x + \frac{9}{5}$. The slope is $\frac{2}{5}$, or 0.4, which means the load time increases by 0.4 seconds for each image on the web page.

11. $\boxed{B}$ The slope is the change in y (daily profit) for each unit change in x (cakes sold).

12. $\boxed{C}$ Notice that the y-intercept is negative. It is the bakery's profit when no cakes are sold. Therefore, anything that varies with the number of cakes sold is incorrect. For example, answer (D) is wrong because the cost of the cakes that didn't sell depends on how many the bakery did sell. It's not a fixed number like the y-intercept is. The best interpretation of the y-intercept is the cost of running the bakery (rent, labor, machinery, etc.), which is likely a fixed number.

13. $\boxed{A}$ The solution $(5,0)$ means that the bakery's daily profit is zero when 5 cakes are sold. Therefore, selling five cakes is enough to break-even with daily expenses.

14. $\boxed{2.5}$ The slope of the equation is 5, which means the temperature goes up by 5 degrees every hour. So every half hour (30 minutes), the temperature goes up by $0.5 \times 5 = 2.5$ degrees.

15. $\boxed{D}$ Putting the equation into $y = mx + b$ form, $y = \dfrac{1}{2}x + 7$. The slope of $\dfrac{1}{2}$ means that one more turtle requires an additional half a gallon of water. So III is true.

Getting x in terms of y, $x = 2y - 14$. The "slope" of 2 means that 1 more gallon of water can support two more turtles. So I is true.

16. $\boxed{C}$ Because this question is asking for the change in "x" per change in "y" (the reverse of slope), we need to rearrange the equation to get x in terms of C.

$$C = 1.5 + 2.5x$$

Dividing each element in the equation by 2.5,

$$0.4C = 0.6 + x$$

$$x = 0.4C - 0.6$$

The slope here is 0.4, which means the weight of a shipment increases by 0.4 pounds per dollar increase in the mailing cost. So a 10 dollar increase in the mailing cost is equivalent to a weight increase of $10 \times 0.4 = 4$ pounds.

Chapter 15: Functions

CHAPTER EXERCISE:

1. $\boxed{D}$ Check each answer choice to see whether $f(0) = 20, f(1) = 21$, and $f(3) = 29$. The only function that satisfies all three is (D).

2. $\boxed{D}$ $f(x) = g(x)$ when the two graphs intersect. They intersect at 3 points, so there must be 3 values of x where $f(x) = g(x)$.

3. $\boxed{B}$ $f(3) = -2$. Now where else is f at -2? When $x = -3$. So a must be -3.

4. $\boxed{C}$ Draw a horizontal line at $y = 3$. This line intersects $f(x)$ four times, so there are four solutions (four values of x for which $f(x) = 3$).

5. $\boxed{C}$ Plug in -3 and 3 into each of the answer choices to see whether you get the same value. If you're smart about it, you'll realize that answer (C) has an x^2, which always gives a positive value. Testing (C) out, $f(-3) = 3(-3)^2 + 1 = 28$ and $f(3) = 3(3)^2 + 1 = 28$. The answer is indeed (C).

6. $\boxed{61}$ First, $g(10) = f(20) - 1$. Now, $f(20) = 3(20) + 2 = 62$. Finally, $g(10) = 62 - 1 = 61$.

7. $\boxed{B}$ $f(-4) = \dfrac{16 + (-4)^2}{2(-4)} = \dfrac{32}{-8} = -4$.

8. $\boxed{C}$ We plug in values to solve for a and b. Plugging in $(0, -2)$, $-2 = a(0)^2 + b = b$. So, $b = -2$. Plugging in $(1, 3)$,

$$3 = a(1)^2 + b$$
$$3 = a - 2$$
$$5 = a$$

So $a = 5$ and $f(x) = 5x^2 - 2$. Finally, $f(3) = 5(3)^2 - 2 = 43$.

9. $\boxed{A}$ Plug in the answer choices and check. $f\left(\dfrac{1}{2}\right) = \left(\dfrac{1}{2}\right)^2 = \dfrac{1}{4}$, which is less than $\dfrac{1}{2}$. The answer is (A).

10. $\boxed{B}$ The x-intercepts of -3 and 2 mean that $f(x)$ must have factors of $(x + 3)$ and $(x - 2)$. That eliminates (C) and (D). A y-intercept of 12 means that when we plug in $x = 0$, $f(x) = 12$. Only answer (B) meets all these conditions.

11. $\boxed{C}$ $g(2) = 2^2 - 1 = 3$. So, $f(g(2)) = f(3) = 3^2 + 1 = 10$.

12. $\boxed{3}$ Draw a horizontal line at $y = c$, passing through $(0, c)$. This horizontal line intersects with f three times. That means there are 3 values of x for which $f(x) = c$.

13. $\boxed{B}$

$$g(k) = 8$$
$$2f(k) = 8$$
$$f(k) = 4$$

Looking at the chart, $f(x) = 4$ only when $x = 3$. So $k = 3$.

14. $\boxed{A}$ $f(18) = \sqrt{18 - 2} = \sqrt{16} = 4$. $f(11) = \sqrt{11 - 2} = \sqrt{9} = 3$. $f(18) - f(11) = 4 - 3 = 1$. Testing each answer choice, $f(3)$ is the only one that also equals 1.

15. $\boxed{D}$ $(1, 2)$ cannot be on the graph of y since an x-value of 1 would result in division by 0.

16. $\boxed{D}$

$$g(a) = 6$$
$$\sqrt{3a} = 6$$
$$3a = 36$$
$$a = 12$$

17. $\boxed{D}$ Using the table, $g(-1) = 2$. Then, $f(2) = 6$.

18. $\boxed{B}$ If $g(c) = 5$, then $c = 1$ since 1 is the only input that gives an output of 5. Then, $f(c) = f(1) = 3$.

19. $\boxed{B}$ From the second equation, $f(a) = 20$. So,

$$f(a) = -3a + 5$$
$$20 = -3a + 5$$
$$3a = -15$$
$$a = -5$$

20. $\boxed{A}$ $g(3) = f(2(3) - 1) = f(5) = 2$. We get $f(5) = 2$ from the table.

21. $\boxed{D}$ $f(8) = 4(8) - 3 = 29$. Testing each answer choice to see which one yields 29, we see that $g(8) = 3(8) + 5 = 29$.

22. $\boxed{D}$ The key words are "linear function": f is a straight line. So for what straight line can both $f(2) \leq f(3)$ and $f(4) \geq f(5)$ be true? Only a horizontal straight line. Take a minute to think that through. Now, since f is a flat line and $f(6) = 10$, then all values of f are 10, no matter what the value of x is. Therefore, $f(0) = 10$.

23. $\boxed{B}$ When $x = 0$, $y = 9$, so the y-intercept is 9. When $y = 0$, $x = 3$, so the x-intercept is 3.

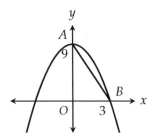

$\triangle AOB$ is a right triangle with a base of 3 and a height of 9. Using the pythagorean theorem,

$$AO^2 + OB^2 = AB^2$$
$$9^2 + 3^2 = AB^2$$
$$90 = AB^2$$
$$3\sqrt{10} = AB$$

24. $\boxed{C}$ The graph of g is 4 units up from where f is, but because the slope of f is -2, the x and y intercepts of g will not increase by the same amount. They'll increase in a ratio of 2:1. So when the y-intercept gets shifted up by 4, the x-intercept gets shifted to the right by 2. The new x-intercept is therefore $1 + 2 = 3$.

Another way to do this is to actually solve for the x-intercept. Using slope-intercept form, we get $f(x) = -2x + 2$. Adding 4 to get the equation of g, $g(x) = -2x + 6$. Setting $g(x) = 0$ and solving for x to get the x-intercept, we get $x = 3$.

25. $\boxed{C}$ The function $g(x)$ is a line with a slope of 1 and a y-intercept of k. If you draw $g(x)$ with the different possibilities for k from the answer choices, you'll see that there's an intersection of 3 points with $f(x)$ only when $k = 1$ as shown below.

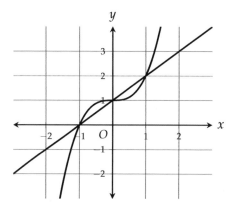

26. $\boxed{3}$ Plugging in $(-a, a)$,

$$a = a(-a) + 12$$
$$a = -a^2 + 12$$
$$a^2 + a - 12 = 0$$
$$(a + 4)(a - 3) = 0$$
$$a = -4, 3$$

Since $a > 0$, $a = 3$.

Chapter 16: Quadratics

CHAPTER EXERCISE:

1. $\boxed{C}$ We factor to find the x-intercepts.

$$y = x^2 - 3x - 10$$
$$y = (x - 5)(x + 2)$$

The x-intercepts are 5 and -2. The distance between them is $5 - (-2) = 7$.

2. $\boxed{A}$ Using the quadratic formula,

$$x = \frac{-4 \pm \sqrt{(4)^2 - 4(1)(2)}}{2(1)} = \frac{-4 \pm \sqrt{8}}{2} = \frac{-4 \pm 2\sqrt{2}}{2} = -2 \pm \sqrt{2}$$

3. $\boxed{.5}$

$$2a^2 - 7a + 3 = 0$$
$$(2a - 1)(a - 3) = 0$$

If you had trouble factoring this, remember that you can always use the quadratic formula. Since $a < 1$, $a = \dfrac{1}{2}$, or 0.5.

4. $\boxed{D}$ Move the 8 to the left side to get $3x^2 + 10x - 8 = 0$. Now, we can either use the quadratic formula or factor. In this case, we'll go with factoring.

$$(x + 4)(3x - 2) = 0$$

So, $x = -4$ or $x = \dfrac{2}{3}$. Since $a > b$, b must be -4 and $b^2 = (-4)^2 = 16$.

5. $\boxed{4}$ Expanding everything,

$$(2x - 3)^2 = 4x + 5$$
$$4x^2 - 12x + 9 = 4x + 5$$
$$4x^2 - 16x + 4 = 0$$

The sum of the solutions is $-\dfrac{b}{a} = -\dfrac{-16}{4} = 4$.

6. $\boxed{A}$ Substituting the first equation into the second,

$$-3 = x^2 + cx$$

$$0 = x^2 + cx + 3$$

The system of equations will have two solutions if the equation above has two solutions. For the equation above to have two solutions, the discriminant, $b^2 - 4ac$, must be positive.

$$c^2 - 4(1)(3) > 0$$

$$c^2 - 12 > 0$$

$$c^2 > 12$$

Testing each of the answer choices, only answer (A), -4, gives a value bigger than 12 when squared.

7. $\boxed{B}$ To find the intersection points, treat the two equations as a system of equations. Substituting the first equation into the second,

$$4 = (x + 2)^2 - 5$$

$$9 = (x + 2)^2$$

$$\pm 3 = x + 2$$

$$x = -5, 1$$

The y-coordinates of the intersection points must be 4 (from the first equation), so the two points of intersection are $(-5, 4)$ and $(1, 4)$.

8. $\boxed{C}$ Because the vertex is at $(3, -8)$, the answer must be either (A) or (C). Because the parabola passes through $(1, 0)$, we can use that point to test out our two potential answers. When we plug in $x = 1$ into (C), we get $y = 0$, confirming that the answer is (C).

9. $\boxed{2.5}$ From the equation $v = 5t - t^2 = t(5 - t)$, we can see that the t-intercepts are 0 and 5. Because the maximum occurs at the vertex, whose t-coordinate is the average of the two t-intercepts, $t = 2.5$ results in the maximum value of v. You can confirm this by graphing the equation on your calculator.

10. $\boxed{400}$ To find the minimum number of mattresses the company must sell so that it doesn't lose money, set $P = 0$.

$$m^2 - 100m - 120,000 = 0$$

$$(m - 400)(m + 300) = 0$$

$$m = -300, 400$$

Since it doesn't make sense for the number of mattresses sold to be negative, $m = 400$. If you had trouble factoring the equation above (it's tough), the graphing calculator and the quadratic formula are both good alternatives.

11. $\boxed{A}$ Substitute the first equation into the second,

$$-3 = ax^2 + 4x - 4$$

$$0 = ax^2 + 4x - 1$$

For the system to have one real solution, the equation above should have only one real solution. In other words, the discriminant, $b^2 - 4ac$, must equal 0.

$$(4)^2 - 4(a)(-1) = 0$$
$$16 + 4a = 0$$
$$4a = -16$$
$$a = -4$$

12. $\boxed{B}$ We need to complete the square. First divide everything by -1,

$$-y = x^2 - 6x - 20$$

Now divide the middle term by 2 to get -3 and square that result to get 9. We put the -3 inside the parentheses with x and subtract the 9 at the end.

$$-y = (x - 3)^2 - 20 - 9$$

Now simplify and multiply everything back by -1.

$$y = -(x - 3)^2 + 29$$

13. $\boxed{D}$ One of the x-intercepts is 3. Since the x-coordinate of the vertex, 5, must lie at the midpoint of the two x-intercepts, the other x-intercept is 7. Therefore, $k = 7$, giving us $y = a(x - 3)(x - 7)$. We can now plug in the vertex as a point to solve for a.

$$-32 = a(5 - 3)(5 - 7)$$
$$-32 = a(2)(-2)$$
$$-32 = -4a$$
$$a = 8$$

14. $\boxed{C}$ Substituting the point $(3, k)$ into both equations,

$$k = 2(3) + b$$
$$k = (3)^2 + 3b + 5$$

This is a system of equations. Substituting the first equation into the second,

$$2(3) + b = (3)^2 + 3b + 5$$
$$6 + b = 9 + 3b + 5$$
$$6 + b = 3b + 14$$
$$-8 = 2b$$
$$b = -4$$

From the first equation, $k = 6 + b = 6 - 4 = 2$.

Chapter 17: Synthetic Division

CHAPTER EXERCISE:

1. $\boxed{C}$

$$x - 2 \overline{\big)\, 4x}$$
$$\underline{4x - 8}$$
$$8$$

This result can be expressed as $4 + \dfrac{8}{x - 2}$

2. $\boxed{B}$

$$2x + 1 \overline{\big)\, 6x^2 + 5x + 2}$$

with quotient $3x + 1$:

$$\underline{6x^2 + 3x}$$
$$2x + 2$$
$$\underline{2x + 1}$$
$$1$$

This result can be expressed as

$3x + 1 + \dfrac{1}{2x + 1}$, from which $Q = 3x + 1$.

3. $\boxed{6}$ This question is asking you to divide the expression by $2x - 1$ and write the result in the form of
Dividend $=$ Quotient $\times$ Divisor $+$ Remainder.

$$2x - 1 \overline{\big)\, 4x^2 + 5}$$

with quotient $2x + 1$:

$$\underline{4x^2 - 2x}$$
$$2x + 5$$
$$\underline{2x - 1}$$
$$6$$

Therefore, $4x^2 + 5 = (2x + 1)(2x - 1) + 6$.
$R = 6$.

4. $\boxed{C}$ Using the remainder theorem, the remainder when $g(x)$ is divided by $x + 3$ is equal to $g(-3) = 2$.

5. $\boxed{7}$ $z - 1$ is a factor only if the polynomial yields 0 when $z = 1$ (the remainder theorem). Therefore, we can set up an equation.

$$2(1)^3 - kx(1)^2 + 5x(1) + 2x - 2 = 0$$
$$2 - kx + 5x + 2x - 2 = 0$$
$$-kx + 7x = 0$$

From here, we can see that $k = 7$.

6. $\boxed{B}$

$$3x - 2 \overline{\big)\, 3x^2 - 8x - 4}$$

with quotient $x - 2$:

$$\underline{3x^2 - 2x}$$
$$- 6x - 4$$
$$\underline{- 6x + 4}$$
$$- 8$$

This result can be expressed as

$x - 2 - \dfrac{8}{3x - 2}$, from which $A = x - 2$.

7. $\boxed{D}$ This question is asking you to divide the expression by $x + 1$ and write the result in the form of
Dividend $=$ Quotient $\times$ Divisor $+$ Remainder.

$$x + 1 \overline{\big)\, 2x^2 - 4x - 3}$$

with quotient $2x - 6$:

$$\underline{2x^2 + 2x}$$
$$- 6x - 3$$
$$\underline{- 6x - 6}$$
$$3$$

Therefore, $2x^2 - 4x - 3 = (2x - 6)(x + 1) + 3$.

8. $\boxed{D}$ This question is asking you to divide the expression by $x - 2$ and write the result in the form of
Dividend = Quotient × Divisor + Remainder, where $ax + b$ is the quotient and c is the remainder.

$$
\begin{array}{r}
x \;+\; 6 \\
x - 2 \overline{\smash{\big)}\; x^2 \;+\; 4x \;-\; 9} \\
\underline{x^2 \;-\; 2x} \\
6x \;-\; 9 \\
\underline{6x \;-\; 12} \\
3
\end{array}
$$

Therefore, $x^2 + 4x - 9 = (x + 6)(x - 2) + 3$.
Finally, $a = 1, b = 6, c = 3$, and $a + b + c = 10$.

9. $\boxed{C}$ Using the remainder theorem, $p(2) = 0$ means that $x - 2$ is a factor of $p(x)$.

10. $\boxed{C}$ Use the remainder theorem to test each option for a remainder of 0.
$p(2) = 2^3 + 2^2 - 5(2) + 3 = 5$.
$p(1) = 1^3 + 1^2 - 5(1) + 3 = 0$.
$p(-3) = (-3)^3 + (-3)^2 - 5(-3) + 3 = 0$.
Therefore, $p(x)$ is divisible by $x - 1$ and $x + 3$.

11. $\boxed{D}$ If $p(x)$ is divisible by $x - 2$, then $p(2)$ must equal 0 (the remainder theorem). Testing each answer choice, only choice (D) results in 0 when $x = 2$.

12. $\boxed{C}$ Using the remainder theorem, we can set up a system of equations. When the polynomial is divided by $x - 1$ or $x + 1$, the remainder is 0, which means that if we let $p(x)$ denote the polynomial, $p(1) = 0$ and $p(-1) = 0$.

$$
\begin{cases}
a(1)^4 + b(1)^3 - 3(1)^2 + 5(1) & = 0 \\
a(-1)^4 + b(-1)^3 - 3(-1)^2 + 5(-1) & = 0
\end{cases}
$$

$$
\begin{cases}
a + b - 3 + 5 & = 0 \\
a - b - 3 - 5 & = 0
\end{cases}
$$

Adding the equations together,

$$2a - 6 = 0$$
$$a = 3$$

13. $\boxed{A}$ From the remainder theorem, $3x - 1$ must be a factor of $p(x)$ if $p\left(\dfrac{1}{3}\right) = 0$.

Chapter 18: Complex Numbers

CHAPTER EXERCISE:

1. $\boxed{C}$

$$(5 - 3i) - (-2 + 5i) = 5 - 3i + 2 - 5i = 7 - 8i$$

2. $\boxed{B}$

$$i(i + 1) = i^2 + i = -1 + i$$

3. $\boxed{C}$

$$i^4 + 3i^2 + 2 = 1 - 3 + 2 = 0$$

4. $\boxed{A}$

$$(6 + 2i)(2 + 5i) = 12 + 30i + 4i + 10i^2 = 12 + 34i + 10(-1) = 2 + 34i$$

Therefore, $a = 2$.

5. $\boxed{C}$

$$3(i + 2) - 2(5 - 4i) = 3i + 6 - 10 + 8i = -4 + 11i$$

6. $\boxed{B}$

$$3i(i + 2) - i(i - 1) = 3i^2 + 6i - i^2 + i = -3 + 6i - (-1) + i = -2 + 7i$$

7. $\boxed{D}$

$$i^{93} = (i^4)^{23} \cdot i = (1)^{23} \cdot i = i$$

8. $\boxed{A}$

$$(3 - i)^2 = 3^2 - 6i + i^2 = 9 - 6i - 1 = 8 - 6i$$

9. $\boxed{B}$

$$(5 - 2i)(4 - 3i) = 20 - 15i - 8i + 6i^2 = 20 - 23i - 6 = 14 - 23i$$

10. $\boxed{A}$

$$\frac{1}{i} + \frac{1}{i^2} + \frac{1}{i^4} = \frac{1}{i} - 1 + 1 = \frac{1}{i}$$

Multiplying both top and bottom by i,

$$\frac{1}{i} \cdot \frac{i}{i} = \frac{i}{i^2} = -i$$

11. $\boxed{A}$

$$\frac{(1 - 3i)}{(3 + i)} \cdot \frac{(3 - i)}{(3 - i)} = \frac{3 - i - 9i + 3i^2}{9 - 3i + 3i - i^2} = \frac{3 - 10i + 3i^2}{9 - i^2} = \frac{3 - 10i - 3}{9 - (-1)} = \frac{-10i}{10} = -i$$

12. $\boxed{A}$

$$\frac{(2 - i)}{(2 + i)} \cdot \frac{(2 - i)}{(2 - i)} = \frac{2^2 - 2i - 2i + i^2}{4 - 2i + 2i - i^2} = \frac{4 - 4i + i^2}{4 - i^2} = \frac{4 - 4i - 1}{4 - (-1)} = \frac{3 - 4i}{5} = \frac{3}{5} - \frac{4}{5}i$$

Chapter 19: Absolute Value

CHAPTER EXERCISE:

1. $\boxed{B}$

$$|f(1)| = |-2(1)^2 - 3(1) + 1| = |-4| = 4$$

2. $\boxed{B}$ Only the expression in answer (B) can equal -5 (when $x = 1$ or 3). Because the absolute value of anything is always greater than or equal to 0, the other answer choices can never reach -5.

3. $\boxed{B}$ Recall that the graph of $y = |x|$ is a V-shape centered at the origin. The graph pictured is also V-shaped but converges at $y = -2$, which means it has shifted two units down. Therefore, the equation of the graph is $y = |x| - 2$. Note that $y = |x - 2|$ shifts the graph two units to the right, NOT two units down.

4. $\boxed{D}$ Test each of the answer choices, making sure to include the negative possibilities. For example, the answer is not (A) because when $x = 2$ or -2, $|x - 3|$ is not greater than 10. However, $|x - 3|$ is greater than 10 when $x = -8$.

5. $\boxed{5}$ Smart trial and error is the fastest way to find the bounds for x. The lower bound for x is -8 and the upper bound is -4. There are 5 integers between -4 and -8 (inclusive). If we wanted to do this problem more mathematically, we could set up the following equation:

$$-3 < x + 6 < 3$$

Subtracting 6,

$$-9 < x < -3$$

Since x is an integer,

$$-8 \leq x \leq -4$$

6. $\boxed{A}$ If n is positive,

$$n - 2 = 10$$
$$n = 12$$

If n is negative,

$$n - 2 = -10$$
$$n = -8$$

The sum of these two possible values of n is $12 + (-8) = 4$.

7. $\boxed{D}$ In the graph of $|f(x)|$, all points with negative y-values (below the x-axis) are flipped across the x-axis. All points with positive y-values stay the same. Graph (D) is the one that shows this correctly.

8. $\boxed{C}$ Make up a number for x. Let's say $x = 3$. Then $b = |3 - 10| = 7$, and $b - x = 7 - 3 = 4$. Using our numbers, we're looking for an answer choice that gives 4 when $b = 7$. The only one that does so is (C).

To do this question mathematically, we have to realize that when $x < 10$, $x - 10$ is always negative. Therefore,

$$x - 10 = -b$$
$$x = 10 - b$$

Using substitution, $b - x$ becomes $b - (10 - b) = 2b - 10$.

9. $\boxed{C}$ The midpoint of $6\frac{1}{4}$ and $6\frac{3}{4}$ is the average: $\left(6\frac{1}{4} + 6\frac{3}{4}\right)/2 = 6\frac{1}{2}$. The midpoint is $\frac{1}{4}$ away from the boundaries of the accepted range for the length of a hot dog. So whatever h is, it must be within $\frac{1}{4}$ of the midpoint:

$$\left|h - 6\frac{1}{2}\right| < \frac{1}{4}$$

10. $\boxed{D}$ The midpoint of 400 and 410 is the average: $(400 + 410)/2 = 405$. The midpoint is 5 away from the boundaries of the accepted range for the length of a roll of tape. So whatever l is, it must be within 5 of the midpoint:

$$|l - 405| < 5$$

11. $\boxed{B}$ There are two possible values of x, 3 and -1. There are two possible values of y, 1 and -5. We get the smallest possible value of xy when $x = 3$ and $y = -5$, in which case $xy = -15$.

12. $\boxed{C}$ If $|a| < 1$, then by definition,

$$-1 < a < 1$$

This means that III is true. Because a must be a fraction, $a^2 < 1$, so II is also true. However, I is not always true because when a is negative, $\frac{1}{a}$ is not greater than 1.

Chapter 20: Angles

CHAPTER EXERCISE:

1. $\boxed{D}$ Using the exterior angle theorem,

$$k = i + j$$
$$140 = 50 + j$$
$$90 = j$$

2. $\boxed{A}$ The missing angle in the left triangle is $180° - 60° - 50° = 70°$. This angle is an exterior angle to the triangle on the right. So, using the exterior angle theorem,

$$70 = y + 40$$
$$30 = y$$

3. $\boxed{B}$ $a + b + c + d$ is equal to the sum of the angles of the quadrilateral, as shown below.

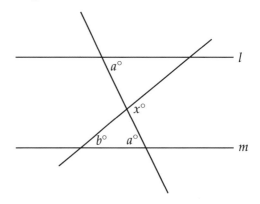

Because the angles of a quadrilateral sum to 360, the answer is 360.

4. $\boxed{B}$

$$x + y + (x + y) = 180$$
$$40 + y + (40 + y) = 180$$
$$2y + 80 = 180$$
$$2y = 100$$
$$y = 50$$

5. $\boxed{A}$ Because alternate interior angles are equal, one of the missing angles of the lower triangle is also a:

Since x is an exterior angle to the lower triangle,

$$x = a + b$$

6. $\boxed{B}$ The angle at the top of the triangle is $180 - 70 - 30 = 80$. If we look at the larger triangle, taking away the top angle gives $a + b$.

$$a + b = 180 - 80 = 100$$

7. $\boxed{C}$ The angles form a circle, which means they sum to $360°$.

$$x + y = 360° - 45° - 80° = 235°$$

8. $\boxed{C}$ Filling out the bottom triangle, the missing angle is $180° - 60° - 40° = 80°$, which means the angle across from it in the upper triangle is also $80°$. Finally,

$$z = 180° - 45° - 80° = 55°$$

9. $\boxed{B}$ The two angles form a line, which means they sum to $180°$.

$$(x + 40) + x = 180$$
$$2x + 40 = 180$$
$$2x = 140$$
$$x = 70$$

10. $\boxed{D}$ We can figure out two angles within the triangle: $100°$ and $50°$. Because y is an exterior angle, we can use the exterior angle theorem to get its value:

$$y = 100 + 50 = 150$$

11. $\boxed{C}$

Shaded Angles = Angles of Rectangle
                + Angles of Quadrilateral
              = 360 + 360
              = 720

12. $\boxed{D}$ The angles of any polygon sum to $180(n-2)$, where n is the number of sides. The angles of a hexagon (6 sides) sum to $180(6-2) = 720$. Because the hexagon is regular, all angles have the same measure. Therefore, each angle is $720 \div 6 = 120°$. Finally,
$$x = 120 - 90 = 30$$

13. $\boxed{D}$ b is an alternate interior angle to the $45°$ angle, which means they're equal: $b = 45$. a and c are also alternate interior angles so $a = c = 180 - 45 = 135$. Using these values, we can see that all three are true.

14. $\boxed{C}$ The two missing angles in the smaller triangle add up to $80°$. The two bottom angles in the larger triangle add up to $180 - 70 = 110$. If we take the two missing angles of the smaller triangle away from the two bottom angles of the larger triangle, we'll end up with $x + y$.

$$x + y = 110 - 80 = 30$$

15. $\boxed{260}$ Angle a is equal to $180 - 60 = 120$. Angle b is equal to $180 - 40 = 140$. Finally, $a + b = 120 + 140 = 260$.

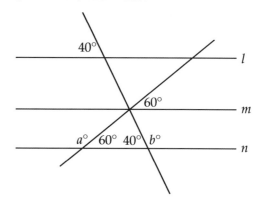

300

Chapter 21: Triangles

CHAPTER EXERCISE:

1. $\boxed{C}$ Because the hypotenuse is always the largest side, $x + 5$ must be the hypotenuse while x and $x - 2$ must be the legs. Using the pythagorean theorem,
$$x^2 + (x - 2)^2 = (x + 5)^2$$

2. $\boxed{B}$ Using the $30 - 60 - 90$ triangle relationship, $DC = \dfrac{1}{2}BC = \dfrac{1}{2}(10) = 5$.

3. $\boxed{C}$ Using the $45 - 45 - 90$ triangle relationship, $x = 6\sqrt{2}$.

4. $\boxed{8}$ Triangles ABE and DCE are similar. Therefore,
$$\frac{CD}{CE} = \frac{AB}{BE}$$
$$\frac{6}{3} = \frac{AB}{4}$$
$$8 = AB$$

5. $\boxed{10 < x < 16}$ To satisfy the triangle inequality theorem (any two sides of a triangle must sum up to be greater than the third side), the third side must be less than $3 + 13 = 16$ and greater than $13 - 3 = 10$.

6. $\boxed{55}$ If two angles have the same measure, then the sides opposite them have the same length. To get the largest perimeter, we choose the third side to be 20. The perimeter is then $15 + 20 + 20 = 55$.

7. $\boxed{B}$ I is invalid because $6 + 7 < 14$. II is invalid because $5 + 5 < 12$. III is the only one that satisfies the triangle inequality theorem (any two sides of a triangle must sum up to be greater than the third side).

8. $\boxed{12}$

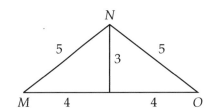

Drawing the height splits the base into two equal parts of length 4. From the $3 - 4 - 5$ pythagorean triple, we know the height is 3. The area is then $\dfrac{1}{2}(8)(3) = 12$.

9. $\boxed{A}$ The side length of the square is $\sqrt{4} = 2$. Draw the height of the triangle to create two $30 - 60 - 90$ triangles:

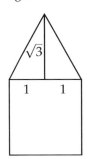

The area of the triangle is then
$$\frac{1}{2}(2)(\sqrt{3}) = \sqrt{3}$$

10. $\boxed{B}$ Let the height of the bottom piece be x. The height of the cone and the radii of the circles form two similar triangles as shown below.

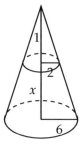

Using the similarity,

$$\frac{1}{2} = \frac{1+x}{6}$$

Cross multiplying,

$$2 + 2x = 6$$

$$x = 2$$

11. $\boxed{A}$ To satisfy the triangle inequality theorem (any two sides of a triangle must sum up to be greater than the third side), $x + y$ must be greater than whatever z is. z cannot be 8, because then $x + y$ would add up to just 2. In fact, z cannot be 5, 6, 7, or 8 because in all those cases, $x + y$ does not exceed the value of z. The greatest possible value of z is 4 (x and y could both be 3).

12. $\boxed{2.5}$ Triangles GEF and GHC are similar. Solving for EF,

$$\frac{EF}{EG} = \frac{HC}{HG}$$

$$\frac{EF}{2} = \frac{10}{5}$$

$$EF = 4$$

Triangles ADF and GEF are also similar. So,

$$\frac{AD}{DF} = \frac{GE}{EF}$$

$$\frac{AD}{5} = \frac{2}{4}$$

$$AD = \frac{5}{2} = 2.5$$

13. $\boxed{C}$

$$225° \times \frac{\pi}{180°} = \frac{5\pi}{4}$$

14. $\boxed{C}$ The sides of triangle DEF are $9 \div 6 = 1.5$ times longer than the respective sides of triangle ABC. Therefore, $EF = 9 \times 1.5 = 13.5$ and $DF = 5 \times 1.5 = 7.5$. The perimeter of triangle DEF is then $9 + 13.5 + 7.5 = 30$.

15. $\boxed{B}$ Because of the triangle inequality theorem, the third side must be less than $8 + 20 = 28$ but greater than $20 - 8 = 12$. So $12 < p < 28$. There are 15 integers from 13 to 27.

16. $\boxed{D}$ We can use the pythagorean theorem to find BC:

$$AC^2 + AB^2 = BC^2$$

$$12^2 + 9^2 = BC^2$$

$$225 = BC^2$$

$$15 = BC$$

Note that this is a multiple of the $3 - 4 - 5$ triangle.

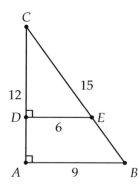

Now $\triangle CDE$ is similar to $\triangle CAB$.

$$\frac{CE}{DE} = \frac{CB}{AB}$$

$$\frac{CE}{6} = \frac{15}{9}$$

Cross multiplying,

$$9(CE) = (15)(6)$$

$$CE = 10$$

302

17. $\boxed{C}$ If $\overline{BC}$ is the shortest side in the isosceles triangle, then $AB = AC$ and $\angle A$ is the smallest angle. At the same time, we want to maximize $\angle A$ so that $\angle B$ is minimized. Now if all the angles were $60°$, then the triangle would be equilateral and $\overline{BC}$ wouldn't be the shortest side. So we need to decrease $\angle A$ to the next highest option, $50°$, which minimizes $\angle B$ to $130 \div 2 = 65°$.

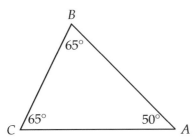

18. $\boxed{B}$ Draw the extra lines shown below and use the $8 - 15 - 17$ right triangle.

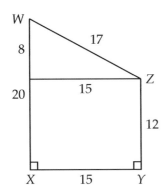

19. $\boxed{C}$ Draw an extra line to complete the rectangle. Then use the $7 - 24 - 25$ right triangle.

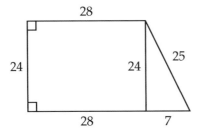

$$24 + 28 + 25 + 7 + 28 = 112$$

20. $\boxed{15}$ Using the pythagorean theorem,

$$8^2 + x^2 = (x + 2)^2$$
$$64 + x^2 = x^2 + 4x + 4$$
$$64 = 4x + 4$$
$$60 = 4x$$
$$15 = x$$

21. $\boxed{C}$ Label what you know.

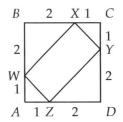

All triangles in the diagram are $45 - 45 - 90$, which means $WZ = XY = \sqrt{2}$ and $WX = ZY = 2\sqrt{2}$. The perimeter of $WXYZ$ is then $\sqrt{2} + \sqrt{2} + 2\sqrt{2} + 2\sqrt{2} = 6\sqrt{2}$.

22. $\boxed{B}$ From the coordinates, $AB = 7$ and $BC = 7$. Because $\angle ABC$ is a right angle, triangle ABC is a $45 - 45 - 90$ triangle. Therefore, the measure of $\angle BAC = 45°$, which is $45° \times \dfrac{\pi}{180°} = \dfrac{\pi}{4}$ radians.

23. $\boxed{C}$ The smaller triangle in the first quadrant is a $3 - 4 - 5$ triangle and is similar to triangle AOB. Using the similarity,

$$\frac{OB}{15} = \frac{3}{5}$$
$$OB = 9$$

Therefore, $n = -9$.

24. $\boxed{A}$ The radii extending to the corners of the triangle split the circle into three equal parts, so the measure of angle ADB is $360 \div 3 = 120°$. In radians, this is $120° \times \dfrac{\pi}{180°} = \dfrac{2\pi}{3}$.

25. $\boxed{C}$ Because triangle ABC is $45 - 45 - 90$, $AB = 2\sqrt{2}$. Because triangle ABD is $30 - 60 - 90$, $AD = \dfrac{2\sqrt{2}}{\sqrt{3}}$ and DB is twice that:

$$DB = \frac{4\sqrt{2}}{\sqrt{3}}$$

We can rationalize the fraction by multiplying both the top and bottom by $\sqrt{3}$:

$$DB = \frac{4\sqrt{2}}{\sqrt{3}} \times \frac{\sqrt{3}}{\sqrt{3}} = \frac{4\sqrt{6}}{3}$$

26. $\boxed{B}$ Because the triangles are $45 - 45 - 90$, $BC = \dfrac{2}{\sqrt{2}}$. The radius of the circle is half BC: $\left(\dfrac{1}{2}\right)\left(\dfrac{2}{\sqrt{2}}\right) = \dfrac{1}{\sqrt{2}}$. Finally, the area of the circle is

$$\pi\left(\frac{1}{\sqrt{2}}\right)^2 = \frac{\pi}{2}$$

27. $\boxed{C}$ To satisfy the triangle inequality theorem, the third side must be less than $5 + 11 = 16$ and greater than $11 - 5 = 6$. So the minimum perimeter is $5 + 11 + 7 = 23$ and the maximum perimeter is $5 + 11 + 15 = 31$. II and III are the only values in this range.

28. $\boxed{B}$ Let $AD = x$. Because ADE is a $30 - 60 - 90$ triangle, $DE = x\sqrt{3}$ and $AE = 2x$. Note that $\triangle ADE$, $\triangle BEF$, and $\triangle DCF$ are all congruent.

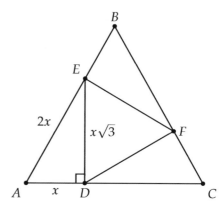

The side length of outer triangle ABC is $3x$. The side length of inner triangle DEF is $x\sqrt{3}$. Because the two triangles are similar, the ratio of their areas is equal to the square of the ratio of their sides:

$$\frac{\text{Area of } \triangle DEF}{\text{Area of } \triangle ABC} = \frac{(x\sqrt{3})^2}{(3x)^2} = \frac{3x^2}{9x^2} = \frac{1}{3}$$

29. $\boxed{D}$ To satisfy the triangle inequality theorem (any two sides of a triangle must sum up to be greater than the third side), a must be greater than $7 - 5 = 2$ and less than $5 + 7 = 12$. b must also be greater than 2 and less than 12.

$$2 < a < 12$$

$$2 < b < 12$$

$|a - b|$ cannot be 10, because the difference between a and b can never be that large, no matter what values you pick.

30. $\boxed{D}$ Because the equilateral triangle lies on a side of the square, all their sides are equal, which means $\triangle ABE$ and $\triangle DCE$ are isosceles.

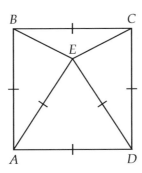

$\angle AED = 60°$, $\angle BAE = \angle CDE = 30°$, which means
$\angle ABE = \angle AEB = \angle DCE = \angle DEC = 75°$.
Finally,
$\angle BEC = 360° - 75° - 75° - 60° = 150°$.

31. $\boxed{D}$ Draw a straight line down the middle. The length of this line is 9 because the top part is simply a radius of the semicircle, whose length is half the side of the square, $6 \div 2 = 3$.

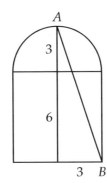

Using the pythagorean theorem,

$$9^2 + 3^2 = AB^2$$
$$90 = AB^2$$
$$\sqrt{90} = AB$$
$$3\sqrt{10} = AB$$

32. $\boxed{D}$ Draw the height from A as shown below. $\triangle ADB$ turns out to be a $30 - 60 - 90$ triangle.

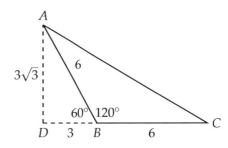

The area is $\dfrac{1}{2}(6)(3\sqrt{3}) = 9\sqrt{3}$

33. $\boxed{D}$

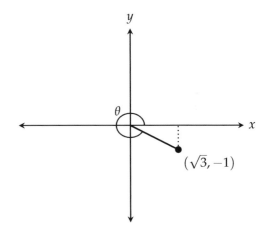

Draw the extra line shown above to form a $30 - 60 - 90$ triangle (the sides are in a ratio of $1 : \sqrt{3} : 2$). The acute angle the line segment forms with the x-axis is $30°$, which makes $\theta = 360 - 30 = 330°$. In radians, this is
$330° \times \dfrac{\pi}{180°} = \dfrac{11\pi}{6}$.

34. $\boxed{3.75}$ Because $DBCE$ is a square, $DB = 3$ and triangles ABD and DEO are similar (their angles are the same). Using the pythagorean theorem, $DO = 5$. Using the similarity,

$$\frac{AD}{DB} = \frac{DO}{OE}$$
$$\frac{AD}{3} = \frac{5}{4}$$
$$AD = \frac{15}{4} = 3.75$$

35. $\boxed{C}$

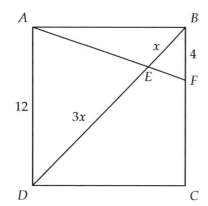

Triangles ADE and FBE are similar. The sides of triangle ADE are 3 times longer than the respective sides of triangle FBE. Because triangle ABD is a $45 - 45 - 90$ triangle, the length of BD is $12\sqrt{2}$. If we let $BE = x$, then $DE = 3x$.

$$x + 3x = 12\sqrt{2}$$

$$4x = 12\sqrt{2}$$

$$x = 3\sqrt{2}$$

36. $\boxed{7.2}$ Triangle ABC is a $5 - 12 - 13$ triangle ($BC = 5$). Triangle ABC is similar to triangle AED (the angles are equal). Using this similarity is tricky because the two triangles have different orientations. The following is one example of a correct setup:

$$\frac{AE}{DE} = \frac{AB}{BC}$$

$$\frac{AE}{3} = \frac{12}{5}$$

$$AE = \frac{36}{5} = 7.2$$

Chapter 22: Circles

CHAPTER EXERCISE:

1. $\boxed{B}$ The circumference of the circle is $2\pi r$. The square divides the circle into four equal arcs. Therefore, the length of arc APD is $\dfrac{2\pi r}{4} = \dfrac{\pi r}{2}$

2. $\boxed{D}$ Finding the radius of each of the small circles,

$$\pi r^2 = 9\pi$$
$$r = 3$$

The radius of the outer circle is equivalent to three radii of the smaller circles, $3 \times 3 = 9$. The area is then $\pi(9)^2 = 81\pi$.

3. $\boxed{C}$ First, find the radius.

$$\pi r^2 = 36\pi$$
$$r = 6$$

The circumference of the circle is $2\pi r = 2\pi(6) = 12\pi$. The perimeter of one region is made up of two radii and one-eighth of the circumference.

$$6 + 6 + \frac{1}{8}(12\pi) = 12 + 1.5\pi$$

4. $\boxed{D}$

$$\pi r^2 = 49\pi$$
$$r^2 = 49$$
$$r = 7$$

The standard form of a circle with center (h, k) and radius r is $(x - h)^2 + (y - k)^2 = r^2$. So the equation of the circle is $(x + 2)^2 + y^2 = 49$.

5. $\boxed{C}$ The arc measure of $\overarc{AB}$ is twice the measure of the inscribed angle. Therefore, $\overarc{AB} = 60°$, which is $\dfrac{60°}{360°} = \dfrac{1}{6}$ of the circumference.

6. $\boxed{60}$ Because $\angle BAC$ is formed from the endpoints of a diameter, its measure is $90°$. Since $AB = 1$ and $AC = 2$, $\triangle ABC$ is a $30 - 60 - 90$ triangle and $\angle BAC = 60°$.

7. $\boxed{C}$

$$\pi r^2 = 36\pi$$
$$r = 6$$

The circumference of the circle is $2\pi r = 2\pi(6) = 12\pi$. Because the equilateral triangle splits the circumference of the circle into 3 equal pieces, arc $\overarc{AB}$ is one-third of the circumference: $\dfrac{1}{3} \times 12\pi = 4\pi$.

8. $\boxed{C}$ The area of the circle is $\pi r^2 = \pi(6)^2 = 36\pi$. The shaded sector is $\dfrac{10\pi}{36\pi} = \dfrac{5}{18}$ of the entire circle, which means central angle ACB must be $\dfrac{5}{18}$ of 360.

$$\frac{5}{18} \times 360° = 100°$$

Converting this to radians,

$$100° \times \frac{\pi}{180} = \frac{5\pi}{9}$$

We could've gotten this answer directly by sticking to radians. The area of a sector is $\dfrac{1}{2}r^2\theta$ when θ, the measure of the central angle, is in radians.

$$\frac{1}{2}r^2\theta = 10\pi$$
$$\frac{1}{2}(6)^2\theta = 10\pi$$
$$18\theta = 10\pi$$
$$\theta = \frac{5}{9}\pi$$

9. $\boxed{4, 5, 6, \text{ or } 7}$ The arc length can be determined by $r\theta$ when θ, the measure of the central angle, is expressed in radians. Therefore, the arc length must be greater than $5\left(\dfrac{\pi}{4}\right) \approx 3.92$ and less than $5\left(\dfrac{\pi}{2}\right) \approx 7.85$.

We could've done this question by converting radians back to degrees but the process would've taken a lot longer.

10. $\boxed{D}$ Draw a square connecting the centers of each circle:

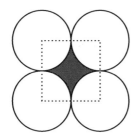

To get the shaded region, we need to subtract out the four quarter-circles from the square. The square has an area of $8 \times 8 = 64$. The four quarter-circles make up one circle with an area of $\pi(4)^2 = 16\pi$. The area of the shaded region is then $64 - 16\pi$.

11. $\boxed{C}$ Unraveling the cylinder gives a rectangle with a base equal to the circumference and a height equal to the height of the cylinder:

The surface area of the cylinder is equal to the area of this rectangle plus the areas of the two circles at either end.

$$2\pi rh + 2\pi r^2 = 2\pi(4)(5) + 2\pi(4)^2$$
$$= 40\pi + 32\pi$$
$$= 72\pi$$

12. $\boxed{D}$ Circle P and circle U each have an area of $\pi(3)^2 = 9\pi$. To get the shaded region, we need to subtract out the unshaded portions of both circles. Because $\triangle PHU$ is equilateral, $\angle HPU$ and $\angle HUP$ are both $60°$, which means the unshaded sectors are each one-sixth of their respective circles ($60°$ is one-sixth of $360°$).

$$9\pi + 9\pi - \frac{1}{6}(9\pi) - \frac{1}{6}(9\pi) = 15\pi$$

13. $\boxed{B}$ Let y be the angle at the top of the triangle.

$$\pi r^2 - \frac{y}{360}\pi r^2 = 24\pi$$

$$\pi(6)^2 - \frac{y}{360}\pi(6)^2 = 24\pi$$

$$36 - \frac{y}{10} = 24$$

$$12 = \frac{y}{10}$$

$$120 = y$$

If y is 120, then x and x have to add up to 60. Therefore, $x = 30$.

14. $\boxed{C}$ From the information given, $AB = 8$, $BC = 4$, and because AC is tangent to circle B, $\angle ACB$ is a right angle. Using the pythagorean theorem to find AC,

$$AC^2 + 4^2 = 8^2$$
$$AC^2 = 48$$
$$AC = 4\sqrt{3}$$

The area of
$$\triangle ABC = \frac{1}{2}(AC)(BC) = \frac{1}{2}(4\sqrt{3})(4) = 8\sqrt{3}$$

15. $\boxed{B}$ The circle has center $(-2, -4)$ and radius 2. If you draw this circle out, you'll see that it's tangent only to the y-axis.

Chapter 23: Trigonometry

CHAPTER EXERCISE:

1. $\boxed{A}$ Since $\cos x = \sin(90 - x)$,
$\cos 40° = \sin 50° = a$.

2. $\boxed{.8}$ Since $\tan x = 0.75 = \dfrac{3}{4}$, we can draw a right triangle such that the opposite side is 3 and the adjacent side is 4.

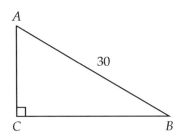

Using the pythagorean theorem, the hypotenuse is 5 (this is a $3 - 4 - 5$ triangle). Therefore, $\cos x = \dfrac{4}{5} = 0.8$

3. $\boxed{D}$ Since $\sin \theta = \cos(90 - \theta)$ and $\cos \theta = \sin(90 - \theta)$,

$$\sin \theta + \cos(90 - \theta) + \cos \theta + \sin(90 - \theta) =$$
$$\sin \theta + \sin \theta + \cos \theta + \cos \theta =$$
$$2\sin \theta + 2\cos \theta$$

4. $\boxed{25}$ Drawing the triangle,

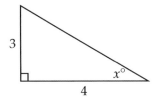

$$\cos A = \frac{5}{6}$$
$$\frac{AC}{30} = \frac{5}{6}$$
$$AC = 25$$

5. $\boxed{C}$ After drawing the right triangle, we let the opposite side be m and the adjacent side be 1.

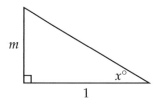

Using the pythagorean theorem, the hypotenuse is $\sqrt{m^2 + 1}$. Therefore,
$$\sin x = \frac{m}{\sqrt{m^2 + 1}}.$$

6. $\boxed{1.4}$ The fact that $AB = 5$ is irrelevant since the ratios of the sides will always be the same for proportional triangles. Instead of actually trying to figure out the lengths of the sides, let's use a triangle that's easier to work with.

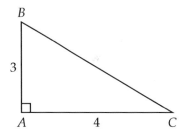

Using the pythagorean theorem, $BC = 5$ (it's a $3 - 4 - 5$ triangle).

$$\sin B + \cos B = \frac{4}{5} + \frac{3}{5} = \frac{7}{5} = 1.4$$

7. $\boxed{12}$

$$\sin x = \frac{1}{4}$$
$$\frac{3}{BC} = \frac{1}{4}$$

Cross multiply to get $BC = 12$.

8. $\boxed{\dfrac{5}{13}}$ Since $\tan B = 2.4 = \dfrac{12}{5}$, we can let

$AC = 12$ and $AB = 5$. Using the pythagorean theorem, $BC = 13$. Since the two triangles are similar,

$$\cos N = \cos B = \frac{AB}{BC} = \frac{5}{13}$$

9. $\boxed{14}$ Since $\cos x = \sin(90 - x)$,
$\cos 32° = \sin 58°$. Setting up an equation,

$$\sin 58 = \sin(5m - 12)$$
$$58 = 5m - 12$$
$$70 = 5m$$
$$m = 14$$

10. $\boxed{D}$ From the coordinates, $AB = 5 - (-3) = 8$ and $BC = 12 - (-3) = 15$. Using the pythagorean theorem to find AC,

$$AC^2 = AB^2 + BC^2$$
$$AC^2 = 8^2 + 15^2$$
$$AC^2 = 289$$
$$AC = 17$$

Finally, $\cos C = \dfrac{BC}{AC} = \dfrac{15}{17}$.

11. $\boxed{D}$ $\angle ABC$ measures $90°$ because it's inscribed in a semicircle. Therefore, triangle ABC is a right triangle. Let the height be AB and the base be BC. Since the hypotenuse $AC = 1$,

$$\sin \theta = AB$$
$$\cos \theta = BC$$

$$\text{Area of triangle} = \frac{1}{2}(BC)(AB)$$
$$= \frac{1}{2}(\cos \theta)(\sin \theta)$$
$$= \frac{\sin \theta \cos \theta}{2}$$

12. $\boxed{C}$ This question is basically asking for the quadrants in which $\sin \theta$ can equal $\cos \theta$. For them to be equal, they must have the same sign. That rules out option II since sine is positive in the second quadrant while cosine is negative. In quadrant I, sine and cosine are both positive, and sine is equal to cosine when $\theta = 45°$ (remember your $45 - 45 - 90$ triangle?). In quadrant III, sine and cosine are both positive, and sine is equal to cosine when $\theta = 225°$ (this is the third quadrant equivalent of $45°$ in the first quadrant).

Chapter 24: Reading Data

CHAPTER EXERCISE:

1. $\boxed{C}$ We estimate the total commute time for each point:

Point	Commute Time
A	$25 + 60 = 85$
B	$38 + 40 = 78$
C	$45 + 80 = 125$
D	$80 + 20 = 100$

Even though the times were estimated, it's clear that C represents the greatest commute time.

2. $\boxed{C}$ The vertical distance between the points at 2004 and 2006 is the smallest among the answer choices.

3. $\boxed{C}$ The points corresponding to July through September are the highest in both 2013 and 2014.

4. $\boxed{C}$

$$\frac{150}{250} = \frac{3}{5} = 60\%$$

5. $\boxed{A}$ San Diego is the only city for which the estimated bar is lower than (to the left of) the actual bar.

6. $\boxed{A}$ Both line graphs go downward every year.

7. $\boxed{B}$ The lowest point with respect to the y-axis is at a little under 40 years of age.

8. $\boxed{A}$ The graph's minimum, 16, must be the weight of the truck when empty. The graph's maximum, 30, must be the weight of the truck at maximum capacity. Subtract the two to get the truck's maximum capacity, $30 - 16 = 14$.

9. $\boxed{C}$ From 2010 to 2011, the percent decrease was

$$\frac{30 - 40}{40} = -\frac{1}{4} = -25\% \text{ (percent decreases are negative)}$$

From 2013 to 2014, the percent increase was

$$\frac{25 - 20}{20} = \frac{1}{4} = 25\%$$

10. $\boxed{\dfrac{2}{3}}$ $\dfrac{120}{180} = \dfrac{2}{3}$

11. $\boxed{B}$ Console A generated $250,000 \times 100 = \$25,000,000$. Console B generated $225,000 \times 150 = \$33,750,000$. Console D generated $125,000 \times 250 = \$31,250,000$. Console E generated $50,000 \times 300 = \$15,000,000$. Console B generated the most revenue.

12. $\boxed{C}$ In Quarter 3, Company Y's profit was about 6 million and Company X's profit was about 12 million (twice Company Y's). In no other quarter was Company X's profit as close to being twice Company Y's.

13. $\boxed{C}$ Alabama spent a combined $15 + 2.5 = 17.5$ billion. Alaska spent $7.5 + 7.5 = 15$ billion. Arizona spent $12.5 + 7.5 = 20$ billion. Arkansas spent $10 + 5 = 15$ billion. Arizona spent the most.

14. $\boxed{44}$ During the first two hours, Jeremy answered 4 calls per hour for a total of $2 \times 4 = 8$ calls. During the next three hours, Jeremy answered 8 calls per hour for a total of $3 \times 8 = 24$ calls. During the final two hours, Jeremy answered 6 calls per hour for a total of $2 \times 6 = 12$ calls. He answered a total of $8 + 24 + 12 = 44$ calls.

15. $\boxed{A}$ From the graph, we can see that it takes Greg's glucose level 2.5 hours to return to its initial value (140 mg/dL) after breakfast and $8 - 4 = 4$ hours to return to its initial value (also 140 mg/dL) after lunch.

$$4 - 2.5 = 1.5$$

16. $\boxed{6}$ At 30 miles per hour, Car X gets 25 miles per gallon. Driving for 5 hours at 30 miles per hour covers a total distance of $5 \times 30 = 150$ miles.

$$150 \text{ miles} \times \frac{1 \text{ gallon}}{25 \text{ miles}} = 6 \text{ gallons}$$

Chapter 25: Probability

CHAPTER EXERCISE:

1. $\boxed{C}$

$$\frac{\text{Stop sign violations committed by truck drivers}}{\text{Stop sign violations}} = \frac{39}{90} \approx 0.433$$

2. $\boxed{D}$

$$\frac{\text{Plumbers with at least 4 years of experience}}{\text{All plumbers}} = \frac{40{,}083 + 45{,}376}{183{,}885} \approx 0.46$$

3. $\boxed{B}$

$$\frac{\text{Plumbers with at least 4 years of experience}}{\text{Workers with at least 4 years of experience}} = \frac{40{,}083 + 45{,}376}{182{,}410 + 208{,}757} \approx 0.22$$

4. $\boxed{D}$ The percentage of silver cars is $100 - 20 - 33 - 10 - 14 = 23$. Red and silver make up $20 + 23 = 43$ percent of the cars.

5. $\boxed{C}$

$$\frac{\text{Games won as underdogs}}{\text{Games played as underdogs}} = \frac{10}{45} = \frac{2}{9}$$

6. $\boxed{C}$ Filling in the table,

	Week 1	Week 2	Week 3	Week 4	Total
Box springs	35	40	20	55	150
Mattresses	47	61	68	22	198
Total	82	101	88	77	348

$$\frac{\text{Box spring units sold during weeks 2 and 3}}{\text{All box spring units sold}} = \frac{40 + 20}{150} = \frac{2}{5}$$

7. $\boxed{B}$ For the USA, the probability is $\frac{29}{104} \approx 0.28$. For Russia, the probability is $\frac{32}{82} \approx 0.39$. For Great Britain, the probability is $\frac{19}{65} \approx 0.29$. For Germany, the probability is $\frac{14}{44} \approx 0.32$. The country with the highest probability is Russia.

8. $\boxed{A}$

$$\frac{\text{Cartilaginous fish species in the Philippines}}{\text{Total fish species in the Philippines}} - \frac{\text{Cartilaginous fish species in New Caledonia}}{\text{Total fish species in New Caledonia}}$$

$$= \frac{400}{400 + 800} - \frac{300}{300 + 1{,}200} = \frac{1}{3} - \frac{1}{5} = \frac{2}{15}$$

9. $\boxed{C}$ Filling in the table,

	Lightning-caused fires	Human-caused fires	Total
East Africa	55	65	120
South Africa	30	70	100
Total	85	135	220

$$\frac{\text{Human-caused fires in East Africa}}{\text{Fires in East Africa}} = \frac{65}{120} = \frac{13}{24}$$

10. $\boxed{B}$

$$\frac{\text{Defective from Assembly Line } A}{\text{Defective}} = \frac{300}{800} = \frac{3}{8}$$

11. $\boxed{D}$

$$\frac{\text{Duplex with 2 family members or less}}{\text{Duplex}} = \frac{22 + 12}{46} = \frac{17}{23}$$

12. $\boxed{B}$ The total number of samples contaminated with Chemical A is $(450 \times 0.08) + (550 \times 0.06) = 69$.

$$\frac{\text{Contaminated samples}}{\text{All samples}} = \frac{69}{1,000} = 0.069$$

13. $\boxed{B}$ The test is incorrect when it gives positive indicators for patients who don't have the virus and negative indicators for patients who do, a total of $30 + 50 = 80$ occurrences.

$$\frac{80}{1000} = \frac{8}{100} = 8\%$$

14. $\boxed{B}$ The number of patients cured by the sugar pill is $90 \div 3 = 30$. The number of patients who weren't cured by the sugar pill is $30 \times \frac{5}{2} = 75$.

	Cured	Not cured
Drug	90	25
Sugar Pill	30	75

$$\frac{\text{Given a sugar pill and cured}}{\text{Given a sugar pill}} = \frac{30}{30 + 75} = \frac{2}{7}$$

15. $\boxed{240}$ Let the number of seniors who prefer gym equipment be x.

$$\frac{x}{x + 160} = \frac{1}{3}$$

Cross multiplying,

$$3x = x + 160$$
$$2x = 160$$
$$x = 80$$

There are $80 + 160 = 240$ seniors at the school.

Chapter 26: Statistics I

CHAPTER EXERCISE:

1. $\boxed{C}$ The sum of the heights in the first class is $14 \times 63 = 882$. The sum of the heights in the second class is $21 \times 68 = 1,428$. The sum of the heights in the combined class is then $882 + 1428 = 2,310$. The average height is

$$\frac{\text{Sum of the heights}}{\text{Total number of students}} = \frac{2,310}{14 + 21} = 66$$

2. $\boxed{C}$ The sum of all five of Kristie's test scores is $5 \times 94 = 470$. The sum of her last three test scores is $3 \times 92 = 276$. The difference between these two sums is the sum of her first two test scores: $470 - 276 = 194$. The average of her first two test scores is then $\frac{194}{2} = 97$.

3. $\boxed{B}$ Because there are 20 editors, the median is the average of the 10th and 11th editors' number of books read. From the graph, the 10th and 11th editors both read 10 to 15 books last year, which means the average must also be between 10 and 15. The only answer choice between 10 and 15 is 12.

4. $\boxed{B}$

$$\frac{(18 \times 6) + (19 \times 3) + (20 \times 5) + (21 \times 4) + (22 \times 2) + (23 \times 3) + (24 \times 1)}{24} = \frac{}{24} = 20.25$$

5. $\boxed{D}$ The standard deviation decreases the most when the outliers, the data points furthest away from the mean, are removed. The outliers here are the Rhone and the Vosges.

6. $\boxed{A}$ Even though the frequencies are the same, the travel times themselves are more spread out for Bus B. The travel times for Bus A are much closer together. Therefore, the standard deviation of travel times for Bus A is smaller.

7. $\boxed{C}$ The median weight is represented by the 10th kayak (47 pounds for both Company A and Company B). The median weight is the same for both companies.

8. $\boxed{67}$ The median is represented by the average of the 14th and 15th days, both of which are $67°$ F.

9. $\boxed{D}$ By definition, at least half the values are greater than or equal to the median and at least half the values are less than or equal to the median.

10. $\boxed{B}$ A range of 3 days means the difference between the longest shelf life and the shortest shelf life among the units is 3. This could be 10 days vs. 13 days or 25 days vs. 28 days. The range says nothing about the mean or median.

11. $\boxed{B}$

$$\text{Mean} = \frac{(5 \times 2) + (6 \times 1) + (8 \times 4) + (9 \times 2) + (10 \times 1)}{2 + 1 + 4 + 2 + 1} = \frac{76}{10} = 7.6$$

$$\text{Range} = 10 - 5 = 5$$

12. $\boxed{B}$ Arranging the scores in order,

$$75, 83, 87, 87, 90, 91, 98$$

The average is $\dfrac{75 + 83 + 87 + 87 + 90 + 91 + 98}{7} \approx 87.3$. The mode is 87. The median is also 87. The range is $98 - 75 = 23$. From these numbers, I is false, II is false, and III is true.

13. $\boxed{D}$ The median in School A is represented by the 10th class (4 films) and the median in School B is represented by the 8th class (also 4 films). The median is the same in both schools. Now we calculate the means:

$$\text{Mean in School A} = \frac{1 \times 2 + 2 \times 3 + 3 \times 4 + 4 \times 5 + 5 \times 5}{19} \approx 3.42$$

$$\text{Mean in School B} = \frac{1 \times 1 + 2 \times 2 + 3 \times 3 + 4 \times 4 + 5 \times 5}{15} \approx 3.67$$

The mean is greater in School B. Intuitively, this makes sense because the distribution for School A has a higher proportion of the smaller numbers 1, 2, and 3 as shown by the chart. These smaller numbers pull down the mean.

14. $\boxed{D}$ Before the 900-calorie meal is added, the median is the average of the 5th and 6th meals (550), the mode is 550, and the range is $900 - 500 = 400$. After the 900-calorie meal is added, the median becomes the 6th meal (still 550), the mode is still 550, and the range is still 400. None of them change.

15. $\boxed{B}$ Before the car is removed, the median is represented by the 8th car (23 mpg). After the car is removed, the median is represented by the average of the 7th and 8th cars (still 23 mpg). So the median stays the same. However, the mean and the standard deviation both decrease. We're removing a data point higher than all the others so the mean decreases. We're also reducing the spread in the data so the standard deviation decreases.

16. $\boxed{A}$ First, it's easy to see that the mean will decrease since we're replacing the maximum data point with a minimum. Now before the replacement, the range is $90 - 45 = 45$. After the replacement, the range is $65 - 20 = 45$, so the range remains the same. Before the replacement, the median is represented by the average of the 9th and 10th cars (57). After the replacement, the median is represented by 10th car (still 57, don't forget to count the replacement as the first value). The median also remains the same. Therefore, the mean changes the most.

Chapter 27: Statistics II

CHAPTER EXERCISE:

1. $\boxed{B}$ There are 2 points above the line of best fit when the value along the x-axis is 19.

2. $\boxed{2}$ Note that the sample size of 400 is irrelevant information. To make things easier, we'll let x be a decimal for now and convert it to a percentage later,

$$3,300x = 66$$
$$x = 0.02 = 2\%$$

3. $\boxed{C}$ The line of best fit gives a y-value of 55 when the x-value is 75.

4. $\boxed{C}$ First, the survey should be conducted with students from the university's freshman class since that's the intended target. Secondly, the larger the sample, the more valid the results.

5. $\boxed{A}$ Using proportions, Candidate A is expected to receive $\dfrac{110}{250} \times 500,000 = 220,000$ votes. Candidate B is expected to receive $\dfrac{140}{250} \times 500,000 = 280,000$ votes. So Candidate B is expected to receive $280,000 - 220,000 = 60,000$ more votes.

6. $\boxed{A}$ The y-intercept is the value of y when the value of x is 0. In this case, it's the average shopping time when the store discount is 0% (no discount).

7. $\boxed{A}$ The slope is rise over run. Because the line of best fit has a positive slope, it's the increase in revenue for every dollar increase in advertising expenses. Note that because both revenue and advertising expenses are expressed in thousands of dollars in the graph, they cancel out and have no effect on the interpretation of the slope. That's why the answer isn't (B).

8. $\boxed{B}$ The slope is rise over run. Because the line of best fit has a positive slope, it's the increase in box office sales per minute increase in movie length.

9. $\boxed{D}$ The y-intercept is the value of y when the value of x is 0. In this case, it's the expected number of mistakes made when the cash prize is 0 dollars (no cash prize).

10. $\boxed{B}$ This question is asking for the slope of the line of best fit. At 20 grams of fat, there are 340 calories. At 25 grams of fat, there are 380 calories. Calculating the slope from two points,

$$\frac{380-340}{25-20} = \frac{40}{5} = 8$$

11. $\boxed{B}$ Apply what you learn from the sample to the larger population. From the sample size, $\dfrac{\text{Car Speeding Violations}}{\text{Total Violations}} = \dfrac{83}{284}$. Now we can apply this same proportion to the state total of 2,000:

$$\frac{83}{284} \times 2,000 \approx 585$$

12. [B] The oat field whose yield is best predicted by the line of best fit is represented by the point closest to the line. That point has an x-value of 350, which is the amount of nitrogen applied to that field.

13. [D] The point farthest from the line of best fit is at an x-value of 7. The total number of seats at the food court represented by this point is $7 \times 80 = 560$.

14. [D] To draw a reliable conclusion about the effectiveness of the new vaccine, the patients must be randomly assigned to their treatment. Only answer (D) leads to random assignment. Note that answer (C) does not because the patients are allowed to group themselves as they desire. For example, three friends might want to remain in the same group, leading to assignment that is not random.

15. [C] Answer (A) is wrong because it's possible that most of the basketballs produced in Week 1 had an air pressure of *over* 8.2 psi. Likewise for Week 2. We don't know for sure. Answer (B) is wrong because it's too definite. Just because the sample means were 0.5 psi apart doesn't mean the true means, which would take into account *all* the basketballs produced in Week 1 and Week 2, were also 0.5 psi apart. That's why there's a margin of error for the samples. Answer (D) is wrong because the samples suggest the reverse: the mean air pressure for Week 1 (8.2 psi) is greater than the mean air pressure for Week 2 (7.7 psi). Answer (C) is correct because the greater the sample size, the lower the margin of error. The sample from Week 1 had a lower margin of error than the sample from Week 2.

16. [D] The lower the standard deviation (variability), the lower the margin of error. Selecting students who are following the same daily diet plan will likely lead to the lowest standard deviation because they are likely to be eating the same number of servings of vegetables. The other answer choices would result in much more variability.

17. [C] Answer (C) best expresses the meaning of a confidence interval, which applies only to the statistical mean and does not say anything about blue-spotted salamanders themselves. Answer (D) is wrong because the study involved only blue-spotted salamanders, not all salamanders.

18. [B] The most that we can conclude is that there is a negative association between the price of food and the population density in U.S. cities (as one goes up, the other goes down). We CANNOT conclude that there is a cause and effect relationship between the two. We can't say that one causes the other.

Chapter 28: Volume

CHAPTER EXERCISE:

1. $\boxed{A}$ Each piece is half the cylinder.

$$\frac{1}{2}V = \frac{1}{2}\pi r^2 h = \frac{1}{2}\pi(2)^2(5) = 10\pi$$

2. $\boxed{B}$ The height of the box is $100 \div 25 = 4$ (dividing the volume by the area of the base gives us to the height). The sides of the base are $\sqrt{25} = 5$ inches long. The rectangular box has dimensions $5 \times 5 \times 4$.

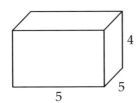

The top and bottom have a surface area of $2(5 \times 5) = 50$. The front and back have a surface area of $2(5 \times 4) = 40$. The left and right have a surface area of $2(5 \times 4) = 40$. The total surface area is $50 + 40 + 40 = 130$.

3. $\boxed{C}$ Let the side of the cube be s. The cube has six faces and the area of each face is s^2. Solving for s in terms of a,

$$6s^2 = 24a^2$$
$$s^2 = 4a^2$$
$$s = 2a$$

The volume is then $s^3 = (2a)^3 = 8a^3$.

4. $\boxed{D}$ The cylindrical tank that can be filled in 3 hours has a volume of $\pi(4)^2(6) = 96\pi$. The tank in question has a volume of $\pi(6)^2(8) = 288\pi$. Using the first tank as a conversion factor,

$$288\pi \times \frac{3 \text{ hours}}{96\pi} = 9 \text{ hours}$$

5. $\boxed{D}$ This question is asking for the volume of the cylinder. The radius of the base is 2 and since the diameter of each tennis ball is 4, the height of the cylinder is $4 \times 3 = 12$.

$$V = \pi r^2 h = \pi(2)^2(12) = 48\pi$$

6. $\boxed{2.5}$ The shortest way to do this question is to pretend that the block is liquefied and poured into the aquarium. How high would the level of the liquid rise?

$$V = lwh$$
$$5,000 = (80)(25)h$$
$$2.5 = h$$

The longer way to do this question is to find the original volume, add the block, find the new height, and then compare it to the original height. While not the fastest method, it is certainly viable.

7. $\boxed{A}$ If you take away all the cubes with black paint on them, you are essentially uncovering an inner cube with a side length of 3. A front view is shown below.

There are $3^3 = 27$ cubes that are unpainted.

8. $\boxed{C}$ Since each small cube has a volume of $2^3 = 8$ and the volume of the outer box is $8^3 = 512$, there must be $512 \div 8 = 64$ cubes in the box. If you take away all the cubes that are touching the box, you are essentially uncovering an inner rectangular box with a square base of side 4 and a height of 6. A front view is shown below.

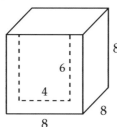

The volume of this inner rectangular box is $4 \times 4 \times 6 = 96$. Since each cube has a volume of 8, there are $96 \div 8 = 12$ cubes that are not touching the box, which means there are $64 - 12 = 52$ cubes that are touching. You also could've taken the straight-forward approach of counting up the cubes along the sides. If you took this route, you should've gotten something along the lines of $16 + 16 + 8 + 8 + 4 = 52$.

9. $\boxed{D}$ The only cubes that have exactly one face painted black are the ones in the middle of each side. For example, the front side has $3 \times 1 = 3$ of these cubes.

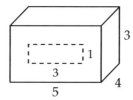

The right side has $2 \times 1 = 2$ of these cubes, and the top has $3 \times 2 = 6$ of these cubes. So far, we have $3 + 2 + 6 = 11$ of these cubes. To account for the back, left, and bottom sides, we double this to get 22 cubes.

10. $\boxed{B}$ Draw a line down the middle of the cone to form a right triangle with the radius and the slant height. This triangle is a multiple of the $3 - 4 - 5$ right triangle: $9 - 12 - 15$. You could've used the pythagorean theorem instead if you weren't aware of this. In any case, the height of the cone is 12 cm.

$V =$ volume of cone $+$ volume of hemisphere

$$V = \frac{1}{3}\pi r^2 h + \frac{1}{2}\left(\frac{4}{3}\pi r^3\right)$$

$$V = \frac{1}{3}\pi(9)^2(12) + \frac{1}{2}\left(\frac{4}{3}\pi(9)^3\right)$$

$$V = 324\pi + 486\pi = 810\pi$$

11. $\boxed{B}$ This question is essentially asking for the volume, or the amount of room, in the crate. The room in the crate can be seen as a rectangular box with a length of $10 - 1 - 1 = 8$ inches, a width of $8 - 1 - 1 = 6$ inches, and a height of $3 - 1 = 2$ inches.

$$V = 8 \times 6 \times 2 = 96$$

12. $\boxed{B}$ Cut the staircase vertically into 3 blocks.

Volume of staircase $=$ Volume of block 1
$+$ Volume of block 2
$+$ Volume of block 3

$$V = (5 \times 2 \times 0.2) + (5 \times 2 \times 0.4) + (5 \times 2 \times 0.6)$$
$$= 2 + 4 + 6$$
$$= 12$$

Mass $=$ Density $\times$ Volume $= 130 \times 12 = 1,560$ kg

Made in the USA
Lexington, KY
27 June 2019